T0113644

"His account of the weeks he spent crisscrossing America is a swiftly unfolding narrative of danger, violence, alienation, and sadness. . . . Realistic, perceptive."   —*American Library Association*

"*Rolling Nowhere* succeeds in its ability to bring out this forgotten world of railyard hoboes. Conover . . . picks up on dozens of fascinating little insights into these men and their way of life."
                                        —*Milwaukee Journal Sentinel*

"Lively and informative. . . . Conover's vivid, personal style makes this well written and well-paced book a worthwhile choice for the general reader. . . . Highly recommended."   —*Library Journal*

"A fascinating account of life in [a] dirty, shadowy, little-known and seldom understood world."   —*Asbury Park Press*

"Interesting. . . . His style in *Rolling Nowhere* reflects wide-eyed wonder and unquenchable curiosity. On the subject of hoboes today, Ted Conover is the best we've got."   —*This Week in Denver*

TED CONOVER

ROLLING NOWHERE

Ted Conover was raised in Colorado and graduated from Amherst College. *Rolling Nowhere,* his first book, has been followed by three others including *Newjack: Guarding Sing Sing,* which won the National Book Critics Circle Award in 2001 and was a nominated finalist for the Pulitzer Prize. He lives in New York City. Further information about Ted Conover is available on his web site at www.tedconover.com.

Newjack: Guarding Sing Sing

Whiteout: Lost in Aspen

Coyotes: A Journey Through the Secret World
of America's Illegal Aliens

ROLLING NOWHERE

Vintage Departures

Vintage Books

A Division of Random House, Inc.

New York

ROLLING NOWHERE

Riding the Rails with America's Hoboes

TED CONOVER

FIRST VINTAGE DEPARTURES EDITION, SEPTEMBER 2001

Copyright © 1981, 1984, 2001 by Ted Conover

A portion of this book appeared originally in *Denver* magazine.

Grateful acknowledgment is made to the following for permission to reprint previously published material:

Don McLean Music: Excerpt from "Homeless Brother," words and music by Don McLean and an excerpt from "The Legend of Andrew McCrew," words and music by Don McLean. Published by Don McLean Music. Administered by Harry Fox (BMI).

Ludlow Music, Inc.: Excerpt from "Hard Travelin'," words and music by Woody Guthrie. TRO—Copyright © 1959 (renewed), 1963 (renewed), and 1972 (renewed) by Ludlow Music, Inc., New York, NY. Reprinted by permission of Ludlow Music, Inc., The Richmond Organization.

Map by Paul J. Pugliese, copyright © 1983 by Viking Penguin Inc. Used by permission of Viking Penguin, a division of Penguin Putnam Inc.

Library of Congress Cataloging-in-Publication Data is on file.

Vintage ISBN: 978-0-375-72786-3

www.vintagebooks.com

For
Ivie Brass, philosopher, seeker, witness, tramp,
and
Lane Sommer (1958–1981)

Acknowledgments

Thanks are gratefully given to: the LaTourettes of St. Louis, Missouri; Lara McIntosh and friends, Olympia, Washington; Jonathan Goldberg, Steve Rubin, and Robin Wright in Portland, Oregon; Mark Curby and Doug Dittman in San Francisco; Brad Segal and Mr. and Mrs. A. B. Bristow in Denver; Christine Evans, Ross McConnell, Peter Engel, and Ira Steven Levine, for manuscript suggestions; Prof. Alan Babb, for his cautious enthusiasm; Mr. Hal Irwin of St. Joseph, Missouri; railroad workers who help tramps in transit; and my parents and sisters.

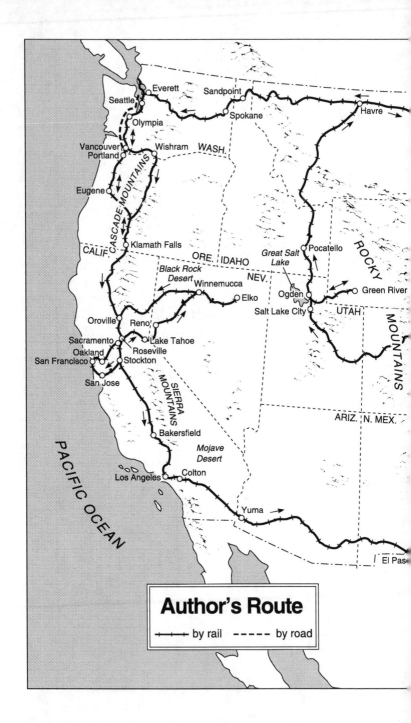

Author's Route

—+—+— by rail   - - - - - by road

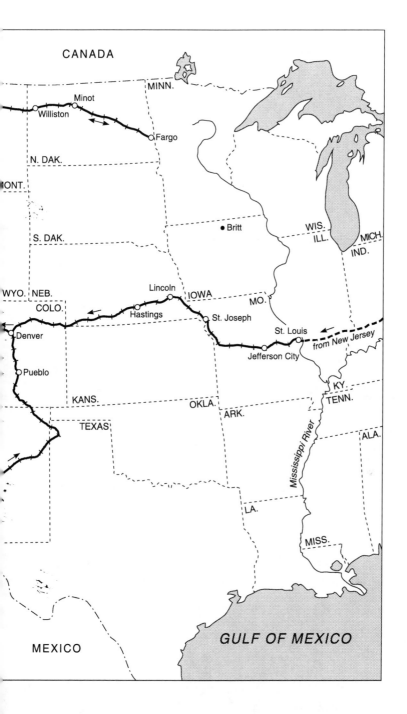

By the time *Rolling Nowhere* came out, I had crossed the country on my bicycle, worked in a Spanish sausage factory, done community organizing as a VISTA volunteer in inner-city Dallas and, of course, spent four months on the rails with hoboes. I thought of myself as experienced and mature. Imagine my surprise, then, when I learned that my editor had appended to my chosen title, *Rolling Nowhere,* the line, "A Young Man's Adventures Riding the Rails with America's Hoboes."

" 'A young man's'?" I asked her on the phone, feeling I'd just been demoted by New York publishing.

"Well, we thought that best described it," I recall her saying. "There's nothing wrong with it—you *are* a young man, you know." And clearly, I was; I was twenty-four.

With this new Vintage Books edition, the subtitle has been improved. But I must admit, as I reread this first book of mine, that the description was accurate. These *are* a young man's adventures. Now that I'm almost twenty years older and have seen more, done more, and written more, this younger man, despite his pretensions of experience, seems a bit callow. And so candid! Most of my first-person writing at the time had been for my journals and diaries, and I think I never really imagined that *anyone* would be able to take this book home from the store or library and read my deepest thoughts.

The world of the railroad hobo has changed considerably in the twenty years since *Rolling Nowhere* was first published. People have been proclaiming his death for years and years now; many were surprised, when my book came out, that there had been any hoboes left for me to travel with. At the time, I guessed there were several thousand railroad hoboes still out there. But now, it does seem there are practically none.

The hobo's death, of course, has long been foretold. Back in 1974, Don McLean sang,

> The ghosts of highway royalty have vanished in the night
> The Whitman wanderer walking toward a glowing inner light
> The children have grown older and the cops have gripped us tight
> There's no spot 'round the melting pot for free men in their flight.

He was premature, but not by much. A different term, "homeless," was gaining currency around the time I wrote *Rolling Nowhere;* if hoboes weren't going to die out on their own, it seemed, they were going to be subsumed into this new concept, which was purely about a social problem, with none of the romance of the railroad world. The wondrous thing about hoboes, who were spawned by the Great Depression, has always been the way we created something romantic out of the inevitable. Freedom of choice—the idea, real or not, that "I'd live this way even if I didn't have to"—is an essential part of the notion, and the reason I wanted to live that life myself.

Of the many changes that have affected hoboes since my sojourn in 1980, some of the greatest actually have to do with trains. When I took my journey, there were still plenty of wooden-floored boxcars, the classic hobo roost. Now these boxcars are all but gone (along with cabooses, whose occupants used to alert the engine crew of wheel trouble or inform them when the end of the train was finally off the main track—jobs now performed by electronic sensors). More and more freight is "intermodal": container boxes go straight from ships to the new "stack" and "doublestack" freight cars, truck trailers are lifted onto piggyback freight cars and unloaded again on the other side of the country. A guy can still catch a ride on those freight cars, but he's more exposed to weather and scrutiny and the rides are less comfortable.

A second change has to do with the freight railroads' attitude toward riders, which has become less tolerant. As recently as twenty years ago, the traditional cat-and-mouse game between hobo and bull prevailed. "As long as you weren't a total jerk, and you got off when he told you to and climbed back on when he wasn't looking—as long as it looked like he was keeping tramps out of the yard—everything was fine," says an old-timer I know named North Bank Fred. "Now it's totally different." Todd Waters, a former marketing executive who goes by "Adman" on the rails— and "free-range human being" in his e-mails—complains that "now they'll even chase you when it's raining!" And, more often than not, send you to jail if they catch you.

Employees who used to help the hobo on his way—brakemen, track crews—now actively turn him in. Citizens sometimes call police or regional railroad offices on cell phones when they spot a hobo at a railroad crossing. I still take the occasional pleasure trip; a while ago I rode with Todd Waters across the Rocky Mountains on the Canadian Pacific. Somehow the engineer of a Canadian National train across the river saw our heads through the windows of the rear locomotive we were in. Soon the train stopped, and Todd and I were busted by a Mountie.

Some blame corporate consolidation for these changes. Over the past few years, the Union Pacific Railroad has absorbed the Southern Pacific, the Western Pacific, and the Denver & Rio Grande Western. Burlington Northern has swallowed up the Atchison, Topeka and Santa Fe. Canadian National is acquiring the Wisconsin Central as I write. These corporations control not just railroads but trucking, high-tech, oil and gas, and hotel companies, and decisions are made by people who aren't a part of the tradition. "Southern Pacific was a railroad, and Union Pacific is a corporation," complains North Bank Fred. That oversimplifies things, but only somewhat.

The hobo's world—not to mention his image—has also been darkened by a couple of serial killers who traveled the rails since the days of my journey. Robert Joseph Silveria—road name "Sidetrack"—is thought to have killed a dozen railroad tramps over fifteen years before he was apprehended in 1996. Worse from a public relations point of view, "Railcar Killer" Angel Maturino Resendiz used the rails to murder up to nine people who lived *near* railroad yards back in the late 1990s, which created tremendous pressure on companies to curb the travels of unauthorized riders.

When I wrote this book, hoboes could still get extra allotments of food stamps by applying multiple times in different train towns—Marysville, California; Everett, Washington; and Havre, Montana, for example. That scam kept a lot of people on the move. But tighter food stamp regulations have changed things. Most able-bodied adults without dependents ("a-bods," in federal parlance) are now cut off after three months, unless they find a job.

But probably the worst thing for modern hobo life has been America's prosperity. "The greatest peacetime economic expansion in history," as Bill Clinton and Al Gore called it, without question shrank the ranks of the homeless and the unemployed. If train crews are a little less helpful to the guys they find in their yards, it may be because when they look at them they don't see themselves, dispossessed, but rather recreational riders (Los Angeles actor Budd Hopkins often hit the rails with a guitar in the late eighties and early nineties, and made it into many newspapers, too) or a newer wave of "nose ring nation people," as North Bank Fred calls them—punks, radical environmentalists, and other disaffected youth "with chains and mohawks and stuff." Scrawled in chalk on the railroad underpass in Seattle is no longer, "Portland Slim was here," but "Anarchy Rules!"

The hobo idea still resonates in articles about these modern-day riders and in memoirs by old-timers, but the world of hoboes with road names who cooked in jungles with "gunboats" (coffee cans) is a thing of the past, and *Rolling Nowhere* is now, I suppose, a historical document.

As for me, *Rolling Nowhere* remains the adventure that changed my life. The week before my college graduation, as I was packing my bags for a job at *The Indianapolis Star*, two calls came in quick succession from people claiming to represent the *Today* show and *Good Morning America;* they had seen a wire story about my travels, they said, and wanted to fly me to New York. It seemed so unlikely that I accused the second caller of playing a prank. But the tickets arrived, I went to New York, and, armed with evidence that people out there might want to read a book about my experience, I found a literary agent, skipped Indiana, and went home to write a book.

Though *Rolling Nowhere* has been hard to find in bookshops, its readers have continued to seek me out—people's interest in the hobo life seems stronger than ever. Maybe that has something to do with the corporate consolidation out there and the regimented quality of modern-day life, with its overwork and structure and the fetish I sometimes think we've made of *safety*.

The only problem with the book being back in print is that now my son, just learning to read, is going to find it easier to get his hands on a copy. Back in the day, I remember secretly rolling my eyes at my professor's admonition that freight-hopping was probably a good way to get my legs cut off, or the tiresome refrain from spokesmen of the American Railroad Association, whenever somebody's freight adventures made it into the newspaper, that hopping trains was illegal and dangerous. What I now admit—and yes, it has to do with parenthood—is that these warnings are reasonable. Enjoy the book, have your own adventures, and be careful out there.

New York
April 24, 2001

R O L L I N G   N O W H E R E

1

I crouched quietly in the patch of tall weeds. Around me fell the shadow of the viaduct that carried a highway over the railroad yards. From the edge of the yards, I squinted as I watched the railroad cars being switched from track to track. As hard as it was for me to look out into the late summer sun, I knew anyone in the sun would have a hard time seeing me in the shade. Cars and trucks were rolling over the viaduct, but what occupied my attention was the dark, cool corridor underneath it, where I hoped to intercept my train.

If the train ever arrived, that was. I was going on three days in St. Louis now, waiting for this train, or any train. Where it went anymore, I didn't really care: I just wanted out. The downtown industrial area of St. Louis was not meant for travelers and was no place to spend the night—or the day, for that matter—yet I had done it twice now. And already today, the sun was on its way down.

How hoboes did this regularly, I did not understand. The railroad yards around St. Louis were fearsome places, enclosed by chain-link fences and patrolled by dogs or guards in unmarked security cars. My plan had been to wait at the end of a yard and jump a train as it emerged from the secured area. But so far the trains I had seen had either rolled out only a tiny bit, then reversed direction and returned to the yard, or had emerged at high speed. Running alongside them, gear bouncing on my back and in my hands, I had realized the futility of trying to grab hold. Even if I managed to snag a ladder, how long would I be able to hold on? Either hoboes had the grip of barnacles, or this was not how it was done.

The railroads were suspicious of telephone calls concerning freight schedules, too. "Who wants to know?" a yardmaster had snarled when finally I found his number in the telephone book. A train buff, I had answered. "Sorry." Click.

This morning, a better ruse had occurred to me. I was going to be a local commercial photographer. I found the name of one in the Yellow Pages and called up the yard, saying I was interested in shooting a westbound freight, headed into the afternoon sun, for a calendar. I wouldn't even have to enter the yard, I said—I could do my shooting from the bridge. After a few tense moments, the yard-master returned to the phone. "Well, we got one called outa here for three-thirty," he said.

This time I scaled a fence into the yard, and at 3:30 I was ready. And at 4:00. And at 4:30. And now at 5:30 I began to lose hope. The night before I had given up on downtown and sought refuge on the suburban back lawn of some family friends a few miles away. They had been very kind, more understanding than most suburban families about discovering a transient asleep in their back yard in the morning. But I couldn't go back—the idea of someone like me riding freight trains to learn about hoboes had seemed quaint and slightly comical to them, and until I had some experience under my belt, some credibility, I didn't feel like doing any more explaining about my riding the rails.

Then finally I saw it. From the crowd of partial trains that cluttered the center of the yard emerged a train that looked to be whole—a train, anyway, that had an engine at the lead end and was quite purposefully leaving the yard, picking up speed. My heart jumped as the engine entered the shadow under my bridge, eight or nine cars visibly in tow. More cars appeared—where could I ride? Stories from friends who had hopped trains always had them comfortably situated in open boxcars—but what few boxcars I could see were resolutely shut. Did you simply hold on to the ladder? I didn't think so, but I was nearing the point where I would give it a try.

I shouldered my small pack and bedroll, hung another bag around my neck, picked up my water jug, and, knees weak, rose to my feet. Now I was visible. I looked down the tracks toward the six-story control tower that the only hobo I had met to date had told me to watch out for. That was earlier this afternoon. He had strode directly up to my hiding spot in the weeds, his "howdy" catching me in the middle of a sentence in my journal. Embarrassed and uncomfortable at being discovered, I returned the greeting, and we talked briefly. I was in the wrong yard for getting to Kansas City, he maintained—the right one was several miles away, and that, in fact, was where he was headed. But as he walked off, he didn't invite me to follow. At first dejected, I realized later that I hadn't asked to tag along, either. Perhaps the time was not yet right for me to join up with a hobo. First I needed some credentials. First I wanted to hop a freight.

The train continued its journey out of the yard. The engine was almost even with the control tower now—plainly in sight of it—and fifteen or twenty cars were visible. Passing underneath the shadow of the bridge took each of them three or four seconds and within that space of time, I knew, I would have to meet the train and climb aboard. No sign would say where to sit, no porter would greet me. If the stories I had heard were true, a railroad cop, or "bull," might be there to toss me back off.

Finally there appeared what looked like a boxcar with the top half missing—a gondola car, I would later learn it was called. Ladders ran up its side, front and rear, and I thought I could make it. The car was a weathered maroon, and it rocked ponderously from side to side as it approached the shadow. I timed my sprint: 4—3—2—1—go! With the gondola still in the sun, I sprang out of the weeds and across the rails, sprinting gingerly over the ties. About twelve tracks separated me from the train; I narrowed the gap as the gondola rolled into the shadow. I slowed down as I approached it, suddenly awed by the immense size of a train up close. I heaved my jug up the twelve or so feet it took to clear the top of the gondola. The train looked impregnable, fortress-like. Out of breath too soon, I began running alongside on the gravel. I ripped my shoulder bag from around my neck, pitched it underhanded into the gondola, and then, both hands free, reached for the ladder. The steel-on-steel sounds of the huge, shining wheels rolling on the tracks underneath cautioned me to keep my distance, and my balance. One hand on, then two, and I hoisted myself up. A few quick steps up the rungs and I was over the edge, just as the train and I emerged into the sunlight.

It was a long drop to the gondola floor. I landed on all fours and quickly gathered up my belongings into a corner on the side of the gondola nearest the tower. If I could press far enough against the wall, I thought, I would not be seen. The train trundled along slowly, and I held my breath. Random pieces of scrap iron littered the gondola floor. The cotton of my pack and shoulder bag seemed out of place here, too soft. My sleeves, I noticed, had become stained with dirt and rust. I pressed against the wall, and the train rolled and rumbled. If they had seen me get on, I thought, now was about when the bull would arrive to make the arrest. Minutes passed. Keep going, I urged the train, *keep going. . . .*

The train stopped with a jerk. A loud blast of air from somewhere underneath the car was followed by silence, and I was more afraid than ever of making a sound. For five minutes I didn't dare to look. My third day out, and already in jail—what an auspicious start!

Stiffly, I rose to my feet, found a piece of junk to stand on, and peered over the side. The tower was nowhere in sight—nor, anymore, were any of the other trains. Woods lined the track on either side, and a dirt road paralleled it. A small wooden shack was set off in the shrubbery, but there were no signs of life there. "Goddamn," I said under my breath, not knowing exactly what had happened but pretty sure it wasn't good.

I gathered up my belongings and prepared to chuck them over

the side and climb out. But just then I heard the sound of tires on gravel. I peeked out and saw a plain-colored sedan with a tiny antenna on top and searchlights near the rear-view mirrors creeping along the length of the train on the dirt road. Quickly I fell back into the car and waited. In time the cruiser passed by; had he been looking for me? I waited a few more minutes, until the coast was clear, and climbed out of the gondola.

Nobody answered my knock on the door of the shack. More and more disconsolate, I gazed at my surroundings. The train was only about twenty cars long. There was no engine anymore, and no caboose: I had been dropped off on a siding. I had gotten nowhere again.

In the distance I heard the noise of cars on a busy street. I sighed and began trudging toward it. I still had my map of St. Louis; with it I could walk to the road, figure out my location relative to my suburban friends, and either hitchhike there or give them a call to pick me up. The thought of conceding defeat was sickening, but not as bad as spending another night in the weed-patch, like two nights ago, or, as on the night before that, on top of a public restroom building in a small park.

At first I thought the rumbling was in my imagination. Hallucinations of passing freights would have been perfectly logical at this point, but this was a real sound, and more: in my chest I felt the deep bass vibrations of diesel locomotives. I stopped walking. Where *was* that noise coming from? It was definitely a train, and it seemed to be moving parallel to my siding, but the thick brush on either side of the track confounded my efforts to pinpoint it. Finally I took a chance and went crashing through the brush on the side that seemed most likely.

I came out in the empty parking lot of a large factory. More shrubbery cluttered its far side, but through gaps in the green leaves and branches I saw bright colors passing. I tore across the parking lot.

The train was huge, somehow made bigger by its greater speed. I caught a glimpse of the engines: four of them hooked together, not just one. This train was longer, already well out of the yard, and already moving rather fast. This train meant business.

Like airplanes, trains often appear to be traveling more slowly than they really are. To gauge the speed of this one better, I ran alongside it for twenty or thirty feet, seeing if I could keep up. Barely, I could. I stopped, caught my breath, and made sure the gravel ahead was free of obstructions. Then I looked back on the monster I was planning to board.

Its speed, I guessed, was fifteen miles per hour. Most of the cars were large boxcars; if the raised track they rode on was figured in, their tops were probably twenty-five feet from the ground. Interspersed with these were big tank cars, grain cars, and flat cars. The ground trembled as they passed over it, and the railroad ties creaked and sagged. Some cars swayed perilously from side to side, so much that I feared they might topple over on me. Ten or twenty cars rolled by, seeming to pick up speed, and again, there was no sign of an empty boxcar, or even another gondola. I began to panic. What if I didn't find a place to ride by the time the caboose appeared?

Then something that looked like a caboose, but wasn't quite, came into view. I regarded it curiously, and the one like it, which followed right behind. These were apparently cabooses-in-progress, caboose bodies of unfinished steel with no upholstery, doors in the frames, or glass in the windows. They were certainly empty, and the ladders at one end of them were actually steps, which extended toward the gravel and had railings up the side. I wanted to board but could not resolve to jump on until it was too late.

My eyes turned back to the cars still to come. Two more boxcars passed, and then—another caboose-in-progress! This was it. I started running before the car even reached me, sprinting in the dimming light over the loose gravel. My flopping pack and shoulder bag pulled at my back and shoulders, uncoordinated with my running, nearly making me lose my balance. The train was now moving faster than I could run. The caboose appeared at my side, slowly gaining on me. I saw its railings out of the corner of my eye and, feet pounding the gravel, swung an arm wildly out and grabbed on. Being attached to all that energy panicked me at first, but then I realized I was also more stable. Twisting my body, I grabbed on with the other arm and, in the same motion, pulled myself onto the steps. The train's greater speed caused me to swing backward, and my packs swung perilously over the back of the caboose. The straps held, though, as did my hands, and I was on. I climbed the steps two at a time, ducked under the chain at the top, and stood on the rear platform of the caboose. It was steady enough here, so I took off my gear, leaned it against the caboose wall, and took a deep breath of relief.

The train speeded up and was soon traveling probably thirty miles per hour. We passed through St. Louis's outlying areas, through crossings where scores of rush-hour drivers were stalled, awaiting passage of the train. I walked into the caboose proper, leaned on a windowsill, and put my head out into the breeze. Now and then my presence in the middle of this train would catch the eye of some pedestrian or bored driver, and in surprise, amusement, or, I imagined, envy, they would turn their heads, wondering what in God's name this kid was doing on the train. Long rows of back yards opened themselves up to my privileged view: many people were out in them this evening, barbecuing or having drinks. Some, especially the young, waved to me, and as I waved back, it finally dawned on me what I had done. I was on a freight! I had hopped it! After weeks of excited anticipation and days of bored, frustrated waiting, my dream was coming true.

A big smile crept onto my face and wouldn't go away; I let out a whoop. To know this feeling, it was suddenly clear, was at least one reason I had wanted to take this trip.

2

The other reasons I never found easy to explain. I know that as a boy growing up in Denver, I had been entranced by the older boys who found their way downtown, jumped the Denver & Rio Grande Western up into the mountains, and returned with tales of courage and narrow escapes. I understood that some men did it professionally, and I grew up with a romantic vision of hoboes as renegades, conscientious objectors to the nine-to-five work world, men who defied convention and authority to find freedom on the open road. "Knights of the road" were subjects of some of my favorite folk songs and short stories. Whenever I brought up the subject, somebody's father, uncle, or brother-in-law had always done some hoboing. No matter if it was in the middle of the Great Depression—they too returned with great war stories. Hopping freights, those mythic behemoths so tied to the growth and exploration of the West, seemed something a red-blooded American boy just ought to do.

Later, my curiosity was sparked by homeless men I met while serving as a VISTA volunteer in Dallas. Drunk or hungry, they would stumble into the storefront office of the community group I worked for—sometimes literally, since the wooden front door had no latch, and those who leaned against it found themselves sprawled across our floor the next instant. We fed them soup, and they went on their way. Perhaps they interested me because they seemed so unlike me, so devoid of ambition and unconcerned about any moment but the present. An overdose of the opposite was one thing that had made me want to take the volunteer year away from school: status-consciousness, competitiveness, and clubbiness seemed the rule at my small New England college. Perhaps I came up with the idea of living with hoboes because it looked like a way of escaping the limiting habits and attitudes of my own social class, of getting an outside perspective on who I was. Perhaps it was the challenge of seeing if my tender, college-bred self could make it in their tough world: did I have it in me? Or maybe it was simply through wondering what life for them was like: was theirs, as one sociologist suggested, "a world of strangers who are friends"? Was there a brotherhood of the rails?

The idea of hoboes in this age of postwar affluence seemed a paradox. Most people told me that freight-hopping hoboes had gone out with the Depression, the "Java men of industrial time." Most of the books on hoboes were forty years old. If hoboes still existed, they were invisible; their niche had been filled by bag ladies and hitchhikers.

Still, a Canadian Pacific engineer I met in Alberta one summer swore that he saw them quite often (and offered some tips on how to travel their way and not get caught), and a buddy of mine who commuted daily on a freight from his home on the Washington state line to college in the Idaho panhandle had seen them too. These reports were corroborated by a recent book of hobo photographs I found on a friend's bookshelf.

My only other lead was something called the National Hobo Convention in Britt, Iowa. I had first read of it while folding newspapers for my delivery route, when I was barely a teenager. The brief article, which I clipped, quoted "Steamtrain" Maury Graham, the "King of the Hoboes," as saying he could tell how the nation's economy was doing by the length of the cigarette butts he found on the sidewalk. I thought such a character would be worth meeting.

Authorities in Britt confirmed that the August convention was an annual event, and that it had been going on for eighty years. The Chamber of Commerce sponsored it, they added. The Chamber of Commerce sponsored a meeting of hoboes? It sounded strange, but I knew I would have to attend, as a serious onlooker if not a conventioneer.

A month before I began my hobo trip, I took a long weekend off from my summer job in the East and went to Britt. I flew into Minneapolis, the nearest big city. A map showed a freight line passing south from there to Britt but, still ignorant of how to hop a freight, I chose to hitchhike down. I had good luck until I was only twenty miles away. The narrow country road leading from the interstate to Britt was choked with motor homes full of hobo fans, on their way to watch the convention. Good news, I thought: the driving would be slow, but I would get plenty of ride offers. The hobo fans expressed plenty of interest in me but, to my dismay, almost nobody stopped. It took me five more hours to get to Britt, past the illuminated welcome sign with its cartoon hobo.

The annual Hobo Day parade was just starting. Down Main Street came the American Legion, high school baton twirlers, gargantuan farm machines, and then, to my disbelief, a hobo float! Seated upon it were maybe fifteen men, all bearded, most with floppy hats, many holding walking sticks. They wore trousers that were heavily patched but spotlessly clean and flashed big, toothy smiles to the crowd. These are hoboes? I asked myself.

I looked for the men in the long lines of people waiting for free mulligan stew after the parade, but few were in evidence. I asked a server where they might be found.

"Probably over in the jungle," she said.

"The jungle? Where is that?"

"Over by the grain elevators," she said, pointing to the town's tallest structures. "It's really a park."

The jungle was easy to find. A large open boxcar had been rolled into its middle—presumably for hobo accommodations, to judge by the sturdy wooden ramp that had been built up to the entrance. Next to this was a cooking area, with folding chairs and stumps for seats around it, and on the other side was a large party tent, set up to protect the hoboes from the weather.

But at that moment it was being used for a hobo press conference.

"So are there really many hoboes anymore?" a newspaper reporter inquired of a gentleman I would learn was Steamtrain Maury Graham.

"Nooo, not many," intoned Steamtrain, sipping from a can of Mountain Dew and whacking flies with a swatter. "Reckon what you see here is just about the last of 'em. Hoboes are a dyin' breed, y'know." Stout, with a flowing white beard, Steamtrain would have made a good Santa Claus. Dark suspenders, stark against his gleaming white shirt, held up his old canvas pants. *Reader's Digest* had once run an article about him: the author had searched night and day over miles of train track to catch up with the mythical Steamtrain. He had apparently been looking in the wrong place: Steamtrain's pickup truck and camping trailer, just in from his home in Toledo, Ohio, were parked a few yards away from the tent, not far from the pair of San-O-Lets thoughtfully provided by the town for any hobo in need.

Further questions were cut short, because it was time for the annual election of the King and Queen of the Hoboes.

All the hoboes assembled on a stage erected near the site of the mulligan stew fest, and the media people crowded around to get it on film. The names of the hoboes filtered through the audience: there was Lord Open Road, the Arkansas Traveler, Portland Gray, Sparky Smith, Hood River Blackie, the Shadow, the Pennsylvania Kid, Virginia Slim, and others. There were even a few women. Cards were circulating through the crowd; "Vote for Hood River Blackie," said one.

First to the microphone was Steamtrain himself, who announced that, due to health considerations, he would be unable to run for a sixth term. Disappointment rippled through the crowd of several hundred, among whom Steamtrain was evidently an old favorite.

Then began the "election." One by one the hoboes got up and told the crowd why they were most deserving of the title King of the

Hoboes. "Why, I bin on the freights since before most of you was born," a typical harangue began. "I remember the days of the coal-burnin' locomotive and ridin' the rods. I had dicks pull me off a train rollin' forty miles an hour, and I've pushed some of them offa trains goin' even faster." The brief speeches were typically followed by an ovation; an emcee had explained that whichever hobo received the loudest applause, in the opinion of a three-judge panel, would be named the new King of the Hoboes.

I was about to go look for a bar when one of the contestants caught my attention. He was a massive, bearded, dangerous-looking man, younger than most of the others, wearing a railroad engineer's cap, and he had something different to say. Stepping up to the podium, the man calling himself Portland Gray related his qualifications—"I rode twelve thousand miles on boxcars last year"—and then told the crowd something it had probably not expected to hear. "People get muddled in their image of hoboes," he said. "Most guys you see on the road ain't like us, all fat and sassy. Most guys on the road are sick and broke. They're hurtin'. Hoboes built this country, and it's workers you see on the rails—only most of 'em's too old or sick to work anymore, or there ain't jobs for 'em. And what do we do? We throw 'em on the scrap heap! Are we going to throw away our people, our resources, those who made us strong?" He took his seat to spotty applause.

Now this, I thought, was something new. When the speeches finally ended, I pursued this man, who seemed the lone truth-teller, back to the jungle.

I introduced myself, told him of what I was about to do, and we set off on a long walk down the railroad tracks. Portland Gray knew more about hoboes than anybody I had met. Here, at last, was someone who had ridden the rails and, more, was still riding them.

"Yeah, there's still hoboes," said Portland Gray to me, "but you ain't gonna see any of them here. This is fun, but it's fake. Nine out of ten of these guys have never been on a freight in their lives—they just come to have a little fun, get a little publicity.

Why, that Steamtrain's got a head that's three boxcars long! This isn't the place to learn what you want to know."

Gray told me what was: "Division points—the towns trains stop in to change crews—that's where you'll find the real tramps." He mentioned a few places—Oroville and Stockton, California; Wishram, Washington; Havre, Montana—names I had never heard of, the capitals of tramp culture.

He himself had gone to college three years, he said, before realizing "I wasn't getting too good a return on my investment." A student of hobo lore, he took to the road just to see what it was like. He had read most of the good books on hoboes, and when we returned to the "jungle" he also showed me two reference books he carried, listing railroad timetables and routes.

We leaned back against a shade tree to enjoy the cool six-pack of beer we had bought. Across the jungle, Steamtrain Maury Graham ascended the boxcar ramp and executed a jig for a television camera crew. Later in the evening we would see him posing next to a bonfire, kids on his knee, for a *National Geographic* photographer, and autographing glossy portraits of himself boarding a train.

I felt cynical about the whole thing—the convention was a fake, as Gray had said. But it was fun, too. The convention was a celebration of an American myth. The hobo, scorned and outlawed during his golden age of the Great Depression, had somehow retained the affection of Americans. As Lady Bo had told the audience, "You all wouldn't be here if there wasn't a little bit of hobo in you!" The "hoboes," most of whom had now retired to the shade of Steamtrain's trailer, out of sun and limelight, understood what that meant. They represented not the scrap-heap hoboes alluded to by Portland Gray, but the footloose, vagabond, ruggedly individualistic hoboes celebrated by Whitman, Kerouac, Dos Passos, London, Steinbeck, and other American writers—the hoboes that some of us, sometimes, might wish we could be. Like the illuminated "Welcome to Britt" sign, the Britt hoboes were caricatures. They replicated rather well the things people like to see in hoboes—the iconoclasm, the freedom, the brotherhood of the road.

In the shade of Steamtrain's trailer the hoboes told stories, keeping alive another American tradition. Meanwhile, a pair of motor homes slowly cruised the perimeter of the jungle. The windows were up, but faces peered intently out, steaming up the glass. I noticed a boy through one window. Somehow, he reminded me of myself. Suddenly he raised his hand, pointing excitedly to the knot of hoboes he had spotted in the shade: "Hey, hey, look!" I could see him say. "There they are! There's the hoboes!"

My college professors, too, had been excited by hoboes, but in the wrong way. "Why, you could lose your legs," my advisor pointed out, adding that sadism by railroad detectives, bulls, was not unheard of, that many tramps were criminals, and that the activity was, after all, illegal. All considered, my college thought the project was not the kind of research an anthropology undergraduate "ought properly to be engaged in." Still, I thought I could learn much more on the rails than back in the library—and maybe, too, I would discover things no one in college knew anything about. Credit was an impossibility, which meant I would have to take more time off, but in a way that was for the best. If I were to enter the world of hoboes thoroughly, college would have to be the last thing on my mind.

My summer job finished, I drove in August to my aunt and uncle's house in New Jersey. Buying used clothing was my first priority for the impending trip. I'd frequented charity stores before, in search of cool vintage clothing, but this felt different. When the cashier sorted through the old slacks, flannel shirt, belt, and overcoat I had chosen, my eyes fell to the floor. A healthy young man must have set his standards pretty low to do his shopping here, I imagined her thinking.

She studied me briefly. "Five dollars," she announced. I dug a crinkled five out of my pocket, she stuffed the clothes into a paper sack, and I fled out the door. Pretty expensive, I was thinking: she must have seen through me.

Back at my aunt and uncle's, I tried everything on again. When I looked in the mirror I realized that even in Dallas, I had never looked this bad. Blue jeans, sneakers, T-shirt and a decent belt—my workday clothing there—was worlds away from this ill-fitting, grossly colored, out-of-style garb. One pair of slacks was flared and pleated; the other, which I now noticed were old Cub Scout pants, were about three inches too short, even when I pulled the stitching out of the hem. The overcoat had holes in the under-arms and a stain on the front. I wondered if it all was washed. What struck me most, in front of that mirror, was the way the crummy clothes affected not only my appearance but my state of mind. In them I felt downright seedy. The idea that "clothes make the man" had always struck me as silly and superficial, but now I saw there was something to it.

Next I bought one hundred dollars' worth of traveler's checks, for emergencies, and contemplated the irony of taking them on a trip like mine. Finally I assembled a crude bedroll: two blankets rolled up tightly into a bundle and then bound with rope, a leftover loop of which could be slung over my shoulder. Notebooks, eating utensils, and a small pan fit into my canvas army-surplus shoulder bag. The traveler's checks fit in my hip pocket. A plastic gallon jug of water, such as I had seen hoboes use in photographs, rounded out my gear.

Still, I thought, taking one last look in the mirror, I didn't look much like a hobo. My beard, struggling to make its presence known for over a week now, was light and uneven. A baseball cap only partly hid the symmetry of my latest haircut. My speech, certainly, would need adjusting; I looked at my orthodontist-straightened teeth and half-wished a couple were missing. I heard the words of a friend at work, wondering if I would have anything at all in common with the men who rode the rails. "I don't think people are as differ-ent as you suppose," I had answered. I repeated the words quietly to myself, to calm the butterflies in my stomach. Believing in that was the important thing.

My excitement and unease made it hard to eat supper that

night; I knew it was time to leave. Anticipating a restless night, I told my aunt and uncle good-bye when they went up to bed. Then I sat down with a map of the United States. Railroad hoboes, it seemed, were a western phenomenon; hitchhiking would be my means of getting west, and my transition to the rails. I was up when it was still dark, and dawn's light saw me walking down the highway, one arm outstretched in the hitchhiker semaphore and the other holding a sign that read ST. LOUIS.

3

Lightning flashed and was reflected in the Missouri River as the train ran along beside it. I had left the window of the caboose as darkness fell and rain began to splatter in. I tried to keep a match lit long enough to take a closer look at my accommodations, and was slightly horrified to see that, except for a few crossbeams, the floor consisted of rows of upward-pointing nails, like a huge fakir's bed. Given the sometimes violent back-and-forth jostling of the car, I was lucky I hadn't stepped on any. Gingerly I made my way over the nails back to the doorway, pulled in my wet gear, and tried to figure out how to lie down. By spreading out on the floor my blanket, overcoat, and some cardboard I had found, I came up with insulation nearly equal to the height of the nails. Little nail points protruded slightly from the mass but I was able, carefully, to lie down. Lightning flashed again through the window and lit up the car. Thunder must be following it, I thought, but the noise of the car being pulled over the tracks was like thunder itself, and if there was any outside, I couldn't hear it.

I dozed fitfully, fearful that every time the train slowed it was because a report of my presence had finally caught up with the authorities. Flashes of lightning I imagined to be the flashlight beams of cops, or of a tramp who had been hiding in the next caboose down the train, and was sneaking over to knock me on the head and steal my traveler's checks. Then it occurred to me that the big steel box I was riding in was probably a prime target for lightning. If the cops and tramps didn't get me, nature would! How I slept soundly enough for what happened next, I'll never know.

I remember feeling the train stop. This had happened a couple of times already, and I assumed the train had again pulled off onto what hoboes would later tell me was a "hole"—a short siding where one train waited while another, usually traveling the opposite direction, shot past. But this time I heard a monstrous *whoooosh,* the sound of a lot of highly pressurized air being released at once from both ends of the car. In my slumber it sounded vaguely and disturbingly familiar, but I was too tired to get up and see what was happening. Only later would I connect the noise with my first, abortive train ride in St. Louis, and remember it was the sound of the locomotive disconnecting itself from the train. That night, though, the thought that my poor little caboose was being abandoned never crossed my mind.

It was still dark when I finally awoke. The rain had stopped and the train had, too. I stuck my head out of the window: the "train," now only three steel cabooses long, was parked in some train yard! I tiptoed to the other window, and in my lingering daze saw a great illuminated dome that looked for all the world like the Taj Mahal. Dislocated and disappointed, I sat gently back down on my blankets. I had absolutely no idea of where I was. It was the middle of the night. The yard was silent: no trains would be leaving anytime soon. Dark railroad yards are not the place for tired, inexperienced trespassers, and I decided to get out.

A small-sized town, dominated entirely by the huge white dome, spread out from one side of the yard. I climbed stealthily from the caboose, crossed a wooden rail fence, and started up the street. Immediately on my right was a classy old three-story clapboard building in the process of being renovated. Three balconies, accessible by staircase, looked out over the yards. No lights were on, and since it was the weekend, I felt sure no workmen would be around when dawn arrived. I climbed to the third balcony, untied my bedroll, and fell asleep.

In the morning, hungry and with a growing curiosity about where I was, I walked into town. Daylight made it clear, within a few blocks, that the mystery dome formed the top of a state capitol building, but shed no light at all on the name of the state. The streets were crowded with churchgoers, and many of them gave me—rumpled, unshaven, and sawdusty—a wide berth. One man, though, returned my "good morning!" with a decorous tip of the hat. I decided to break the big, embarrassing question.

"Um, excuse me, sir, but could you tell me what town this is?"

He gave me an odd look, and said, "Why, sure, it's Jefferson City."

I mustered all my courage. "J-Jefferson City, where?" I sputtered. He narrowed his eyes, perhaps trying to assess whether I was from this planet or on drugs.

"Missoura. Jeff City, Missoura. The *capital.*"

"Ooh, hey, thanks a lot!" He walked hurriedly away. I realized then I was going to have to learn a lot of geography before I could profess to be any good at this. My respect for hoboes, who would have either known the town or how to take the situation in stride, jumped a notch.

My next stop was a grocery store. In the checkout line, a caption on the cover of a women's magazine caught my eye: "Expert's Advice to Hay Fever Sufferers." Since I had been suffering lately, I leafed through the article. "Scientists agree that plants release most of their pollen between sunrise and nine A.M.," summed up the expert. "Hay fever sufferers should make a point of staying inside during these hours."

I laughed under my breath, realizing the impossibility of doing that. Soon, I suspected, as a hobo, few magazines would have anything to say to me.

I headed for the gracious lawns of the capitol and sat down to enjoy my brunch. Almost immediately, I felt out of place. The occupants of passing cars stared at me as I leaned back on my bedroll in the sun. Passing policemen looked hard too, but miraculously left me alone. On a bicycle ride I had taken across the country, my friend and I had made use of the parks in almost every town we rode through, for sleeping as well as for eating. If passersby gawked, it was usually just a prelude to coming over and asking us where we were headed and how far we had come. My answers to such questions would have been much more interesting that morning, but nobody stopped to ask.

The absence of a bike, of course, had much to do with that. A bike with packs told people that your grubbiness was temporary, that you were traveling for recreation and had a plan. That was all right. People admired your adventuresome spirit.

Hoboes too had plans, I would soon discover, but often not the means of achieving them. That made everything different. That made hoboes professional wanderers, and the legal term for wanderer is "vagrant." But what is vagrant, I thought that day, other than being poor, in a public place, with no immediate plans? Do the same thing at home and it's simply "laziness."

The difficulty of living in public places is compounded by the need to go to the bathroom. It can be done in the restrooms of restaurants or public buildings on business days—but on a Sunday? I was many blocks from the yards, and, to make things worse, in a nice section of town. There were no woods, no dark alleys— nothing. As my discomfort increased. I recalled having been in the fashionable Georgetown district of Washington, D.C., that summer. I was walking down the sidewalk with a date when out of the corner of my eye I spied an old man, pants around his knees, crouching near the emergency exit of a fancy hotel. How disgusting! I thought.

Today I felt differently. Sure, public restrooms were unappealing—but some people really needed them. For blocks I walked in mild agony, my retention bolstered by the mortifying thought of being seen performing this necessary function. Finally I noticed a bridge over a creek that passed through the neighborhood. I hightailed it to streamside and, in the gloom, found relief.

I languished for much of the rest of the day back on the balcony, vagrant but out of sight. Jefferson City was not a big train town, and the two trains that did pass through stopped only momentarily, not long enough for a beginner to find a place to ride.

The next morning I awoke before dawn to a clamor in the yard below. A switch engine was shunting cars onto a newly arrived train, stopped in the middle of the yards. It was Monday, and within a few hours, I knew, workmen would likely return to the building and discover me. Hastily I rolled up my bedroll and slipped down the balcony stairs and into the yard. I was grateful for the darkness, which provided good cover for a furtive railrider.

But where could I ride? There were no empty boxcars. I felt I *had* to get out on this train, and so began considering other possibilities. The flat cars might work, though they were awfully exposed to wind and the sight of authorities. Most of the other cars were oversized automobile carriers, three levels high. I had heard stories of men riding these, but it seemed impossible: small gaps in the metal sheeting that formed the sides afforded a glimpse of the automobiles, but were way too small to squeeze through; and the ends, through which the cars were loaded and unloaded, had locked doors.

Or did they? In the dimness I gave them a second, careful look. The first two levels were definitely sealed, but there appeared to be just enough room to climb in the third. A narrow ladder led up the side of the car to the lofty roof. Draping my gear over my shoulders and making one last check for observers, I climbed it. The train would be leaving any moment now. I peered in the top opening; except for glints off the polished finishes of the new sedans, it was dark. Keeping hold of the ladder with first one hand and then the other, I removed my gear and tossed it in. I followed; the train designers apparently hadn't counted on agile hoboes.

My eyes grew accustomed to the dark, and I looked at the cars, fresher than those in a dealer's showroom. Price stickers were in the side windows, and plastic covers lay across the velour seats. What comfort! But the doors were locked, and entering such a car would probably be a good way for a hobo to find himself in jail.

The train began rolling almost immediately. I looked out the door as the end of the railroad yards and the outskirts of Jefferson City rolled by. It was a wonderful vantage point—like riding in the high cab of a truck or a bus, but better. For a while, anyway. As the train picked up speed, air began whistling through the opening above the door at the front end of the railroad car, like a wind tunnel. I unrolled my bedroll on the narrow strip of floor next to a car, and lay down.

The cars, their axles chained to the floor, began shaking up and down and side to side. With my head only inches away, the racket was deafening. I chewed up pieces of paper and stuffed them in my ears, but they dried up and fell out. I got up, shivering. This would never do. It seemed all the worse because comfort—the interiors of the new cars—was so near. In a surprisingly short length of time, a criminal was born. Adjusting my balance to the sway of the train, I made my way slowly around several of the cars. The keys must be here somewhere, I thought—it would be a lot of trouble to ship them separately. I checked the wheel wells, under the hood, behind the grille, behind the rear license plate frame, where the gas cap was . . . aha! There they were, wired together and taped to the frame. Elated, I tried them in the driver's door. Success! I dusted myself off and climbed in.

The violent, bouncy ride wasn't exactly the one advertised in magazines. But the car was quiet, and the FM stereo *did* work. I drifted off.

The next thing I knew, the train was backing up again, and outside it was light. Waking upon a change in the train's direction was becoming a reflex for me, and I was glad of it, because a backing-up train always seemed to mean trouble. This time was no exception. Looking out the car carrier door I saw, to my chagrin, that the car carrier was being backed slowly into a huge fenced-in lot filled with new automobiles . . . probably a distributorship. I glanced at the ground, thirty feet below, and noticed a brakeman hanging on the ladder of the car carrier.

"Hey, are you setting this one off?" I shouted down, startling him. It was a phrase I had learned that summer, while reading an old hobo book. He nodded, staring back up at me as I began my exit.

The train's jolts and starts made for a risky descent. I jettisoned my gear just as the car entered the fenced-off area. Dropping off, I recovered it, ran back out of the lot, and watched from a distance as the car carriers were set off. Not recalling any other kind of rideable car on the train, I pretty much gave up hope of reboarding. I had started off on foot down the tracks when the train, minus the car carriers, overtook me.

I moved off the tracks and waved at the engineer as he chugged by. Then I paused to examine the whole train in the daylight. There were tank cars, closed boxcars, grain cars, flat cars, all in a variety of dirty oranges, reds, yellows, greens, and browns, with the logos of what seemed a hundred different lines and companies: Burlington Northern, Lackawanna & Pacific, N & W (Norfolk & Western), Cargill, ARCO, Cotton Belt, Railbox, Chessie System, Feather River Route. Following were the dismal-looking coal cars, solid black, with no logos and no tops . . . no tops. Wait a minute, I thought. Couldn't I? Yes, why not? I did a test run next to the train, to see if it was rolling slowly enough to board. It was, at least for the moment. Would the engineer suspect? It was too early to get arrested yet—I hadn't even met any hoboes. But it was worth the risk. I fixed my gaze on one of the ladders and jumped.

I was up in a flash. The car was loaded nearly to the brim with coal, but I dug myself out a little hole and settled in for a cool, early-morning ride. Near-panic struck when the vibrating of the car caused my hole to cave in, burying my lower body. I decided to brave it on top of the coal pile, and rode gallantly into Kansas City, Missouri, hair blowing in the wind.

The Missouri Pacific yard was bleak. Trains stretched, row after row, for as far as I could see; there was no visible vegetation; and the control tower was very prominent. Uneasy, and also discouraged by not having seen hoboes on the "MoPac," I decided to switch to a larger railroad, one rumored to be more heavily traveled by hoboes, the Burlington Northern.

Unfortunately, the "BN" yards were in the other Kansas City—in Kansas, across the Missouri River. It took me an hour to arrive there by thumb—not bad time for city hitchhiking, especially considering that I looked as though I had just climbed out of a coal car. In my search for a good place to "catch out," I was able to scout most of the BN yard's outlying areas for stray hoboes. To my disappointment I found none, and few traces of where any might have been. Frustration mounted as I missed first one train—it seemed to be rolling too fast; then a second—I couldn't decide where to ride; and finally a third—there were brakemen in the vicinity, and I was afraid of getting caught. I was learning each time I was thwarted, but that afternoon the thought offered little comfort.

Impatience was a bigger problem. Only when I sat down in a small field in a huff, fuming over the inefficiency of the mode of travel I had chosen, did I realize that impatience, too, was a product of my inexperience. I was in a hurry to meet some hoboes, and in a hurry to learn how to ride the rails like a pro. But the rails were not meant for people in a hurry. My summer had been a time of appointments, prearranged meetings, bus and plane schedules, and telephone calls, all efficiently squeezed into as little time as possible. Time was money, and idle moments were wasted moments. On the rails, though, that was not the point. Here one was not a productive unit—hardly a part of the economy at all, in fact—and life was more attuned to watching, thinking, and talking.

Making the transition reminded me of some of my earliest bicycle tours. In the heat of the summer, my friends Ross, Lane, and I would pedal up into the mountains from Denver for overnight or weeklong trips. The climb up some of the steeper grades—over Loveland Pass and the Continental Divide, for example, an extended seven-percent grade—required much more than physical strength.

I didn't learn this until partway up one such climb. I had always been a faster hill climber than my friends—but also, I had noticed, a more tired cyclist at the top. Heat radiated off the blacktop on this day, even at nine or ten thousand feet, and the only wind was created by us as we moved through the swelter. Worse, a small company of the huge, stinging flies that plague unfortunate areas of the Rockies during the warm months had begun to circle me. They buzzed loudly past my ears and would occasionally land on my bike or me, though often I wouldn't know until I felt the bite. I started periodically slapping my back, just in case one might have landed. The siege continued, and in the burning sun I became panicky and feverish. I couldn't wait for the climb up the hill to end.

I started riding too fast. Obsessed with getting to the top, I began pumping more and more quickly. I didn't notice that I had left most of the flies behind. Soon sweat was pouring from my body. My heart and head pounded, and I couldn't see very well. Balance began to elude me for tiny instants, and I would swerve off my careful path onto the road's shoulder. I stopped thinking about anything other than finish, finish . . .

Suddenly Ross was at my side. Sensing something wrong, he had executed a very conscious, careful burst of speed and made his way slowly up behind me.

"Ted, *slow down!*" he breathed. "What are you doing? You're going to kill yourself."

In my delirium I dimly suspected he was simply trying to keep me from beating him to the top. But Ross repeated his warning.

Slowing down required all the willpower I could muster. Somehow, it had become more difficult even than pedaling up the hill. Finally, exhausted, I reined myself in. I dropped behind Ross, but regained my sight and balance and steadiness. The important race, I later realized, was with myself.

Here on the rails, it seemed that dispensing with the poison-ous hurry habit was the key to embracing a new way of life. Anx-iousness over too few hoboes or infrequent trains would make me nothing but unhappy. I resigned myself to living more slowly, lay back in the grass, and closed my eyes.

The whistle and rumble of another outbound train snapped

me from my meditation. I looked up to see a long string of empties, just the thing for me, rolling by my small field on the westbound track.

Shouldering my gear I approached it, chose the car I would try to board, and began to run. As the doorway drew even with me, I began to toss my bedroll in, but reeled back sharply: *there was somebody in there!* The figure of a man standing a few feet back from the open doorway passed in an instant, and I stopped my spring, incredulous. I stared at the car as it disappeared up the line. Had he seen me, and would he look out the door?

A head, small now in the distance, peered out from around the boxcar doorframe, then retreated. I turned, chose another target, broke into a run, then heaved my gear and my body into the doorway as it drew alongside. Torso across the boxcar floor, I kicked my legs up over the edge and rolled in. I was on a hobo train. There *were* still hoboes. The rivers and fields flashed by, and I stood a few feet back from the doorway, watching.

4

The sun had fallen to the point where its hot rays streamed directly through the boxcar doorway, coaxing me from the shade, when the train rolled slowly into a long, dusty yard and squealed to a stop. *Whooooosh*—I heard the noise that means the same thing to hoboes as the flight attendant's "We have arrived at the gate . . ." I dropped out the doorway into the hot Indian-summer afternoon. Moments later, the man I had seen a few hours before did the same. I nodded in his direction, and presently he lifted a hand and waved at me. Slowly, casually, we approached each other. Then I committed my first faux pas: I offered my hand.

He looked at it strangely; his right arm seemed to twitch, but did not immediately rise. "How you doin'?" we kind of said at the same time, and I did not drop my hand soon enough. Awkwardly, he lifted his and quickly we shook. Handshaking, I would learn after reflexively repeating my mistake two or three times with other hoboes, was a foreign mannerism here.

The man followed it by asking where I was headed.

"Oh, Lincoln, I guess," I replied.

"Yeah, I been thinkin' 'bout that too," he said, beginning to walk up the track. I fell into step with him. "Ain't nothin' goin' on here, y'know." Along with no handshake, I noticed, the man had not introduced himself. I held back on offering my name and glanced over at him as we walked.

He was wearing shiny black patent-leather shoes with no socks, dirty slacks, a buttondown short-sleeve shirt, and a soiled brown cap. He carried a water jug and a paper bag, which later I would learn contained some extra clothing. He was black and probably in his forties but looked younger. Very talkative, he was soon telling me how he had been surprised to see me catch the train "on the fly," as he put it, since "most guys just go into the yard, and climb on before it starts moving," as he had done in Kansas City. He stooped over to pick up a partly smoked cigarette someone had discarded.

"But don't they ever catch you?"

"Well, it all depends," he said. "Some lines are hot, like that Santa Fe, Union Pacific, Missouri Pacific—you don't see many tramps at all on them. Then you got the Burlington. They got—what do you call it—a humane attitude. Long as you stay sober, don't start no fires, don't get drunk, you can stay outa trouble on the Burlington."

Ah, so that's it, I thought: the reason why five days of railroading had yielded so few hoboes.

Our present location, he informed me, was St. Joseph, Missouri, on the far west side of the state. He had been here many times before; hoboes, he explained, pretty much had the run of this yard. The statement was borne out by people we met as we reached a road and began to cross the yard.

"Evenin', gents," said a conductor with an overnight bag waiting for his caboose. When my companion asked a brakeman where we could get water, he indicated we were welcome to go into the railroad workers' locker room and fill up at the sink.

Then I saw the hoboes. The first were a pair of old men, bearing their gear and walking slowly down one edge of the yard to a train that I had the momentary illusion was waiting for them. The next were an odd threesome—a gawky-looking guy about my age with a backpack and a belt buckle in the form of a marijuana leaf; a meek-looking, balding, dusty middle-aged man; and a fierce, explosive-seeming tramp with a deeply creased face, who confronted us as we neared the side of the yard.

"Hey!" he demanded of me. "Where's the Sally?"

"Who?" I asked, puzzled.

"Awww, shit." He nearly expectorated, disgusted that I didn't know what he was talking about, and too impatient to explain. But my companion understood.

"You find it about three miles up the tracks," he said. "Turn left when you see the stoplights."

"Three miles!" the old man snarled. "No way!" Turning to his companions, he said, "C'mon, let's go. These guys don't know what they're talkin' about." The young one objected, and nearly had his head taken off by the gruff old man. "You're either with me or you're not," he growled, striding off along the tracks. Reluctantly, the other two fell into file behind him.

On the side of the yard nearer St. Joseph, the man and I found a grass patch to rest in and enjoy the end of the day. A "Sally," he explained to me, was tramp talk for a Salvation Army facility, just as "Willy" was a Goodwill Store, and "St. Vinnie's" was St. Vincent de Paul, a Catholic charity organization. Just before the sun set, I suggested that we walk into town to get groceries. He had some food stamps, he had confided, and I had a small amount of change in my pocket.

But he demurred, "Folks like me ain't welcome in this town till after dark," he said. He was probably referring to his black skin, but he may have meant his poor, train-dirtied clothing and the gear he carried, which identified him as a tramp.

"What about folks like me?" I asked.

The man shrugged. "You can try."

I headed up the sleepy, poor back streets in search of a grocery store. Finally I came upon one and, leaving my stuff outside, I bought milk, cheese, bread, sandwich meat, and a candy bar. Starving after the long train ride, I walked directly to a street corner and took a seat on my bedroll. I wasted no time in guzzling the quart of milk and making several sandwiches. I was so involved in eating that I barely noticed a dirty white pickup truck that slowed down as it turned my corner, and then parked just a few yards away.

The truck door opened. I nearly choked in mid-swallow when I looked up to see a huge overweight man lumber out of the driver's seat and plod toward me. Through the window of the cab, a puffy-faced woman I guessed was his wife was staring at me. The man's boots were heavy and his neck, exposed by a military-type haircut, was red.

Oh, no, I thought to myself as nausea swept over me. My first attack.

The man was walking directly toward me. I glanced again at the pickup. Fortunately, it had no rifle rack. There was a magnetic sign on the door. SAL BRODER, it said, ST. JOSEPH, MISSOURI. I would need that for the police report.

Sal Broder stopped just a few feet away. "Boy," he started, and I thought, here it comes. I noticed he had no teeth. "Boy, I know it ain't none of my business, but I just wanted to know how you're doin'. You broke?"

His words and tone were friendly—was it a ruse? Though I was still suspicious, a small wave of relief swept over me. I answered that I was on the road but no, I wasn't broke.

Sal Broder continued with a number of questions, interrupting himself to explain that he had left his teeth in the truck. "Are you sleeping on the ground?" he asked. "In jails? Did you run away from your parents? Where are you from?" Supposing in turn that I was not dangerous, Sal Broder sat down next to me on the curb. "Are you headed home?" I answered him as truthfully as possible without letting on about the hobo project, but he didn't really seem too concerned with the answers. He just wanted to express his concern.

"You know, I was a cop here when I was younger," he said. "Met a lot of young guys like you. Even took some home with me. Wife and I helped 'em get a fresh start. So when I saw you settin' there, you know what I said to her? I said, 'Honey, I'm going to give that boy a dollar.' " This Sal Broder proceeded to do, taking out his wallet and trying to put the dollar in my hand. But I resisted, insisting that I was not broke and that, though it was very kind of him to offer to help me out, I really was doing okay—and I showed him the food I just bought.

"Nonsense!" said Sal loudly, forcing the bill into my bedroll. "By the way, you ever been in trouble with the police?"

"No, never have."

"Well, keep it that way. If a policeman comes up to ya, tell him he's barkin' up the wrong tree."

A dollar poorer, Sal Broder then got back into his truck, said something to Mrs. Broder, and drove away. As what had happened became clear, I was filled with multiple emotions: incredulity, gratitude, shame for having suspected him, and a secret satisfaction that my mere appearance had prompted his generosity.

I returned to the yard and shared what was left of the food with my companion. Though I didn't smoke, I had picked up some cigarettes as well; the tramp put down the butt he was preparing to recycle when he saw them, and immediately smoked three with great relish. I smoked one, too—the first of too many—to be good company. We retired to a trackside shanty and sat on a wooden bench in the dimming light. I introduced myself, and he told me his name: Lonny. It had been a long time since he had had a good listener, it seemed, for he talked and talked. Since we were still nearly strangers, sizing each other up, talk was limited to simple matters.

"Man, ain't nothing can beat fried chicken when your ribs start showin'," he said. His last good meal had been outside a Kentucky Fried Chicken restaurant in Fort Worth, Texas, a week before.

"A big meal there must cost a lot," I ventured, doing my best to see things from the hobo point of view.

"No, man—I don't *pay* for it," said Lonny, explaining what

must have been to him a very obvious point. "What you do is wait till closin' time, then hit that dumpster out back—or just ask one of the peoples that works there. Every night they throw away all that chicken! Waste it, 'cause it's cooked and it won't be fresh anymore. Corn on the cob, mashed potatoes, gravy, rolls, too—mmmmm. Well, I don't let that chicken go to waste—I put it in my belly!"

The thought revolted me. My whole life I had been taught that what goes into the trash stays there. But then I gave him a hard look—he was bright-eyed, energetic if not actually robust, apparently in good health—and I thought: maybe it can be done.

Lonny traveled constantly, almost always on the rails. Hitchhiking, he acknowledged, was sometimes faster, but he avoided it because of "too many weirdos," especially in New York and California. His railriding often took him in a loop from Reno, the home of his sons and estranged wife, down through California to Yuma, Arizona, then east to El Paso and Fort Worth, north to Kansas City and St. Joseph, Missouri, and back west through Denver and Salt Lake City to Reno—"circle jerk," I had heard this kind of tramp called in old hobo books. Yet despite his fondness for this territory, Lonny apparently traveled all over the country, for he talked of places in the East, the Midwest, and especially the South; Franklin Parish, Louisiana, was where he grew up. Though there are some hoboes on that side of the Mississippi, said Lonny, most stick to the West. "The East can be very bad, peoples can be very malicious. It's partly on account of peoples never seen hoboes, they don't understand about them," he explained. The severity of winter in the East and Midwest, as compared to the West Coast or Southwest, was another reason to stay west, according to Lonny.

Lonny had traveled outside the United States as well—in our country's name, to Vietnam. He served there for several of the nine years he was a Marine. Lifting his shirt, he showed me a souvenir of his tour: a line of round scars slanting diagonally across his chest, from machine gun bullets. Having been just young enough to avoid the draft, I was fascinated by the man, in the manner of one hearing news about a calamity one has narrowly missed. But the otherwise loquacious Lonny, like many other Vietnam vets I had met, did not want to talk much about it. Sometimes, he said, remembering Vietnam made it hard for him to sleep. He was glad to leave. "Man, when you're killing women and children, it does something to your conscience. Blood does something to your conscience."

Soon after getting back from there—seven or eight years ago, I gathered—Lonny and his wife split up. Now, he said, his veteran's check went straight home to her and his two sons, and he had been riding the rails ever since.

Apparently, he almost never worked. A fellow could get along if he simply knew the cities and their free resources, according to Lonny—another good reason to avoid the East, where the resources were scarcer. West of Lincoln and Houston, he explained, the Sallies and the rescue missions were free. And the West had some other notable founts of charity: at the Mormon Bishop's Warehouse in Salt Lake City, said Lonny, a man could get a big sack full of groceries in return for an easy day's work, a sack so heavy, he explained, that "when I got back to the trainyard I was cryin', there was knots on my back! Them Mormons don't help black guys—or any poor guys—get a real start, but they sure are big on that charity!" The Tucson Indian Center was another good food source, and certain town governments—for example, Phoenix and St. Paul—had excellent reputations for offering assistance to those who were down and out. In receiving any kind of welfare, however, Lonny admitted that "the single man got it bad." That was because in many states the lion's share of benefits went to families, especially those with a female head of household. Back when he was living with his family, Lonny related, he would often leave the house for days at a time when the welfare caseworker was expected, since that would put his wife, the "sole provider," in a position to receive more benefits.

We heard locomotive engines approaching, and then through the window of the shanty saw three locomotives pass by, pulling a train very slowly. They stopped. Lonny and I went outside. The train was very long; the lead engine, about six cars up, illuminated the track ahead with a powerful headlamp. "He's gonna go pretty soon," said Lonny. "Let's find out where to."

"How do we do that?" I asked.

"Why, you ask somebody," said Lonny, again having to explain the obvious. We noticed a light swinging back and forth in the hand of someone walking along the train, just a few cars down. "There's a brakey," said Lonny. "You wait here."

I watched as Lonny approached the lone figure in the darkness. Still well away from him, I heard him call out, "Why, hello there! How you doin' this evenin'?" The brakey answered him in low tones. They traded some words and Lonny returned.

"It's called for Lincoln," he announced. "But oooo-eeee, it's cold out here, and I don't see any empties."

"So what do you think we should do?" I asked.

"We wait till he goes away," said Lonny, gesturing toward the passing brakeman.

When he was gone, Lonny said, "Follow me." We walked up alongside the tracks until we were even with the rearmost of the three engines. "Now," he instructed, "we wait."

I decided to trust in Lonny's experience. The brakeman, lantern swinging and bootsteps drowned out by the ubiquitous bass drone of the locomotives, walked by us in the gloom and ascended the stairs to the lead locomotive. Lonny's eyes, however, were on another trainman, this one crossing from one locomotive to the next, lingering in each cabin to check the controls, and occasionally checking under one of the many hoods of the huge machines. His mission completed, he returned to the lead cabin.

The timbre of the engine's whine changed—barely noticeably to me—and Lonny advised in a low voice, "Now, get ready."

Slowly, almost imperceptibly, the train began to move forward. From the spaces between train cars, where the couplings were, a series of bangs rang out from the front of the train to the back as the advancing engines took up the slack between cars.

They had the cumulative effect of a thunderclap. "Let's go," said Lonny tersely.

Gear under his arm and hunched over, Lonny ran toward the third engine. Close on his tracks, I momentarily faltered as I realized what he planned to do: board the engine. I had never heard of hoboes doing this, and had assumed it was so grave a trespass in the eyes of the railroads as to not be contemplated, much less committed. But Lonny was on the stairs, hand on the railing, pulling himself quickly up, and I found myself just steps behind. A tiny door at the top swung open to his touch, and we twisted in and closed it.

"Stay down," he commanded. We were in a sanctuary. The shutting of the door had sealed out most of the engine roar, and we were sheltered from the light rain beginning to fall. Lonny flipped a switch on a small wall heater, and the tiny room began to warm up. Around us were tiny, colored control lights, shining in civilized contrast to the brash spotlight-sized headbeam of the lead engine. Most were on the instrument panel in front of the engineer's seat, one of two upholstered swivel chairs. Thinking it silly to be sitting on the floor with luxury so close by, I rose to place myself in the other chair. But Lonny hissed at me to get back down.

"They'll see you through that window," he said, pointing to the filthy pane next to the seat, on the front side of the train. It seemed very unlikely that they could see through the windows of the intermediate locomotive, and I said as much, but Lonny was adamant.

We laid our gear over the warm floor. Using my bedroll as a pillow, I leaned back and tried to become at ease with my new surroundings. The train was moving quite fast now, but the speed was undetectable from the floor of the weighty, solid locomotive—we had to peer out the windows to tell. What a change from a boxcar! The cabin even had a small refrigerator with drinking water inside, and, down a short and narrow stairway, a tiny restroom.

Over a speaker attached to the control panel we could eavesdrop on radio conversations between the engineer, firemen, and brakemen in the lead engine, and the conductor and brakeman in the caboose. Listening to these, as well as talking with Lonny, I learned that hoboes and trainmen share a language of the rails, an argot peculiar to their railroad-centered lifestyle. The locomotive engines were "units"—we were on a train with three units. The caboose was a "crummy." Empty boxcars were "empties," and refrigerated boxcars were "reefers." Occasionally the train would pull off the "main line" onto a siding—or "hole"—in order to let pass trains going the opposite direction, or express trains ("hotshots") going the same way, such as ones carrying mail, or sleek, shiny, whistle-fast Amtrak passenger trains. Our train, I learned, had been "called for" seven that evening—in other words, the train crew had been instructed to be prepared to leave by that hour. Like most trains, however, its departure had been delayed by mechanical and logistical problems, and its actual departure was after ten P.M.

I asked Lonny what would happen if we got caught. "Well, sometimes they mind," he said. "But sometimes they don't. And it sure is cold out there tonight, and hell if I'm gonna ride a boxcar with these clothes and no bedroll!" And that settled it. Necessity seemed the mother of hobo daring.

Less nervous about me than I certainly was about him, Lonny soon fell into a deep slumber. He seems friendly and all, I thought, but can he be trusted? Now that I had revealed to him how new I was to the rails, would he take advantage of a sleeping greenhorn? Fatigue finally overcame suspicion and I dozed off.

5

Workboots and dungarees greeted my sleepy, floor-level eyes. I followed the legs up to the body and face of a trainman standing in the morning light, looking over us supine hoboes. I stiffened and waited for a swift kick, but that was the last thing on his mind.

"Fellers, we're about ten miles outa Lincoln. The crew's gonna take a sec and get ourselves some breakfast," he told us. "We'll be back in 'bout an hour." He checked some dials and walked out, closing the door behind him.

"Shit," said Lonny.

"What's wrong?" I asked, surprised by his seeming ingratitude.

"We ain't gonna make breakfast at the mission," he said. "We'll get in too late."

"What mission?" I asked. "When's breakfast?"

"That one in Lincoln—Lincoln Rescue Mission. 'Jesus Saves.' And man—it's good! They got sausage and eggs, orange juice, coffee, toast, jam. . . . Breakfast's at seven." He looked out the window. "It must be at least six-thirty."

How does he know all that? I asked myself. Then I remembered that Lincoln was on his circuit, and that, being without a watch, he probably was adept at estimating the time by looking at the sky.

We stepped off the engine as it slowed to enter the yards in

Lincoln and walked the gray, weary way into town. Here and there we saw hoboes still asleep in the grass, or under a bridge. Lonny expressed shock as we came upon a bare field on the edge of the factory-warehouse area, with charred brush pushed into several piles, as though by bulldozers. "This was the jungle!" he cried. "Look what they done!"

Apparently the city fathers of Lincoln had decided a vacant lot suited the town better than one full of shrubs and hoboes, and so they had cleared it. According to Lonny, the trees were still standing and the hoboes still jungling up when he had passed through a month earlier. We walked on.

"Well, good thing this is still here," he said as we approached a huge shade tree abutting a factory. It was so overgrown that its outermost branches touched the ground, creating a dark, doughnut-shaped room around the tree's thick trunk. "Here's where we can eat."

"Eat what?" I asked wryly.

"Well, let's find out," he said, never daunted.

After taking a quick look around for observers and then stashing our gear under the tree's fallen branches, Lonny and I set off into the industrial district. He evidently had been here before, for he wound his way purposefully through the parking lots and wide streets, still empty at this early hour, until we arrived at a long string of loading docks behind a large factory. Two large dumpsters on wheels stood near a door at the end. After giving a quick and furtive look around, Lonny handed me his overcoat, lifted the lid of one dumpster, and climbed in. Before I knew it I was being handed an onion, some apples, and a plastic bag partially full of old potatoes. Out of the dumpster hopped Lonny and into the other one, where he found nothing. "Let's go," he said.

On our way back to the yards area, we inspected the haul. Aside from some scratches, the onion and apples looked about as good as any in a grocery store; the potatoes were a little more battered. "Too old to sell but good enough to eat," said Lonny, and that, evidently, was the plan.

As we neared the tree, I retrieved some old planks from a box-car on Lonny's instructions. Both of us kept our eyes open for a stewpot—a can large enough to hold our victuals—but the ones we saw had holes in the bottom or sides or unpalatable scum of one sort or another adhering to the inside. Clearly, a can expedition was needed. Two blocks away, at the Sealtest Dairy, the silver-tongued Lonny persuaded some loading dock workers to contribute a ten-gallon can to our cause, and even to fill it partway with water. Salt was the only ingredient missing, and that, said Lonny, was something I should get: "Them housewives gonna like you—young dude, personable, innocent face. Just smile at 'em."

It was an easy enough assignment. But it was also my begging debut, and I was amazed at how scared I was. Nobody did this anymore—walk up to a stranger's door and ask for food. I tried to relax. Salt really was a pretty insignificant request, I supposed, and after all, we were neighbors of the hobo tree. On the other side of the factory zone I found a block of modest houses. I chose the most modest, remembering an observation from one of Jack London's old hoboing books, *The Road:*

> The very poor constitute the last sure recourse of the hungry tramp. The very poor can always be depended upon. They never turn away the hungry. Time and again, all over the United States, have I been refused food by the big house on the hill; and always have I received food from the little shack down by the creek or marsh, with its broken windows stuffed with rags and its tired-faced mother broken with labor.

Give me a tired-faced mother!, I prayed, advancing up the crumbling sidewalk to the chosen house. Let there be no German shepherds! London always had a good hard-luck story ready for the skeptical homeowner, and I racked my brain for a credible story that would justify my need for salt. I was just in from the desert . . . for days I had sweated under the burning sun . . . my system was crying for salt. . . .

I rang the doorbell.

"Hi-I'm-just-in-and-am-broke-and-could-really-use-some-salt—"

A guy about my own age, with dirty hair halfway down his back, red eyes, and smelling of marijuana, smiled back at me. "Salt?" he mused. "Salt. Oh, yeah, sure, some salt. Just a sec."

In two minutes he had returned, a Baggie-ful of salt at the end of his outstretched arm. I took it and left. God, how easy.

Back at the tree-jungle, Lonny had started the water heating over a small fire, and was just getting out the potatoes.

"Say, you got a knife?" he asked. I did not, but Lonny, searching among the debris around the tree, came up with a tin can lid. Grasping the middle of each flat side firmly with his fingertips, he used the sharp edge as a knife, peeling, then slicing, potatoes and onions. I dumped the salt into the concoction.

The kettle of stew took a long while to warm up. When it had, we suddenly realized we had no way to eat it. Lonny scaveneged a "clean" can amid the trash, and handed me a styrofoam plate, the kind that meat is placed upon and then wrapped in cellophane at grocery stores. I scooped up a plateful of stew. Thinking back on the simplicity of its ingredients and the crude preparation, the stew doesn't sound very tasty at all—but that morning, in the cool of the hobo tree, enjoying the company of a friendly, professional urban camper and ravenous, it was delicious. We scraped the can clean.

It was a drizzly day, one fitting, I would learn, for a visit to the rescue mission. As he did the good dumpsters, Lonny knew exactly where it was, and we walked there, our pace a compromise between the fullness of our stomachs and the rain, which was beginning to fall heavily. The mission was announced by a large sign in the shape of a cross, projecting from the side of a building. Within the neon outline of the cross's horizontal bar was the word JESUS; proceeding downward from the middle "S" of JESUS to form the vertical bar was the word SAVES. Some men slightly older than me were hanging around outside the gate, smoking cigarettes and leaning against the wall. They were the kind of guys that, in my other life, I would have given a wide berth when passing on the sidewalk, and it took much determination to look them in the eye, give a nod of the head, and, when Lonny discovered the gate of the mission to be locked, assume my position on the sidewalk as though it were my customary place.

Lonny rang the doorbell. After a long delay an old man came to the gate and told us the mission was closed until the evening. Lonny explained that we were just in, that we hadn't slept in three days, and that we felt a need for the comfort of the Lord. The man cocked a suspicious eyebrow, but eventually produced his keys, turned them in the lock, and said, "Well, come on in." He reminded me of the gatekeeper to the Emerald City, who welcomed Dorothy and her friends after they had explained they were there to see the Wizard of Oz.

Several derelict men stared at us as we passed through a small courtyard leading to the indoors, and the inspection was slightly unnerving. Later I would learn that pairings of blacks and whites on the rails were often homosexual; perhaps that had been suspected of us. Inside, a mission staffer signed us up by writing our names and birthdates on cards, and recited the mission rules: three nights at the mission allowed per man per month, to be taken consecutively; attendance at the sermon required before eating dinner or receiving a bunk assignment; no swearing, no weapons, no coming in drunk. The Emerald City it was not. Lonny explained we were only in to clean up and have some lunch, and the man waved us in.

The atmosphere in the main living room was somber. Six or seven men, mostly old and white, were lounging around. Some read paperbacks and some stared blankly ahead. All of them, it seemed to me, were interested in watching us, though none in meeting my eyes. Just as we were leaving the room, an ancient black-and-white television in the corner flashed dimly on, apparently at the command of a switch in the office. It was TV hour.

We descended to a large washroom in the basement. In one of the mirrors above a row of sinks I caught my own eye. I stopped and stared. It had been a long time. The eyes looked a bit brighter blue (was it the dinginess of my surroundings and clothing?) than the last time I looked. But the change in the rest of my face was arresting: My beard was fuller and nearly half an inch in length; seeing it was much more striking than feeling its daily, incremental growth. My teeth, fuzzy and dull, needed brushing, as did my hair. It lay unwashed, flattened, and close to my scalp, changing the contour of my head. I thought of Sal Broder, the last non-hobo—myself included—to take a real look at me.

Lonnie received permission from the man cleaning up to take a shower. Filthy from riding the trains, I was going to join him, until I realized the showers were merely a corner of the room where the floor slanted down to provide a drain, and there was no shower curtain. I looked around me as Lonny stripped down and noticed four or five guys had arrived; they were seated on benches along the wall, watching the half-naked Lonny with interest. I went and sat in one of the bathroom stalls instead.

Finished, Lonny received a new set of recycled clothes from the bathroom man, and tossed out the old—shoes and everything. As we climbed the stairs he gave me a dime he had found and told me to go bum a few cigarettes for us. It was unlike Lonny to ask me to do something he could do himself, but I realized that, being young and white, I would probably get a warmer reception from cigarette owners than he would. The dime went to the first man I asked, who was sitting on a bench with what appeared to be a mission counselor. The counselor seemed deep in conversation, but the man looked anxious to start talking with me instead.

"Sure, buddy," he responded, with enthusiasm uncharacteristic of life in the mission. "Share 'em when you got 'em, that's what I say. Y'never know when a guy'll need to ask for one hisself." He looked piously at his benchmate, who gave a nod of approval.

Lunch, I hoped, would provide an occasion for some spirit of community, would get people talking to each other. But instead, the twenty men partaking ate almost silently. We were fed thin soup, bread, and sugar cookies. On each table sat a large bowl of old grapes. Everyone was solemn and silent, eyes down, reminding me of punished kids. An odd man across the table from me interrupted the silence to announce to me that the Cisco Kid, of Europe, had died. He then started mumbling to himself. Nobody looked. Dishes were cleared.

Lonny was anxious to get out, and so was I. "Those places do somethin' to guys," he said as we left. "If we were stayin' tonight, we'd have to go to the sermon—then you'd see what I'm talkin' about. Missions are like communism. They take their message and try and force it down on you."

He then asked why I didn't take a shower, and I told him. Also on my mind, I explained, was his story of the day before, relating how once, in prison for trespassing on railroad property, he had witnessed the gang rape of an inmate across the corridor from him. Nine men attacked the guy, said Lonny, and he had to have his rectum sewn up at a hospital. The screaming, he said, was awful; I confessed that echoes of it were in my ears in the washroom.

My fears were not misplaced, said Lonny. Many of the men in missions and on skid row had spent a lot of time in prison. Just the same, he said, I probably did the worst possible thing under the circumstances: act scared.

"What you can't do is fear it, 'cause when you do, certain guys gonna get the idea you feel like they want a piece of your ass. And when they know that, well, they're gonna try and get it.

"I learned one thing out here on the road," said Lonny, "and that is when you run from one thing you run into another thing. Don't you do that. If you weak they gonna take advantage of you—size ain't got nothin' to do with it. You gotta show spunk, gumption, show you's a man. Then they leave you alone.

" 'Course you gonna be scared some time. But don't you show it, don't run. Keep walkin', steady and slow, and you be okay."

We walked to the railroad yards. I was cautioned that these had a dangerous reputation: one tramp had murdered another here recently, and the railroad bull was very tough. Intensifying the "heat" were the fields just west of the yard, said Lonny—they were full of marijuana plants, and this was the best time of year to harvest them. A passing brakeman told us we wouldn't be able to catch out until late afternoon, and then confirmed Lonny's warning. "The bull's been pickin' up all kindsa guys," he said. "Watch out."

We kept low as we crossed over trains on our way to the side of the yard Lonny said was best for waiting. I had reason to doubt this judgment when finally we arrived, however: on one side of the dark wooden shack where Lonny indicated we could wait were spray-painted, in foot-high white letters, the words BUMS KEEP OUT!

"That don't mean us," Lonny reassured me, tongue-in-cheek. "We're tramps."

Despite the joke, I had heard there was a serious distinction, and I asked Lonny what it was.

"Well, you see, the tramp travels, and he works. You work sometimes, dontcha?" I nodded. "Well then, that's like us. Now the hobo, he travels, but he don't work. Just likes driftin'. The bum ain't gonna do nothin', work or travel—that bum don't do *shit!*"

This hierarchy, with the tramp preeminent, would be repeated to me by men down and out all over the West. Nearly all, though, even if they really fit the definition of "bum," claimed to be "tramps," and said it with pride. "Hobo" was usually an acceptable synonym of tramp, but not the term they preferred. Another term, "home guard," meant basically the same as bum, but was always used to refer disparagingly to down-and-out men who had settled in one place and generally acted like they owned it, competing with real tramps for the resources there and causing trouble. If gear was stolen, yards were hot, or the mission was full, the home guard were generally to blame. I researched the term later and found it had originated in World War I, when it referred to the men who stayed home, while others fought the war.

Anyway, we obviously weren't "bums," and the ignorance of whoever had painted the warning on the shack wall was, in Lonny's judgment, just another reason we should rest our feet there.

We reclined on crude wooden benches. The door, slightly ajar, allowed in a sliver of light, but otherwise the room was dark. Tired, I started to drift off, but Lonny wanted to talk. Realizing that it was a good opportunity to learn more about him, I forced myself awake and broached some questions that had been nagging me.

Most tramps were white men, I had noticed; most were older, and many came from the South and rural areas. I asked Lonny, "Ain't it tough to be a tramp and be black at the same time?"

"I don't like to look at things that way," he said. "I mind my own business and do my own thing."

"But don't some tramps give you shit because you're black?"

"Yeah, well . . . man, you always gonna find the assholes and the pricks, yeah, always, but don't you worry about that. You can't worry about it and keep your head straight. The Bible tells about a fool—if you can't talk with a fool, get away from him, or you find yourself as foolish as he is.

"Uptight bastards—you just don't let 'em get to you. It's all in how you manage your life." Lonny dealt with prejudice not through confrontation, it seemed, so much as through trying to ignore it.

But it was not a subject Lonny enjoyed talking about. Women, especially famous white women, were a subject closer to his heart. Jackie Kennedy, Marilyn Monroe, actress Angie Dickinson—he knew something about them all.

"That Jackie—she's somethin' else. She never shoulda done that to John—marry that Greek dude, ol' what's-his-name. I mean, I seen a lot of hoboes, but she takes the platter. That woman knows how to make money. Ten million dollars for a trick—goddamn, it musta been something special!

"Angie Dickinson—that woman looks gooo-oo-oo-d! Whoo. You seen her in that movie, what's it called—she's in that elevator, loses her clothes. Man. And Marilyn Monroe—oh, what they done to Marilyn. Made her so famous, made her so unhappy. Poor, poor woman.

"But you know? I been noticin' something. Women used to have big tits, you know what I mean? Like Marilyn. But nowadays, they don't have 'em anymore! Where'd all them big tits go, any-ways?"

He went on and on about women, filling his conversation with this half of the human race so absent from his life, even as he filled the shack with conversation that, alone, he could not have had.

Ever since I met him, I had also been wondering what animated Lonny's wanderings, what kept him on the perpetual cycle in which today's destination is tomorrow's point of departure. An economic explanation, I hypothesized, was that by keeping on the move, Lonny could best exploit the free resources available to him—missions, food stamps, other welfare, church handouts—and therefore avoid work. When he had used up his three nights at the mission or his monthly allotment of food stamps at a certain town, he would go on to the next one. But this raised the question of why he chose to avoid work in the first place. Laziness, many people would have said—weakness of character. But there seemed more to it than that. Along with a life free of work, Lonny had gotten one free of security, free of a wife and a place to go home to at night, free of respectability, free of personal safety, free of a future. His idleness came at quite a cost. Something more than laziness, I speculated, kept Lonny from working. Was it memories of the Vietnam War? Was it the experience of breaking up with his wife and having his family fall apart? Was it too much drinking, a result of the above two? I could only guess. Those certainly were not the reasons Lonny gave to explain his life on the road.

"Livin' this a-way broadens my mind," he explained. Other questions—about his home life, about his war experience—prompted only curt replies, but his reasons for riding the rails were almost a celebration: "I likes to be in different towns with the peoples, know what's goin' on. How do people live? There's all kinds—that's what makes that world spin, makes it somethin' else to live in!"

How do people live? That was one of my questions in making this trip, too.

He continued. "Learnin' the road is hard when you don't

know it. But being on the road teach you to take care of yourself. Learn to be strong and stand up on your own. It's a good experience, and you gotta benefit from it. I think a fool is a man who drifts and his mind is a waste.

"It's like an experiment: every time I try something different, learn something new."

Then Lonny asked about me. From the first, when I had been unable to answer the cranky tramp's questions about the location of the St. Joseph Sally, I had known I would never be able to give Lonny the impression I was a seasoned tramp. So I had decided to be honest: I had just started riding the rails, I told him, and had a lot to learn. I tried to make Lonny my teacher, and fortunately, he accepted the role. Today, he wanted to know a little bit more about the tramp-initiate.

"Where were you before you started trampin'?" he asked.

Before, I explained, I had been a student at college in the East. Tired of that life, I had been looking for a change. I had heard that there were still guys riding the rails, and they had always seemed pretty interesting to me, and so I decided to try it myself for a while.

"And how does it look to you now?" he asked.

"Not quite as romantic as I thought at first," I said.

Lonny laughed and laughed. "Young man," he said, "*this* will be your education! I want to hear what you think about it in a few months."

I offered him one of the last cigarettes, talk subsided, and I stepped outside to check on the train situation. The sun was setting as I found a brakeman, who indicated to me that the "hotshot" to Denver was now "made up" and would be leaving soon from Track 5. I counted five tracks over from the side of the yard and spotted our hotshot. We would have to climb over two trains to get to it.

The train was all piggybacks, long flat cars with two semi-truck trailers secured atop each one. Many carried mail, Lonny explained, which was why this was an express train. It would probably stop only twice between Lincoln and Denver—at Hastings and McCook, Nebraska. The speed was also a disadvantage, though, for as Lonny pointed out, piggybacks ("piggybanks," he pronounced them) offered the hobo little protection from the weather. The best place to sit, he showed me as we tossed our gear aboard and climbed the ladder at the end of the flat car, was on the leeward side of a trailer's large wheels, with your back against the wheels. That way, the wheels would block some of the wind, and the trailer itself would be a roof—albeit a leaky one—if it started to rain. "But it's a cold ride any way you approach it," warned Lonny. "Get out your jacket if you have one."

In fact, the wind began to blow before the train even started. The coolness prompted Lonny to tell me a story of building a "piggybank house" one night on a train from Oakland to Stockton, California. He had found four large pieces of cardboard and had wedged them among the trailer's four wheels and two axles, defying the wind. "That's what I call fun," he said.

He then told a tale of a less fun "piggybank" trip without a house, on a frigid fall night. He arrived in Lincoln with frostbitten feet—"they felt like ol' lumps a' wood on the end of my legs." At the veterans' hospital they were injected with a fluid that somehow saved them.

We heard the hiss of air from the units' compressors entering the brake system, a signal that soon the train would pull out. "Now as we leave this yard I want you to watch real careful," Lonny told me. "Look out in them fields, and I tell you you ain't never seen so much marijuana in your *life!*"

The great midwestern marijuana fields had always been something of a legend in my high school, but I had never had a chance to see one. The train started forward with a jolt. I looked out with anticipation as our car gathered speed, clearing the ends of other trains. At first the plants looked like corn, or just patches of tall weeds. Lonny shouted over the growing din of the quickly accelerating train: "Sometimes you see dudes out there pickin' it." He pointed to one such fellow, ducking furtively behind some shrubs with a gunnysack in hand. It was definitely marijuana, I realized. Amazing.

What happened next was almost too sudden to recall. The train had accelerated to easily twenty or twenty-five miles per hour, well beyond the speed at which I could ever have boarded it, when in the waning light I saw three large figures emerge from the tall plants on my side of the train. All three immediately heaved large white sacks onto our car, further toward the back. Then, to my amazement, they began running hard alongside the train, and one by one, they grabbed onto the edge of our flat car. Since the track was elevated through the field, these edges were at shoulder level, and as each man seized one, his body from the shoulders down was torn from the ground and swung toward the back of the car.

"My God, Lonny, look!" We watched transfixed as the frontmost two, dangling perhaps fifty feet away from us, swung their legs back and forth in order to get enough momentum to kick one over the edge and onto the flat car. With each swing, their legs went perilously far underneath the car and over the tracks, feet sometimes bouncing off the gravel. The men were scant inches from dismemberment. I looked for the third, but he was no longer visible; either he had fallen off or, what seemed very unlikely, he had been able to climb on immediately. What desperation would prompt someone to try a thing like this? The question kept me from scooting down the car and lending a hand.

Finally the front guy got a leg up and then pulled the rest of his body on. Exhausted, he lay for a while on the edge of the flat car. Then, still on his stomach, he recovered his duffel and started shimmying toward us, guerrilla-style. He was a black man, quite stocky, and as he approached I noticed that his eyes were very red. Lonny noticed it too, and leaned over toward me to ask "You got a knife?" I nodded, and put my hand into my trouser pocket. Lonny muttered something about getting off at the next stop. A flat car traveling forty miles an hour and gaining speed is no place to meet desperate men.

The man reached us. Very worried that he had been seen, he warned us to stay low as we passed through an upcoming highway crossing. We all crawled into the space between the two axles to minimize our visibility. There the man told us he had just gotten out of jail. Five days ago the railroad bull had had the train stopped, "Oh, 'bout right here," after he spotted the man and five others aboard. The train whizzed through the intersection he indicated. This evening, it seemed, we were safe. But I had not caught on yet: "So what were all you guys doin' on the train together?" The man, annoyed at my denseness, gestured toward his duffel bag. The top was not closed, and I could see its contents. Some was spilling out. It was marijuana.

We extracted ourselves from the cramped space between the wheels, returning to our seats against them. Soon the second man arrived at our wheels with his duffel. Equally powerful-looking, nervous and red-eyed, he was friendlier than his partner, whom he called Vernon. Vernon offered cigarettes to the other two, conspicuously omitting me. I felt it was because I was white—my skin color was a disadvantage. In this situation Vernon had no reason to be friendly to me: I was a tramp like him, not somebody whose goodwill he needed.

The train was now rolling faster than the cars on a nearby highway traveling the same direction, so I guessed our speed was over sixty miles per hour. The wind became very, very cold, and it seemed the men's cigarettes burned themselves up just moments after they were lit.

Vernon's friend (I never learned his name) produced a jar of raspberry jam from his coat pocket and passed it around. Like the others, I dug into it with my fingers, and eating seemed to warm me up. The two marijuana smugglers, now that I had taken a closer look at them, were not at all like the urban blacks I knew at high school; their manners seemed coarse and rural. They were dirty, their clothes were frayed and out-of-date, and their hair was bushy and untrimmed. "What happened to Leon?" the nameless one asked Vernon. Vernon shrugged. "Later we can check for his bag," was his only reply.

I imagined Leon lying by the side of the track twenty miles back in Lincoln. It was dark there, and cold, and nobody for miles around would know he was there.

The scenery became a blur. Seated at the edge of the flat car, inches away from oblivion, I became more uneasy. I imagined Leon, and then imagined myself; there were better ways to go than being tossed off a boxcar by dope smugglers. A glance at Lonny revealed he was at his garrulous best with the newcomers, trying hard to make friends with them. It was a good idea, but I had no clue how to proceed. Then I remembered a lecture I had attended at which the professor discussed the anthropological laws of reciprocity. The gist of the lecture was the piece of folk wisdom that went, "The gift makes beholden the receiver." I'll give the guys something, I thought; if they take it, they'll feel obliged to me. I opened my sack and took out the last of my bread and my remaining peanuts. They were devoured almost immediately. But the men defied anthropology, offering no thanks at all. My uneasiness increased.

Using as an excuse the fact that it was crowded with all four of us sitting against the tires, I took leave of the men, making my way up under the next trailer toward the front of the flat car. There, I knew, I would have plenty of room to myself and also a clear view of anyone who might choose to approach me from their direction. Being alone also meant I could remove my jacket from my pack. Neither Lonny nor the smugglers had one, and worse, I thought, than being the only white person would be to be the only white person with a jacket on.

The train and its wind stopped at Hastings, Nebraska, and Lonny and I jumped off. Unfortunately, we learned, there would be no more westbounds for several hours. Shivering and pooped, I laid out my bedroll in a small park near the tracks to get some rest; Lonny walked into town to find some food. He soon returned with his favorite: fried chicken, begged from the workers at a Jim Dandy. He shared some with me. The pieces were still warm.

Having no bedroll, Lonny preferred to rest in the shelter of a boxcar. He pointed to the one he'd be sleeping in, and we agreed to meet there when the train came.

Several hours later the train was in, and I was searching in the dark for Lonny. The boxcar he had indicated had been moved. Quickly I ran around the adjoining tracks, calling out his name. Time was short: the westbound train was on the main track which, as Lonny had explained, meant it was stopped only briefly, to change crews.

He's probably already on, I thought to myself. Most of the train's boxcars appeared to be near the caboose, so I jogged down fifty or sixty cars to take a look. Finally I found an open empty—but it did not contain my friend. My sprint back to the front of the train was cut short by a jolt and a boom, signs the train was moving. Knowing there might be no place ahead for me to ride, I returned to the empty I had just left and caught it on the fly.

An hour later the train pulled into a hole and I continued my search, walking it front to back, daring even to look in the units. It was with a heavy heart that I concluded the train had no other riders; Lonny was gone.

6

The boxcar on the freight from McCook, Nebraska, rocked from side to side as the train slowed and crossed a section of bad track on its arrival into Denver a day later. Brakes squealed and doors banged, every sound magnified by the huge echo chamber that is an empty boxcar. My fellow passenger had not spoken during most of the trip, which was okay since I probably couldn't have heard him anyway. But now, as we entered the yards, he started to talk.

"Goddamn coal trains," he muttered, surveying the ones we would have to climb over to make our way out of the yard. I stood in the open doorway of the boxcar, surveying the Denver night. "Hey—get back!" he hissed, pointing to the railroad control tower we were about to pass. "They'll put the dicks on us." I retreated to the darkness at the back of the car.

"They got a mission here?" I asked him, wondering where I would spend the night.

"Twenty-third and Lawrence," he said with little pleasure, "but it's too late to check in. You missed the sermon. Hell, you missed dinner too, but that's okay—all they serve is some goddamn beans somebody made fifty years ago up in Laramie.

"What I do—I sleep in one of them bad order [damaged] cars they got lined up on the U.P. [Union Pacific] tracks down there—they don't move 'em to the shop till morning."

I nodded, adding that I was unfamiliar with the routine in Denver.

"Oh, it's a good town for eatin'," he said. "You got the Sally at Twenty-first and Larimer at nine A.M., bologna sandwiches at the Holy Ghost Church at ten, dinner at the Catholic Worker at four. . . ." He went on. A Denver native, I had never heard of these places.

The train stopped with a jerk that nearly knocked us off our feet. I was cautioned to wait until they "broke the air," the signal that the locomotives had disconnected themselves and the train was going no farther. Finally the *whoosh* came. My companion signaled me to follow, and stealthily we climbed down from the box-car and wound our way over the coal trains and out of the yard, entering downtown just north of Union Station. Home looked disturbingly foreign from this angle.

"My name's Ted—" I started.

He kept walking. "Well, Ted, one thing you gotta know about Denver—if you got two pennies in your pocket, separate 'em. I'll prob'ly see you tomorrow," and he turned, bedroll over his shoulder, and vanished down Larimer Street, the heart of Denver's skid row.

I paused. I had been through parts of town like this before, most recently in St. Louis. Yes, they were dangerous, but my experience was that the danger was usually overstated by people from backgrounds like mine—people who only made occasional mistaken forays into them. The risk depended partly on who you were. If you looked like you belonged there, and not like a deacon from Dubuque on a guided tour, you could probably get by all right.

Still, Larimer Street was a place I had been warned against visiting since childhood. I had cruised it with high-school friends, in a car with doors locked and windows up, for the shock effect of seeing human beings in such a degraded state and for the thrill of being in a forbidden zone. Though I saw it more realistically now, an old, irrational fear lingered. Lonny would have scolded me for my first few steps down the street, all too tentative.

Though parking meters lined the curbs, the narrow street was nearly empty of cars. Low, dark brick buildings dating from early Denver pressed in on the sidewalk. Those storefronts that had not been boarded up contained pawnshops, bars, a dirty-magazine shop, a massage parlor, a rundown cafe. Almost all were closed at this early hour of the evening, and many advertised the fact with large metal gratings pulled down over the fronts, keeping thieves out of the display windows and winos from the doorways. I passed the rescue mission, with its neon cross, and also the Salvation Army. The doors of both were locked tight.

I looked for other people. I noticed some men slumped on couches in the dim lobby of the Gold Rush Hotel; walking by an alley, I heard voices and turned to see shadowy figures seated with bottles, and the occasional glow of a cigarette. Two guys shuffled past me on the sidewalk, asking for cigarettes that I didn't have. Several times I passed crumpled figures in doorways, curled up in trash that almost always included wine and beer bottles.

Headlight beams crept up the street from behind me, and I heard a slowly running engine. I looked back and a spotlight beam exploded into my face; squinting in the glare, I could just make out the markings of a police car. I stopped and waited for the cop to roll down his window and say something to me, but he didn't. Finally the light went off and he continued his cruise up the street.

It wasn't the homecoming I had expected. On the train I had been excited in anticipation of my return to Denver, a place where I thought I belonged. But now home was a different part of town, and in my hobo role, I was different from what I had ever been before in Denver.

For several days I had been debating whether to stop in and see my family. My parents, of course, knew about the hobo trip: ever since a friend and I completed a month-long bicycle tour of New England by ourselves at age 15, they had been good about letting me choose my own way. Yet this idea worried them more than most. Always they had tried to make sure I had enough money, good equipment, a set itinerary, and a way of being contacted before I set off. But the hobo trip didn't exactly fit that scheme. Instead, we came up with the idea of posting a map on the kitchen wall to trace my travels, and keeping a log near the phone to record my destinations and companions, if any, when I called. My three younger sisters were trained in the system and sounded excited about the trip. Still, I had been glad to leave from the East, and not from Denver: it spared us all the pain of departure.

Now, though, the family was only a bus ride away. The thought of our house became so comforting, so warm and secure. But my appearance and state of mind would make staying in our neighborhood awkward. Worse was the prospect of leaving: safe, loving home was, in many ways, such a welcome contrast to the risky, solitary life of the rails. Would I be able to say good-bye?

No, I had to stay downtown. Some hoboes ached for a home, others cringed at the prospect; I would have to *resist* home.

Turning off Larimer Street, I headed for the taller buildings of downtown proper. Nestled among them was a short, nondescript church, one I had always admired simply by virtue of its location. The land it sat on had become valuable with the growth of downtown, but the church had stayed, apparently confident of the role it had to play amid the skyscrapers. Tonight for the first time I noticed its name: the Holy Ghost Church, the same one my boxcar companion had recommended for free sandwiches. A sign on the side door confirmed this: SANDWICHES DISTRIBUTED AT 10 A.M. MONDAY THROUGH SATURDAY ONLY, it said, and penned beneath the sign, in crude letters, was a tramp's protest: DONT GET HUNGRY ANY OTHER TIME.

According to the tramp on the train, the line here stretched all the way around the block in the mornings. Tonight, though, there was only me and a guy sitting on a sidewalk planter box a few yards away. He was about six feet tall and had red hair cut Prince Valiant-style. Dressed in mission clothes—an old overcoat and black oxfords—and carrying no gear, he was apparently a home guard. He was eating from a can of cold Campbell's Chunky Soup with a spoon.

"Evenin'," I said.

"How's it goin', man?" he replied, between ravenous spoonfuls.

"Oh, not too bad. I could do without the cops shinin' their lights on me, over on Larimer."

"Yeah, them streets is hot at night," he said. "Here you're okay, though." I had been with hoboes long enough to construe the remark as an invitation. I took a seat next to him on the planter.

"Hungry?"

"Yeah."

"Here, you got a cup? Have some of this."

I removed a cup from my shoulder bag, and he spooned some out for me. "Got a ten-dollar voucher from the Sally," he explained.

Before I could move the conversation toward places to sleep, an old man, obviously drunk, approached us. "Hey-buddies-either-you-got-a-cigrette?" He seemed to be looking mostly at me. I reflexively replied that I didn't smoke.

"You don't? Well, good," he slurred. "Don't you ever start, 'cause iss a terrble, terrble habit."

Prince Valiant and I laughed, the remark having lightened what had been for me a serious and disquieting evening. He then offered the drunk some rolling tobacco from a pouch in his pocket, and we watched while, standing unsteadily, he pulled a piece of paper bag from his pocket, tore off a small, uneven square, and rolled a wet cigarette. Lighting the thing with his wavering hand seemed to take him forever, but finally smoke issued thinly from his nostrils and lips, and he turned and staggered off.

Prince Valiant turned back toward me. "Buddy, you look beat," he said, in an accent I had tentatively placed as backwoods Southern. He glanced at my bedroll. "You just in?" I nodded. "Well, lookee here, I'll gitcha some coffee."

Entering the basement of the church, we went to the men's room, where the man rinsed his spoon and I my cup. Then, producing his own cup and a jar of instant coffee from deep in a pocket, he sprinkled some coffee into the cups, turned on the hot water, and filled them. Like Lonny's mulligan stew, it tasted awfully good. We walked back outside.

"Say, I'm wonderin' where guys can sack out around here," I said. "I been thinkin' about down on Cherry Creek, or the Platte River." The two bodies of water bordered the downtown area.

"Oh, don't you do that!" he advised. "There's guys down there that'll kill you for a nickel, especially now, in this cold weather. Don't take that bedroll with you," he said, gesturing toward it. "I can guarantee you you won't have it in the morning."

"Well, is there anyplace else, besides the mission?"

"There's St. Andrew's," he said. "You been there yet?"

No, I replied, I hadn't. "Well, it's mostly for young guys—I'd be there now, 'cept my three nights was up yesterday. But if you hurry you might still make it. They take twenty-five guys a night."

"Does it cost anything?"

"No man—'course not. You just gotta show up on time."

"Guess I better go now, huh?"

He half shrugged, though the answer was obviously "yes." I guessed that, like me, he wanted some company. Suggesting we'd see each other the next day, I set off across town to St. Andrew's.

I completed the ten or fifteen blocks quickly, turned the corner, and walked right by. This part of town I knew better than the other, and I had dismissed the church as simply the place in whose lot my dad used to park his car. Looking again, I saw a number of young men lounging around on the lawn outside the place, and all of a sudden remembered similar scenes from days when I had passed the church with Dad. He worried about the safety of his car with guys like those around, and had intentionally looked away from them. That had frightened me.

Tonight, though, I exchanged greetings with some. Most had eaten dinner inside a couple of hours before; now the monks who ran St. Andrew's (it was actually an Episcopal abbey) were having their evening services, and would let the men back in when they were done. There were about twenty of us, so I figured I would get a spot. Three or four conversations were going on, and I joined in one I judged to be the most animated. Six men—three whites, two Chicanos, and an Indian—were passing around a pair of good used boots, each man taking off his own shoes to see if they fit. "Here, see if you're Cinderella!" one of them said, tossing me the boots. I gave it a try, since the boots I was wearing had worn through in the sole and let water in. The boots fit. "Cinderella it is!" cried somebody, but satisfaction, not envy, came to the faces of my evil step-sisters—that somebody could make use of the boots was the important thing. I tossed my old boots in the trash can and hoped the nickname wouldn't stick.

Another group of men passed to us a half-eaten bag of Cheetos. "Hey, are these fit for human consumption?" asked the fellow to my right who had received them, articulating the normally unspoken fear of those among us who visited dumpsters.

The man ate a handful and passed them on. "I can see the headlines tomorrow," he said. " 'Mass Suicide at St. Andrew's'!"

A well-thumbed back copy of *Playboy* magazine followed the Cheetos around the circle. Everybody was smoking, almost all, I noticed, from trial-size packages of Vantage cigarettes.

"Free samples downtown today," explained the man on my right. "Weren't you there?"

"Nope—just got in this evening."

"Well then, here," he said, reaching into a deep pocket of his Army fatigue jacket, one fairly splitting with the sample boxes of cigarettes. He fished one out for me.

"Thanks."

A noise from the locked door brought everyone to his feet, and the crowd pressed down the stairwell to the basement of the abbey. A shaven-headed monk, dressed in a hooded robe made from old Levi's, forced open the door and counted men as they went in. More had joined the throng since I arrived. The uncertainty this caused about who would get in resulted in a scene like New York City subways at rush hour. "Twenty-four!" he called out as I entered the basement, and I breathed relief.

St. Andrew's was a world of difference from the Lincoln Rescue Mission. For reasons I did not understand, "patrons" under 30 years of age could stay three nights a month, while older men were allowed only one. One result seemed to be an atmosphere much brighter than at Lincoln. Men were talking to each other, making jokes—I even heard someone singing in the shower. Some had bedrolls, but this was not really a place for railroad tramps; the men were too young, too unseasoned at transiency, too frivolous and full of themselves. Another reason seemed to be all the clerics around—monks bustled here and there, all dressed in their funky robes, making sure everyone was inside and preparing supplies of towels and blankets. They weren't scornful or morose like the Lincoln mission workers, and this had an effect on everyone. Soon a man in a priest's collar entered the room and asked everyone to be quiet. Introducing himself and the monks, he explained there was no sermon here: "We're not interested in converting you. If you become interested in our way, that's terrific, but we're not pushing anything down your throats." Next we all had to introduce ourselves, telling where we were from, and where we were going. The variety of origins was wide: Arkansas, Texas, California, Nevada, Mississippi, New York, Mexico, South Dakota—the list went on and on. Before leaving, the priest assigned the two couches to the men from farthest away—New Hampshire and Alaska. The rest would sleep on the floor.

The television was left on for a while, and a stocky guy with a pockmarked face, long brown hair, and an earring watched a boxing match with me. We bet twenty-five cents on the outcome but sadly (my guy was ahead), the head monk switched off the set before the fight ended.

Monks passed out blankets, and men began to stake out their pieces of floor. Over numerous objections, an Indian succeeded in setting the alarm clock for five A.M., so that he could get to the "slave labor" office—a temporary manual-labor employment agency—in time to get a job. I lay down on the cold concrete floor near some bookshelves, and found myself in agreement with a young Oklahoman across the aisle who was wishing out loud he had a girl to lie on the hard floor with. My bunched-up jacket provided a good pillow. Just as I laid down my head, a cockroach skittered by. The monks hit the light switch.

Hours later, I awoke with a start. My movement startled the abbey cat, which had been resting next to me, and it bounded away. I touched my nose; it was wet. Then it all came back—the cat had been licking my nose, but in my dreams it was a giant cockroach, crawling on my face. . . .

I slumbered some more, until a pounding at the door, and the ringing of the brass bell in the vestibule. A rope leading to the outside allowed the bell to serve as a doorbell. Somebody wanted in. I contemplated getting up and cutting the cord in two with my pocket knife.

Finally a grumpy monk answered the door. The callers claimed they had left their bedrolls inside, but the monk refused them entrance. When he left, they resumed their knocking. The police were called. Moments later, it seemed, the alarm clock rang to rouse the Indian, and the monks decided everyone might as well get up. The men, seldom afforded the luxury of sleeping late, were awake and up quickly. I sat and listened to the day's first words:

"See these goddamn boots? They got fifteen hundred miles on 'em!"

"I'm gonna catch a fast freight outa here—*fuck* this town!"

"When are you goin' to Georgia?"

"Whenever I decide to."

"Well, when you do can I go with you?"

"Yeah."

"I just know I ain't goin' back through Oklahoma—man, the pigs'd get me."

Breakfast, like every morning, was thin coffee and a bowlful of thick, heavy porridge. "Eat it quick, before it sets," the monk advised all comers, spooning it from a cauldron into the bowls in our hands.

"You don't have to chew it," the guy next to me advised, "because it comes back together before it goes down your throat."

The oatmeal joke contest was on.

"If you can't finish it, just take it out and put it in your pack—it stays like a little ball."

"—or patch the sole of your shoe with it."

"What don't get et they give to the street repair crew."

"Hey, pour me some of that coffee," said another, changing the subject. "Let's get the old plasma flowin' so it'll come out easy!"

One by one guys filtered outside. At the last possible moment, I followed.

Downtown, the day had barely started. Newspaper boys were making their deliveries to office buildings, shopkeepers were sweeping their sidewalks, crews in large yellow trucks were picking up trash, and people passed in and out of the 24-hour cafés. There was, I realized, a whole side of the city I hadn't seen, and I devoted the early morning to a walking tour of downtown's periphery.

Later I returned to the central business area. It was the morning rush hour and traffic and pedestrians choked 17th Street, the "Wall Street of the Rockies." I was back in the downtown I knew, but the familiarity was not at all reassuring. Instead, all of the secretaries, businessmen, and lawyers on the sidewalk made me feel out of place. They stared at my bedroll, my clothing, and, until I looked back at them, my face. Always before I had felt welcome here; my father's firm worked high up in one of the buildings, and his name was on the office door. But always before I had been dressed up, and had a reason for coming. Now I was wearing entirely the wrong clothes and had nowhere in particular to go.

I walked the main streets for a couple of hours, self-conscious but also hopeful that perhaps some businessman who was a family friend would favor me with a brief glance, and then, recognition lighting his face, would stop in astonishment and ask what in God's name I was doing. Better yet, he would fail to recognize me at all. But here came Mr. Stone, and Mr. MacDougall, and Peter Foster—

and try though I did to catch their eyes, all looked studiously in the other direction. I couldn't believe it; I felt like Rip Van Winkle.

Then I remembered the men I had seen on Larimer Street the night before, especially those lying on the sidewalk. People like these could be found all over a city, I realized, but until recently I had been in the habit of not seeing them. Maybe it was because they were not normally considered people of consequence, people worth noticing. Perhaps I had been disgusted by them, or embarrassed, or at a loss about how to help. Maybe it was simply that, unlike theirs, my eyes were not trained to the sidewalk, and I just didn't notice people on the ground. But I didn't think so. When it comes right down to it, the sight of a grown man lying on the pavement is very strange, indeed, and the sight of a guy like me, dirty, unshaven, and with a bedroll, is also unusual. Yet people wouldn't look, especially directly, at me. Why not? I asked myself. What don't you—what don't *we*—want to see?

The question confounded me as I moved through the tide of business people. Idly, half in a daze, I looked up and across the street and noticed one of my closest high-school friends, a woman who had finished college early and was already working downtown. She was wearing pumps, a dress, and an overcoat. A tall fellow I didn't recognize accompanied her.

"Hey, Jen!" I called out. "Jennifer Ross!"

She looked up, unable to tell at first who had called her name. Her eyes finally stopped on me. I waved. A look that could only be translated as "What the hell—?" crossed her face. "It's Ted," I called. "Me, Ted Conover!"

"Come on, let's go," said the guy, pulling on her arm, glaring at me like some real pain-in-the-ass crackpot.

"Ted?"

"Yeah!" I smiled, crossing the street, as recognition seemed to cross her face.

"Ted, what are you *doing?*" she asked, as though she had just seen me injecting heroin into my arm.

"I'm riding the rails—living with hoboes."

"Oh, I heard about that!" she said suddenly. "Wait a minute—you mean you're really living with them, not just interviewing them on trains or something?"

"Right—slept at a mission last night, 'bout to go pick up some free sandwiches!" God, I thought that sounded amazing and adventuresome.

The excitement left her eyes. It seemed like more than she really had wanted to know.

"Come on, Jen, we gotta get going," urged the pillar of propriety at her side, making no secret of his disgust.

"Wait—are you doing it *with* somebody?" she asked me. "I mean, is anybody with you?" One person doing such a thing conceivably was crazy, I guessed she was thinking; two probably were not.

"Well, I'm with people when I meet up with them, other guys on the road. But really, I'm alone. I thought it was important to do it by myself."

She smiled, sort of. "Well, guess we gotta go," she said, beginning to retreat. "Hey, but give me a call sometime, okay? Or look, I'll call you," she added, as a concession to my look of disappointment.

"Uh, that might not be too easy," I said, finally smiling.

"No . . ." she trailed off, yielding to her friend and moving back into the stream of people.

I left for the Platte River. Prince Valiant's warning of the night before was not enough to keep me downtown, among the home guard and the executive set. I wanted to be back with the real railroad tramps, where, it unsettled me for a moment to think, I belonged. Cutthroat or not, they had something to teach me; all I was getting in town was anxious.

Cherry Creek and the Platte River meet just west of downtown Denver. The city's founders built their first settlement at the confluence, and, until as late as my boyhood, the bushy banks of both streams, which wind through the middle of several large railroad yards, provided shelter for large numbers of westbound migrants and modern-day transients. When I returned there, though, the downtown area was booming due to Denver's newfound prominence as the energy capital of the West. The city suddenly realized that the streams it had ignored for the past several decades, letting the water become polluted and the banks become littered, could in fact be an attractive natural resource for ordinary citizens. Boom met bust west of downtown, and the result was a kayak course at the turbulent confluence, a general cleanup, and a miles-long bicycle and jogging path, offering a circuit of calisthenic stops. The streams became pretty again, but the hoboes began to get bumped out. A late claim had been made for the spaces they had inherited by default.

I arrived at the confluence, where there was actually a park now, to take a close-up look. Trying to overcome the contradictory feeling of being a hobo on the bike path, I then took a walk down the Platte. Several helmeted cyclists whizzed by on their ten-speeds, and business people on lunch-hour breaks jogged by in expensive exercise suits. I knew hoboes camped out here when I was growing up—I had seen them—and I had even read a Depression-era book by a hobo who passed through Denver regularly, always finding a pleasant, grassy spot to sleep under a bridge on the stream I was on. But after walking a mile without seeing anyone with an annual income under $30,000, I began to get skeptical.

Then I heard the noises. There was a clank on the other side of a cement wall supporting a bridge ahead of me, and laughter. It would not be a meeting of joggers, I knew—they never seemed to leave the bike path. Stepping cautiously over the low shrubbery and sandy soil, I peered around the wall.

A large sandy beach extended down to the water, and in the shade of the bridge I saw something spinning through the air. *Thunk*—it hit the sand at the feet of a tall, gaunt man wearing a floppy hat, spraying his boots. He slowly picked up the horseshoe and flipped it back in the direction from which it had come. It hung in the air a moment and then, *clank,* bounced off a metal rod projecting from the sand at the feet of another man, this one wearing a cap and old jacket. "Nothin'," said the second guy, referring, I guessed, to the points earned by the throw. Picking it up, he tossed it back. They were playing horseshoes! Horse*shoe,* anyway. Two other tramps watched from an embankment against the wall, sipping cans of beer.

I walked discreetly out from behind the wall, through the shrubbery and out onto the sand. I took a seat on the embankment, a comfortable distance from the two seated men. "Howdy," I said matter-of-factly, nodding slightly toward them when they looked over at me. One dipped his head back, but the look was brief, just an informational glance, and the game resumed.

They were playing something like a round robin, with a player on the sand occasionally trading places with one on the embankment. The game progressed slowly, due to the single horseshoe, and because the stakes were set at funny angles. They weren't really stakes at all, I discovered later, but the ends of rebar set in concrete, left over from the construction of the bridge. Tramp imagination had seen an opportunity for diversion in something others might sprain their ankles over.

"Ringer!" cried the capped one, to the multiple clangs of the horseshoe circling the far stake. His opponent responded by getting off a leaner. I just sat and watched, and the contest went on for about an hour. Mostly I was ignored, but during one of his sits I was able to start a bit of conversation with Floppy Hat. He looked at me critically when I asked if many guys still jungled on the river, as though to say "You don't know?" but then said gruffly that, well, *he* did. When I said where I had come from, he started a detailed discourse on the different trains between Denver and Lincoln—the "Daytime Man" and the "Nighttime Man" he called them—and recited the entire schedule. His questions to me about the configuration of the yard sounded like a test, and it seemed he doubted that I had really come the way I said I had. Then, though,

I related the story of the marijuana fields, and the men who had boarded our train. He was the first one I had told about it, and for some reason I guess I expected him to be impressed by the tale of adventure and danger. But all he said was, "Ayup, them niggers like that grass all right, s-u-u-re do."

The beer was gone and the game broke up. Frankly, I had not understood how a game of horseshoes played with one horseshoe could last more than a few minutes. But they felt lucky to have found the one—"That guy picked it up in the dump," said Floppy Hat, when I asked where it had come from—and rather than looking at it as I did, from the perspective of one who is used to having four horseshoes, they looked at it from the perspective of men who were used to having *no* horseshoes. It had been a good midday diversion. No one ever invited me to join the game or share in the beer, though the man I had gotten to know somewhat asked if I wanted to toss the horseshoe a few times before he hid it.

I was reasonably good at horseshoes, but walking forty feet after every throw wore me out. I handed it back.

"Say," I said, after the horseshoe was stashed, "if you're walkin' up the river, I'll go with you."

The man shrugged, and I fell into step with him. We walked the bike path to the next bridge—one of a score the railroads had erected in order to run their yards as though the river didn't exist. The man evidently did not care to stay on the bike path, and soon we were on a parallel dirt path on the river's other side. Here and there we passed evidence of former homes of the homeless: cooking cans and garbage in the sand, a grate that had gone over an old cooking fire, ashes. My companion's long, loping gait moved him in slow motion over much more ground than I was covering with nearly twice as many steps; he seemed a professional walker. Five bridges later we came upon a clearing in the brush on the bank. Our arrival was met by the hysterical barking of a small mongrel dog. It confronted us at the edge of the jungle, snarling savagely. I came to a dead halt, but the tall tramp didn't even hesitate, striding confidently by. Presently, a tarpaulin hanging from some small trees and fixed to the ground quivered, and a shorter man appeared behind the dog.

"Shuddup, goddamnit, I said shut up. Lady, shut up!" The man yelled some more, whacked the dog once on the rear end, and then, grudgingly, it became quiet. "Mind if I come in?" I asked. Still hovering over the dog, the second tramp all but ignored me. Since he didn't say no, I walked into the clearing and set down my gear. As the tall tramp disappeared into the tarpaulin tent, I explained I was recently in, trying to get my bearings, and more than a little hungry besides. The man, like almost all tramps with extra food, was quick to oblige. He handed me a cellophane-wrapped ham-and-cheese sandwich from a box full of them, and I took a seat on an overturned bucket.

The jungle's main feature was the tentlike shelter made from heavy green canvas and plastic sheeting, suspended from linden and cottonwood. A wooden spool table, the kind found in college dormitory rooms and near telephone line crews, sat next to this, covered with condiments; the end of a mattress projected from the shelter's door. The river flowed slowly by, just a few feet away. Presently the shelter and mattress moved again, and the tall, floppy-hatted hobo rose stiffly to his feet and headed toward the bushes to relieve himself. Later, I would hear the second tramp address him as "Tree," and later still "Treetop," a name that fit. Hearing Tree address the man as Al was also how I learned his name. They never asked mine.

When Tree returned to sit on the mattress I relocated my bucket nearer to him. "Hungry, huh?" he asked, watching me swallow the sandwich nearly whole. I nodded. We listened to country-and-western music on a transistor radio, powered by a large square battery with a railroad's name on it, with wires leading from the spiral wire terminals on top to the open back of the radio. Occasionally Tree would remark on a song coming over the radio, or would wave at a jogger passing by on the path across the river. We talked about trains, about the "slave market" downtown, about the dog and the weather.

Tree looked about sixty. White whiskers lent his face a ragged outline, and the hillbilly hat hid his bald scalp. He wore old boots, loose canvas pants, a heavy shirt, and a jacket. Al, the other tramp, was over at the river's edge, washing some clothes—a chore of questionable effectiveness, given the murkiness of the water, but the pollution didn't seem to bother him. I even saw him chuck an old bag of trash into the water; most of it sank, bubbling, to the bottom. He looked about twenty years younger than Tree, wore an open shirt and no socks. Al declined my offer of instant coffee, and didn't smoke, either. He and Tree enjoyed occasional sips from a bottle of wine in a bag and traded jokes. As with the beer at the horseshoe game, I was not offered the wine—but now I was beginning to suspect that this was less because I was a newcomer than because I had not contributed to its cost. Food seemed plentiful around Denver, and was easily shared, but alcohol was a scarcer resource, and tramps were stingy with it. Soon, though, a collection began for the next round, and I pitched in a handful of change. Then all three of us embarked on a supply expedition.

The first stop was a mammoth dumpster behind the Burlington Northern offices. Though tall, the aging Tree needed a boost. I obliged, and was soon being handed a pair of shoes, which luckily fit Al, and a number of batteries like the one that powered the transistor radio.

"What're these from?" I asked.

"Brakeys' lanterns," Al said. "You know, those big flashlights they tote around." Al tested them by holding his tongue to the two terminals. "If you feel it tingle, then there's juice left," he explained.

Next, we stopped at a catering concern which, Al and Tree knew, daily threw out all the sandwiches, yogurts, pies, salads, and so on that had passed their expiration date. Our timing was perfect: the last of the employees' cars was leaving the parking lot, and the big green dumpsters sat clustered alone at the back. Al and Tree's nonchalance as we lifted the lids made me feel like a real coward— I couldn't help looking around to see if anyone was watching. Again, Tree did the digging, and Al and I sorted the cellophane-wrapped haul into three large plastic bags from the dumpster, which later we shouldered and hauled back toward the jungle.

En route, we stopped to rest on a crumbling, out-of-the-way street corner. Al disappeared around the corner.

"Where's he gone to?" I asked Tree.

"It's Miller time!" was the grinning reply.

In a few minutes Al reappeared, carrying three tall-boy beers in a paper sack. Tree found himself another small sack in the debris around our feet and placed his can in it; I did the same. In the opinion of Tree and Al, this made our drinking more discreet. The beers tasted wonderful in the hot afternoon, I couldn't help imagining what kind of commercial the scene would make—Al, Tree, and I and our huge plastic trash bags, seated on a shady stoop on a ramshackle street corner, sipping beers from paper bags and grinning widely. Tree had no teeth. Al had about five. "After a hard afternoon of dumpster hunting," the announcer would say, "nothing quenches a man's thirst like a Miller."

Tree warned me against discussing the location of the concessionaire's dumpster. He sounded like a trout fisherman who had just revealed the location of his best stream. "It's out of the way, and ain't nobody gonna find it less you got loose lips."

I promised not to, and asked how he had found it in the first place. It was, after all, a long way from the jungle, and the company certainly did not advertise the fact that there was a miniature canteen in the dumpster. But explaining annoyed Tree. "Just found it, that's all," he said.

There was no dinnertime at the jungle; each man ate the recycled food—some of it stale but most of it perfectly fine— when he was hungry. Later, to the light of crooked, broken candles sunken into the sandy soil of the tent floor, we listened to a football game on the radio. Al and Tree bitterly contested the merits of the two teams. It became late. "Okay if I stay here tonight?" I asked. "Do what you want," answered Tree. I cleared a space for my bedroll and slept out under the stars, a quarter mile from downtown Denver.

The next day at the jungle went slowly. With more to learn about Denver, and beginning to tire of the steady diet of cellophane sandwiches, I decided to brave downtown again. I took my gear with me, not yet certain of the trustworthiness of my hosts, and told Al and Tree I'd be back in the afternoon.

Back on downtown streets, I recognized a lot of the faces of the down-and-out from the day before. It was still strange being as one of them in my hometown. I worried less that day about my appearance to people like my father than about what would happen if I bumped into another young down-and-outer, a dropout I had known from my years in the Denver public schools. I could just imagine him eyeing me, former overachiever, and saying with smug satisfaction, "Ahh, look who's here!"

Yet I would find as I left downtown that day, full of vegetable soup, old corn on the cob, watermelon, and tea from the Catholic Worker house, that old dropouts were really the last thing I needed to be worried about.

7

"Hurry up, asshole," yelled the policeman.

I looked up, startled. I was walking west over a viaduct that spanned railroad yards, the Platte River, and an interstate highway. My goal was Al and Tree's jungle, on the other side, and I had thought that by taking the high road I would avoid having to trespass on the hot Union Pacific property underneath. Seeing this policeman fifty feet ahead of me, I was not so sure. His patrol car, lights flashing, was straddling the center line of the road. He stood next to it, waving his arms irritably and ordering the drivers of passing cars to hurry up, too.

Unaware that I had done anything wrong, I continued at the same pace toward the end of the viaduct.

"Hurry up and get your ass off the bridge!"

"Why?" I asked, still walking. "What's going on?"

Pointing a finger at me, he cried, "I said get your ass off the damn bridge—now *move!*"

Disturbed, I complied and then looked back and jotted down the license number of his car. He noticed this and shouted, "Go ahead and write it down—if you can read!"

Once off the bridge, I paused. Had I been better groomed, I thought, wearing a coat and tie, this would never have happened. I had never been in trouble with the law—never even received a traffic ticket—and suddenly one point about police treatment that hoboes had made to me was driven home with force: it's different when you're poor.

Knowing I would probably need the policeman's badge number to make a credible complaint, I mustered my courage, stepped back onto the bridge, and asked for it.

"I told you to get off this bridge!" he yelled.

"Please tell me your badge number, and I'll get off the bridge," I said.

"I'll arrest you!"

"What is your badge number?"

"You'll get it on the summons if you don't move your mother-fuckin' ass off this bridge!"

I knew that department policy required a Denver police officer to disclose his number when asked, and so I persisted: "What is your number?"

"Mister, you're getting arrested."

The particular combination of rage and fear I felt then was new to me. He spoke briefly into his car radio, slammed the door shut, and stopped the traffic. A city bus packed with commuters stopped just a few feet away from me, and I noticed a dozen faces staring out the front windows. Unsnapping the holster of his service revolver, the policeman strode briskly over to me, twisted my arms behind my back, and handcuffed me.

"Take it easy," I said. "I'm not resisting."

Holding me by the handcuff chain, he shoved me forward, lifting the chain high so that the cuffs dug into my wrists. Then he opened the front passenger door of the cruiser. As I bent down to take a seat, he pushed me in. My head hit the metal door frame.

He frisked me inside the car. "How old are you?" he asked.

"Twenty-two."

"Good, then you'll go to jail," he said. "I'm sure you been there before."

As we drove off, we passed my gear, lying by the side of the road. He refused to pick it up. Nor would he answer my questions about why I should not have been on the bridge, or give me his name. It was only by listening to his car radio that I remembered the President had been speaking in town that day, and learned that we had been on the viaduct near the time when members of the President's party were supposed to be driving on the highway underneath it.

Another police car joined him in a parking lot on the way, and we proceeded to a police substation. As the cop pushed me toward the substation door, I realized how powerless the handcuffs had left me. It was as though half of my body was immobilized, incapable even of resisting mistreatment. I remembered how trappers always try to bind an alligator's mouth shut as soon as possible, because then the alligator gives up. My arms and fists must be like the alligator's jaws, or the lobster's claws, I thought, for I felt utterly helpless.

Inside, I was taken down a long white hall, past a roomful of tables and lockers filled with people in the same uniform as my captor. They regarded me incuriously—another hood. Finally the cop stopped me in front of two gray metal doors, opened one with a key, removed my handcuffs, pushed me in, and slammed the door.

The room was the size of three phone booths, outfitted with a toilet and a metal shelf along one wall, apparently designed to be laid upon. I rubbed my wrists; they were skinned and sore. A fluorescent light buzzed overhead, and I sat upon the shelf.

Outside doors opened and closed, and footsteps clicked down the corridor. Presently I heard the policemen talking. "Heard you got somebody up on the bridge," said a voice. "What happened?"

"Aaaa, it was just some shitheel."

Shitheel? The word provoked the most primitive reaction in me: desire for revenge. Man, I thought, would I love to tell him a thing or two—where I went to college, for starters, then where I'd worked that summer, where my dad worked, where we lived. Then see if he thought I was a shitheel! My dad's law partner oversaw the police department for the mayor—let me use the telephone, and then stand back and watch this cop's head roll.

It took a while for me to cool down and realize how stupidly I was reacting. I'd been happy to experience the fun side of hobo life—the clandestine travel, the freedom—but now that the system was treating me like a real hobo, I was acting like a little brat. Pulling social rank on the policeman would prove only that I wasn't what I appeared to be. Things had gotten a bit tough, and I was ready to fold. No. I felt my beard. I was proud of that beard, my hobo beard, and wouldn't betray it now. I tried to put aside my anger, and remember the reason I was here, after all: to learn.

I reached for the notebook in my hip pocket to record these thoughts and the details of what had happened—but it wasn't there! My record of the past two weeks had disappeared. Had it fallen out of my pocket in the scuffle, to be mashed by the wheels of that bus? No, now I remembered—the cop took it when he frisked me, along with everything else in my pockets—wallet, traveler's checks, pen, change. I worried, for he would surely be looking at it, especially since he had seen me writing down his license number. I had also quoted, verbatim, his first remarks to me—"Hurry up, asshole!" A thousand important observations, including those taken during my time with Lonny, gone into some police station wastebasket.

I lay down, discovering that I couldn't even stretch out on the "bed." The room pressed in on me. I remembered being at summer camp, and being pushed into a small wooden locker in a cabin when the counselor wasn't there. Older boys had locked the latch and I had panicked, banging the door and screaming. Laughing, joking, afraid of getting caught, they had let me out after a few minutes. The main difference between then and now seemed to be that the police weren't afraid of getting caught. With all my might, I tried to stay calm.

After a while, I noticed that a carbon copy of some form had been slipped under the door. I picked it up. My name was on it, as well as the name and number of the arresting officer—both illegible—and then a section describing what I had been charged with. "Disobeying the lawful order of a police officer," it said. Well, that figured. Then I noticed another charge underneath.

"Pedestrian in roadway where sidewalk is provided." But I had been on the sidewalk all the way across the bridge. At least until . . . until the policeman had announced he was going to arrest me! He had stopped the traffic and, to show him I wouldn't cause any trouble, I had stepped off the curb, hands in front of me to show I was prepared to be handcuffed, and walked calmly toward him. . . .

Steps sounded outside, and I stood up. The door opened to two new policemen. Hands resting on the butts of their revolvers, they looked hesitant, as if, like a tiger, I might leap out and attack.

"Let's go."

Handcuffs again linked my sore wrists behind my back; they again frisked me and then led me out to what they called the squad car. It was a van with benches in the back and bars between the cab and rear compartment.

"Hey, what's going to happen to the stuff the other policeman took from me?"

"You'll get it back when they let you out," said one. I was glad to hear release was a certainty. They drove me to the city jail.

Like the other parts of Denver, the jail was new to me. Actually, I had driven by the modern brick building a thousand times but had never stopped to imagine what was inside. As the van turned into a driveway, the passersby stopped and gawked. They seemed to know my destination.

We went down a ramp and stopped in a dark basement. The back doors of the squad car opened, the cops again looking as though they might have to restrain me. I was escorted to a small lighted room with elevator doors. A female guard was there, and she smiled as she saw the officers. Her finger pressed the elevator button.

"Hey, Gena, what's goin' on?"

"Nothin' Roy, how are you, baby?"

Roy, to my surprise, took Gena in his arms and gave her a long, passionate kiss. His wife? I wondered, but not for long.

"Hey, what about me?" asked the other cop.

"Oh, all right, Stu," said Gena, spreading her arms and sharing with Stu a more-than-friendly embrace. The elevator arrived. I was shown into a caged-off area in the back of it. Gena sat upon the operator's stool, waved bye-bye to the cops, and took me to the fourth floor.

There I was searched for the third of what were to be five times—they even checked inside my shoes. The contents of my pockets were confiscated, as was my belt (suicide prevention, I supposed); and then the sheriff's deputies who ran the jail placed me in a succession of tiny holding cells, as booking proceeded through fingerprinting, photographing, and my one phone call.

I called home, and Mom answered.

"Well, you'll never guess where I am," I said.

"Let's see, last we heard you were leaving Nebraska on your way to Colorado. You must be in Denver."

"That's right—can you guess where?"

"Well, let's see—the train station?"

"Ma—that's where passenger trains stop! Here's a clue: this is my only phone call."

There was a long silence. "You're kidding!"

"Nope."

Mom responded as though the possibility of this happening had crossed her mind before. "Well, I'm sure it will be a good learning experience," she said, cheering me considerably. "Do you want me to come bail you out?"

It was a terrific temptation. Bond had been set at only $90, a little more than what I had left in traveler's checks, and seeing her and the family would be about the most wonderful thing I could imagine right now—I might even make it for dinner. But a hobo would not be able to call his mother and have her spring him from the jail. So I explained my decision to her quietly, so that the officer in attendance could not hear—and agreed to keep her posted. She wished me love and, hanging up, I felt strong.

The next destination was the main holding cell. It was Friday night, and the hard metal benches that lined the room were crowded. All of the prisoners were men, most black or Chicano; whether drunk or disconsolate, most just stared at the floor when the electric door whirred open and I was ushered in. The main topic of conversation among those who talked was what they had been busted for. Often, when a man got around to telling the man next to him what he was in for, the other conversations kind of hushed, out of curiosity. A Chicano kid younger than me had been arrested for failing to pay traffic tickets, and was worried about what his mom was going to say when she found out this time. A black man who worked at the airport was nabbed for being late with alimony payments, and was worried that he'd be fired if he didn't show up for work in the evening. I was waiting for somebody to awe the rest of us with the news that he had shot and killed his worst enemy, but nobody would confess, or lie. Most of the men looked more bored than worried. Finally one next to me, from whom I had coaxed the information that he had broken his parole, and was headed to the state prison—"the joint," as it was known here—asked me what I was in for.

"Crossing a bridge," I confessed.

"*What?* What were you, crossin' it with no clothes on?"

Everyone hushed to hear this story, and so I told it. In a way telling it worried me: I wished I could have been the murderer, or had the guts to pretend I was, because these guys looked altogether pretty tough, and I needed some toughness credentials. Being an illegal bridgewalker didn't really qualify.

"Oh, man, that's bullshit!" said an older black man from across the room. "Man, you just tell that to the judge, just like you told us, and you be out. You been in before?"

I shook my head.

Other men nodded, and it seemed to me the prisoners were by and large a supportive group. Old-timers, and there seemed to be quite a few, answered questions about what the meals were like, about the court session scheduled the next day, about the jailers. A man with a puffy jaw and a wary eye appeared to speak with the most expertise on the last topic—he had failed to laugh at a deputy's joke on the way up in the elevator, he said, and had gotten a sock in the jaw. I saw no reason to doubt him; from what I had seen, the jailers were a macho, dispassionate bunch with larger-than-average mean streaks. Every man listening shook his head. "You gotta be a savage to be a jailer," said one ruefully.

Everyone seemed to take for granted being locked in a pretty small room, and this calmed me. What did worry me was whom I might get stuck with as a bunkmate. Though probably no one in the room was completely benign, some seemed less dangerous than others, and I prayed I wouldn't get stuck with a savage. Lonny's stories about homosexual attacks in jail gnawed at me. One fellow I was particularly worried about was white, in his late twenties, about six feet tall, with long, stringy hair. His beltless pants had fallen halfway down his butt, he had on no shoes or socks, and he had chosen the toilet as a seat instead of a bench. He seemed to live entirely in his own world, reacting to none of the words of the men around him, peering oddly out at us when the spirit moved him—please, don't let him look at me!—and sporadically bursting into loud, rude laughter for no apparent reason. Clearly, he had problems, and I wondered why he was in jail instead of in a place where someone could help him. After a couple of hours, when a jailer opened the door and called my name, I told him I thought the man was crazy, and asked to be put with someone else.

He laughed. "All we gots is singles in this hotel," he said with a smirk. He led me back to the elevator. Lonny's advice about appearing confident lingered in my mind. Though apprehensive, I tried not to look it; as long as things kept happening to me, as long as I was not forgotten about in some corner, as long as the jailers couldn't tell I was scared, I would be all right.

The elevator opened onto the sixth floor, and I entered a small fluorescent-lit waiting space. The tallest, toughest-looking jailer I had seen yet was standing there, waiting for me.

"Hands against the wall, feet spread," he barked.

I was frisked for the fifth time.

"Sit down, take off your shoes." He gestured toward a wooden chair. Satisfied the shoes were empty, he told me to turn around and drop my trousers.

"What?" I said, surprised.

"Drop your pants and bend over!" he growled, knowing I had heard him the first time. Feeling the combination of anger and fear I had earlier that day, I did so. What's this for? I wondered. Didn't they know from the earlier frisks that I had no weapon there? The real objective here seemed to be ritual humiliation, putting a shitheel in his place, expressing the guard's absolute power.

Without telling me when I could hoist the pants back up, he ordered me to follow him. We passed a laundry room with a pile of gray towels at the door. "Take one of those."

"Say, have you all got anything to read, like maybe a Bible?" I asked, seriously.

"Nope, nothin' to read."

We passed down a bleak white corridor, monitored by cameras, and then past a control center of some kind, with banks of red and green lights. Probably to control the opening of the doors, I guessed. Two such doors opened as the jailer arrived at them, and I went over in my mind the number of locked doors between my location and the outside world. At least eight came to mind. Escape, I thought half-seriously, would be very difficult.

Finally we arrived at a corridor connecting many small cells. As I followed him down it, I looked through the thick panes in the doors and saw that many were filled with men lying down on metal bunks, such as I had been on several hours before. The doors all had numbers on them. The guard stopped in front of 4W 17.

"Open Seventeen!" he yelled.

Within a few seconds, there was a loud click from the latch area of the door, and slowly the door slid aside.

"Any dinner tonight?" I asked as I entered.

"You missed it," said the jailer. "Close Seventeen!" The door slid shut and again clicked.

The room was small and bare. It had four main features: the

door, solid steel with a thick Plexiglas window; a toilet and sink combined in one small stainless-steel unit; a metal shelf, of the type I had in the room at the substation but embellished by a wafer-thin mattress pad; and a window, about the size of a cereal box, which looked out at a dark black wall six inches away. Fluorescent bulbs shone from the ceiling.

I examined the cell from wall to wall. A boyhood passion of mine had been reading tales of escape from prison, and I couldn't help pretending I was the imprisoned Benvenuto Cellini, or the character known only as "The Brain," whom no prison could hold. Besides their enormous intellects, however, the characters had always had some extra resources at their disposal—the inside parts of a toilet, wires from a bedspring, screws from some fixture, an accomplice waiting outside. John Dillinger, I recalled, had sculpted a pistol from a lump of soap, blackened it with shoe polish, and fooled a timid jailer. But I didn't even have soap. The cell had no removable parts: all the screws were one-way; the toilet was flushed by a button. A canny prisoner, I surmised, could probably get the door to his cell opened by yelling out of the two-inch space at the bottom, "Open Seventeen!" in just the right tone and at just the right moment. But even if that worked, it was doubtful he could make it through the remaining seven doors without a hostage, and the hostage tactic called for a desperation I most certainly didn't have.

Bored, I peered idly under the bed pad. There was nothing but dirt, and some scratchings in the painted surface of the bed shelf. I looked more closely. It was graffiti, a prisoner's message, written not with pen or Magic Marker—those would have been confiscated—but scratched in the paint with a small piece of metal. ARIZONA BUCKY, it said 9-19-80. Beneath it was a testimonial:

A.B. is in love w/a girl from Chi-town.
Her beauty puts to shame a mountain
sunrise, her hair blows like silk in the

wind . . . many men long for her heart,
even the legendary *Arizona Bucky*!

Bucky, I thought, what was a romantic like you doing in jail? Like many a tramp on the rails, his thoughts while in solitary confinement had turned to the things he didn't have: love, a woman, a legend surrounding his name.

I scoured the walls for more sayings, but besides various initials, there was only this morsel of jailhouse philosophy: "I'm gonna do it again but I ain't gonna get caught." That's the spirit, I thought.

I pulled the roll of toilet paper out of its holder, placed it on the bed as a pillow, and lay down. There was a lump in my back pocket, and I discovered that they had left me my cigarettes and matches. Thank God, I thought—something to do! I lit one and pulled luxuriously on it. I would ration them, one every couple of hours. That would help me keep my sanity. It was very cool in the cell, and so I threw the blanket over me. It was too small. If I turned it diagonally, one corner came to my calves and the opposite one to right between my shoulder blades. Assuming the fetal position, or as near to it as I could come, I tried to make it cover me. I snuffed out my cigarette butt on the floor and drifted off to sleep.

A faint, insistent voice awakened me. "Hey, Seventeen!" it called, muffled. "Hey, Seventeen!" I sat up. Yes, I thought, I was Seventeen—that's what the jailer had called out to open and close my door. Maybe it was him.

"Seventeen!" I got up and walked to the door. The hall was empty, but the thick windows of three cells were visible, and through the window of Number 15 I saw a new inmate. About my age, he held two fingers up in a "V" in front of his mouth, as though he were smoking, then disappeared downwards. Again I heard the voice: "Hey, Seventeen—got a cigarette?" He was speaking through the space between the bottom of the door and the floor. He rose again and repeated the smoking gesture. He must have seen my smoke.

I nodded, and went to get a cigarette for him. I ripped a pack of matches down the middle, bound matches and cigarette with a rubber band left in my pocket, and bent down and tossed it through the opening under my door toward the opening under his, perhaps fifteen feet away. It bounced and skidded to a stop three or four feet from the target.

Soon an arm had extended itself out from under the door and into the hall. Number 15 groped around, but his arm was several inches too short. He had played this game before though. Presently the arm reappeared, this time holding a blanket.

"Tell me which way!" he called, throwing the blanket out into the corridor and then dragging it in, in hopes the cigarette would be underneath.

"More toward me," I instructed him. But again he missed, and again. Finally, losing patience, Number 15 tossed the blanket out too far, and lost that as well.

"Shit," he said.

The blanket, I thought, would be very conspicuous to whomever was looking at the closed-circuit hall monitor camera. Sure enough, within a few minutes the tall, tough guard turned the corner into the hall.

"All right, quit fuckin' around out here," he said with irritation, kicking the blanket back into Cell 4W 15. I pulled my head back from the window so that he wouldn't see me. "What're you shits tryin' to pull?"

"I just wanted a cigarette," said 4W 15 defensively.

"You'll get more than that if you don't quit fuckin' off," said the guard. He mashed the cigarette bundle with his boot and kicked it in under the door, too.

"Thanks a million," said 4W 15 sarcastically.

I lay back down. There were no clocks around, but after a while one of the three fluorescent bulbs on my ceiling flicked off, as did one in each of the other cells around me. That, I thought, must mean it is nighttime. I slept fitfully.

When the lights came on again, we were released one by one to eat breakfast in a central area, and then it was back to the cells. Much later during what I guessed was the same day, we were released again and herded into an elevator waiting room, to go to court. Court, conveniently, was downstairs, and one by one the prisoners, trying to keep our beltless pants up, smoothing over hair which we had no means of combing, and striving to remove the rumpled appearance from our slept-in clothes, filed into the gallery of the courtroom.

It was a different crowd from the original group in the holding cell, most of whom had probably been bonded out. Among the prisoners were some tough-looking women, two of whom, I learned, were in for beating up a garbageman who had whistled at them; another for prostitution; another for shoplifting. Among the men were transgressors of the law against public urination, one quite embarrassed; guys behind on alimony payments; barroom brawlers; and a pimp.

Some discussed strategies with which to impress the judge. The fellow next to me, a kindly-looking older man with flaming red hair who said he had been busted for falling asleep in a park, asked me if it was daytime or nighttime. The courtroom had no windows.

"Daytime, I think," I said.

I had gone over what I was going to tell the judge a hundred times. It would be the truth, minus the fact that I was a college student trying to learn about what happened to guys who had landed where I had. Of course, I would plead not guilty, because I would never have been arrested if the policeman had treated me properly.

The judge's instructions, however, made me think twice. We could enter a plea of guilty, no contest, or not guilty, he said, patiently explaining what those meant so that everybody—except the Mexicans sitting to my right, who spoke no English—could understand. A not-guilty plea, he was at pains to explain, would require him to set a new trial date, probably ten days to two weeks in the future. Unless the prisoner were bonded out between then and now—and that was unlikely for all these men, who had spent at least a night in jail already—he would have to stay in prison until the trial. This news angered me, and I really expected that at least some of the twenty-five or thirty men who preceded me to the podium would feel the same way and defiantly proclaim their innocence. But not a one did.

"What do you think you'll plead?" I asked the red-haired man.

"Oh, guilty. Always plead guilty," he said. "That always works the best. Then they like you—they can see you want to get the whole thing over with right away, too. Otherwise, well—you heard what he said: ten days to two weeks! Not me, no way. How 'bout you? You're the guy that walked across the bridge, right? Sheeit, that ain't nothin'. Don't be crazy!"

Sacrificing principle for my freedom, I pleaded no contest. After hearing my account of the arrest, the judge lectured me about how the police were under a lot of pressure when the President was in town, advised me to "change my attitude," threw out the "pedestrian in roadway" charge, and gave me a fifty-dollar fine on the disobedience charge, suspended on the condition I didn't do the same thing in Denver within a year.

"Not much chance of that," I confessed to the red-haired man as we walked out of the jail a few hours later. "I'm gettin' out of Denver as soon as I can."

"Hell, I'm leavin' sooner than that!" he said, parting company with me as I went to reclaim my property from a different police building.

Wallet, pencils, change—except for the bedroll, it all seemed to be there, I thought, as I opened the "Prisoner's Property" envelope with my name on it. But then I came to my reporter's notebook, which I had half expected not to be there at all, and discovered that the last few pages—the ones upon which I had quoted the cop and written down his patrol-car number as I left the bridge—had been ripped out. Furious, I marched directly upstairs to the Denver Police's Staff Inspection Bureau. Denver, unlike many cities of similar size, has no independently elected commission to oversee the operations of the police department, and so the police do it themselves: the foxes watch over the foxes. The office was staffed by a variety of lieutenants and sergeants, who seated me near a window overlooking the jail building to fill out a lengthy report of my version of the incident. Almost merrily, the officer in charge accepted it, offered me some coffee, and assured me I would hear from the bureau about the disposition of my case "within a few months."

Frustrated by the charade and by the system that had just scooped up and disgorged me, and sick and tired of being enclosed by four unfriendly walls, I punched the first-floor button of the elevator so hard I hoped it would break and fled the police building.

The Denver & Rio Grande Western yards: a mythic, imagined place of my childhood. Here the trains that climbed from plains to mountains, winding their way through canyons and tunnels, over passes and trestles like muscular, writhing snakes, were set out uniformly, equidistant, arrow-straight. Here, momentarily, they were in suspended animation, resting from the last trip and getting readied for another. Switch engines pulled apart newly arrived trains, car by car, and remade them into new trains. Brakemen walked their length, connecting the air hoses between each car, and "car knockers"—railroad inspectors—checked the cars for damage. The units, nerve centers of the trains, disconnected themselves for refueling and repairs; when they returned, making the train whole, one knew which way the train was going and, more important, that it was about to leave.

Here, also, was where men boarded the trains, secretly, without benefit of ticket or conductor, in violation of the law. Today, that last part scared me. I sat under a bridge over which an interstate highway ran, and under which tracks led south out of the yard. All the way from downtown, I had painstakingly obeyed the law, crossing only in the crosswalks, obeying DON'T WALK signs as though they, too, had the power of arrest. Yet it was hard, as walking was the thing I most wanted to do in the world—walk and not stop, walk and get out of town, walk and be free.

It took a moment to become reaccustomed to brightness and shade, to wind blowing and clouds coming and going, to a temperature that moved up and down, not holding steady at a deadening sixty degrees. But after my enforced hibernation, I welcomed the outdoors—recklessly, for though I had emerged from jail with my jacket, my bedroll and other survival tools were gone. I didn't know what I would do; but I did know Lonny had been able to make do in circumstances much rougher than my own, and that I should be able to, too.

Yet my exhilaration at being out was undermined by my anger. President nearby or not, people should not be treated that way in America. And compared to what happened to other people, what happened to me was probably nothing. In Dallas, again and again I had heard poor people complaining about police brutality. Why had I always questioned them, assuming the real problem was a lack of respect for policemen?

Possibly worst was that the arrest had interrupted my daydream. The hobo trip, in other words, was in ways a lived-out fantasy. Entering the hobo world, I fancied I had entered a world free of responsibility and unjust authority. And even as the hobo subculture stands as a reproach to the dominant culture, I could reproach academe by doing schoolwork and *enjoying myself*.

But the cops had reminded me that the hobo's life was not a game. I realized I had not predicted the fright of it. Hoboes themselves, I supposed, could treat each other even worse than the cops did. Armed with a new realism, I took long, Treetop-style steps back to the jungle on the Platte, en route to the D & RGW yards. I wanted to say good-bye to Al and Tree.

But they had vanished, along with the dog and the tarpaulin. A new tramp was there now, making use of the spool table and enjoying a lunch of a few leftover concessionaire's sandwiches. He said he didn't know where Tree and Al had gone, though he had heard from tramps down the river that cops had been there looking for "a real tall guy" the night before. He probably caught out on the "Nighttime Man," I thought to myself.

Earlier that week, on the way back from our dumpster hunt, Al had spied an old sleeping bag stashed in woods adjoining the river. Claiming finder's rights, he had hidden the bag in brush behind the tent. I checked the spot, told the surprised tramp it was mine, and had myself a new bedroll. By commandeering one of several surplus water jugs that littered the site, I had nearly a full complement of gear. I asked the tramp for directions to the Denver & Rio Grande yard, and hiked there in the hot afternoon sun.

It was not a fun place to be. For company there was only an empty bottle of white port, ant lions beneath the sand, and a thousand FUCK YOU's scratched and painted on the beams of the bridge. FUCK YOU TOO, read one response. It could have been mine.

The yard's tower was tall and prominent, and I didn't dare venture into the yard to gather intelligence on train departures. Finally, though, dusk began to fall, and I scrambled down to ask a passing switchman for directions to a westbound train. There was one called for soon, he answered quickly, glancing at the tower, and told me what track it was on. I found an empty and, as night fell, left Denver.

The train wound its serpentine way up into the mountains. I planted my feet firmly near the doorway and looked out over the plains, doing an about-face to see out the other door every time the train did a hairpin turn and changed direction. Denver sparkled with the variously colored lights of buildings, houses, and streets, and all of a sudden I felt very sad. Back there were cops and the jail but also, a million times more important, back there was my family. In Jack Kerouac's *On the Road,* which I had read over the summer, I had been struck by the frequent use of the word "sad" to describe almost anything connected with his travels—the "sad highway," the "sad town," the "sad American night." Why, I had wondered, did it have to be sad? Life on the road for me had always been adventuresome, unpredictable, exciting, more fun than sad. But tonight, the sad made sense. It could have been used to describe almost anything around me—the city view, the boxcar, the mountains ahead. It was my sadness, the sadness of moving alone, to destinations unknown. And I realized that night what must be common knowledge among hoboes: it's easier to be on the road when home is something you don't feel too good about.

But as the train climbed higher, and the air grew cooler, I steeled myself. Misgivings about leaving home and friends I had had before. But for now, I had resolved, I had to be tramping. Now I was a son and brother to one family; later, I might be husband and father to another. My own family would depend on me more heavily, and the risks I took would in a way be theirs.

And, of course, I had to tramp sometime, to have my own stories to tell, not those of someone's uncle, or the big kids, or a movie. Even if I didn't return to tell the stories . . . well, long ago I had decided that I'd rather go by falling off a freight into a bottomless gorge than by dying of heat prostration in some big city's rush-hour traffic.

Slowly now, the train climbed steeply. Moonlight shone through the boxcar doors, illuminating my breath and making the snow-capped mountaintops glow. Already the train had passed through a number of short tunnels, plunging me into darkness and a self-imposed paralysis, for I knew that the slightest imprudent move could send me through the doorway and into oblivion. Soon the train would pass through one of the longest railroad tunnels on the continent, the six-mile-long Moffat Tunnel, which cuts beneath an 11,500-foot-high automobile pass and the Continental Divide. The Moffat was one of the Goliaths of the older, railriding boys of my childhood—the black hole of the rails, an endless, fume-filled tube. The best survival strategy against the hot, acrid smoke, I had heard, was to place a wet handkerchief over the mouth. Since my bandanna had disappeared with my bedroll, I unbuttoned one of my cuffs, soaked it with water from my bottle, and using that as my gas mask, emerged at the end only slightly woozy.

The tunnel opened up on the Winter Park ski area, and suddenly I was back in familiar territory. I had spent countless weekends up here learning to ski, and many times I had cross-country skied on the railroad right-of-way between the mountain and the house of some friends in the nearby town. I had waited at the crossing I would soon be passing through and marveled at the train, the only one I ever got to see up close.

Soon we chugged through the crossing, to the flash of red lights and the jangling of the warning bells. I gazed out the door at the familiar road, with the familiar pines and spruce and, now that the exhaust had blown away, the familiar mountain smell. I thought of jumping off: the embankment was steep, but I could make it. I could take our friends' house key from its hiding place, go inside, and take a shower and lie between warm sheets.

But I turned the other way. There was no such thing as home to hoboes—or if there was, it was only a memory—and I resolved it was time to get the idea out of my mind.

8

Lying on my belly on the jiggling boxcar floor, I watched dawn reveal the bare landscape. Drifting in and out of sleep all night, I had been vaguely aware that the country outside was Utah; now that I could see it, I sat up and rubbed my eyes. The soil, chalky and the color of cream, lay dry and uncovered except for a few cowed, thirsty-looking shrubs and small trees. It spread in large pastel expanses, punctuated by randomly placed towers of stone, and sometimes by an eroded, mid-sized mountain or ridge. The powdery soil looked as though it would turn to sticky mud at the first drop of rain; at night, a person walking across it might feel like an astronaut on the moon. Now, except for the raucous, directed energy of the train, all was very still. Already it looked hot. Later, I thought, I would value the shade provided by my boxcar. I lay back down and dozed.

The warning bells of a highway crossing sounded through the boxcar door. I sensed the train was slowing and awoke completely. Bells rang out again: more crossings. It was going to be a fairly large town. I sat just inside the doorway, waiting for a clue to my location, and pondered the jangling of the signal bells. Not only did the volume change as my boxcar whizzed by, loudest at the exact moment the flashing red lights shone through the door, but the pitch rose to its highest at that same moment. The Doppler effect. I remembered my teacher explaining why the noise of a passing automobile did the same thing. The sound waves emitted by the car as it approached hit the eardrum faster and faster, resulting in a change in the frequency. The closer the car got, the higher the note—until the car passed and sped away, and the note traveled back down the scale. The same thing was going on with those signal bells, only now it was my ears that were moving, not the source of the sound.

Now here, I thought for a happy instant, was something I could tell the tramps about a feature of their life, to improve their understanding of it as they were always improving mine . . . but then again, no. Some knowledge alienates; school-learned knowledge, shared on the rails, seemed to almost always. I would keep the Doppler effect to myself.

More crossings, and finally the sighting of an interstate highway and of distant tall buildings against a backdrop of dusty hills convinced me this was not a train town of the usual order of magnitude; it was Salt Lake City. The route in to the central city, however, was like the train's way into many towns: lined with warehouses and factories, storage lots and vacant lots, and rusty, overgrown sidings jumping off the main track to terminate a few yards away at the loading docks of factories. Old boxcars often sat on these rickety rails, waiting for a locomotive to remember them and pull them back into circulation.

My boxcar became noisier, the tracks underneath it multiplied. The engineer changed tracks, maneuvering for a good position in which to enter the yards. Actually, I had learned that "maneuvering" had nothing to do with it: the train's course was navigated not by the engineer, but by the main tower, via radio and electric signal impulses. The tower sent out the signals, and little motors switched tracks from one position to another. The difficulty of the engineer's prestigious job eluded me—he had nothing to do with steering the train; he only made it go faster or slower. It could probably all be accomplished with a single knob. I entertained a daydream of taking a train for a little spin—how hard could it be?

The train finally braked to a stop on the edge of the yard, a brusque brakeman pointed me in the direction of downtown, and I set off down the tracks.

The space underneath bridges, in Norse mythology, is often the dominion of fierce, hairy trolls, and perhaps it was no coincidence that under the first bridge I came to that morning stood the first tramp I had seen in Salt Lake City. Tall, dark, heavy, and bearded, he was as forbidding as any troll. But this tramp seemed uncomfortable with the role, and called out to me from across the tracks as I approached.

I headed slowly toward the man, sizing him up. He appeared to be in his thirties. I was struck by the new nylon-frame backpack he wore, a piece of equipment more characteristic of middle-class hitchhikers than of tramps. Contrasting more sharply, though, with the man's sheer bulk, rough features, and gravelly voice, was a tiny puppy sitting pertly next to his thick-soled work boot. It yapped at me as I approached.

"Hello."

"How you doin'?"

"Nice puppy," I said, bending down to pat it. The tramp stiffened but said nothing. The pup was a German shepherd, by the looks of him, but I asked the man to make sure.

"He's a poodle . . . no, er, I mean a Chihuahua," he said.

"I don't think so," I replied, raising an eyebrow. "He's furry and dark. You sure?"

The question wasn't answered. Instead, the man asked me, "Say, is this where the P.U. trains leave from?"

"The what kind?"

"P.U."

"Wait—you mean U.P.?"

"Yeah, that's it."

"Well, I'm just in, so I don't really know, but from the looks of it, this here's the end of the Rio Grande yards. The U.P. must be somewhere else."

"Oh."

There was a long silence, while I tried to figure out what this guy was all about.

"Are you hitching, or are you riding trains?" I asked him.

"Trains," he said. "I'm headin' for Vegas. Hey, I know where there's some water. Want some?"

Fresh water sounded good, and so I followed him to a clump of bushes near the bridge. Water flowed from a pipe, and as he stooped to drink from it, I noticed he seemed stiff, in pain.

"Something the matter?" I asked as he paused, half down to his knees.

"I got a rupture, see?" He cupped his hands around his genitals, displaying an oddly placed bulge. "It's intestines down in my nut-sack."

I whistled.

"I ain't feelin' too good," he said. "Say, would you go buy some food for me?"

"Okay. You got some money?"

"Yeah, but you buy it, and I'll pay you back."

"I don't think so."

"Hey, don't worry about it. You leave your gear here, and I'll watch it for you."

If he thought I would go for that, too, he was crazy. Tramps almost never entrusted their gear to other tramps, especially new acquaintances. How dumb did he think I was? More to the point, how dumb was he?

I walked away, without his money, bought some milk, and returned to the bridge. "Want a drink of this?" I asked, holding out the quart.

"Sure," he said, taking it from me.

We climbed into the shade under the bridge and sat for a while. The wide array of Rio Grande tracks to the south narrowed to just two sets by the time they reached the bridge; to the north of the bridge, the two tracks ran down the center of a long, sandy corridor, bounded by steep barbed-wire fences, forty feet from each track, which marked the beginning of industrial property. A number of tramps were out walking along the corridor. We watched as one older, fat tramp shuffled slowly down the line, eyes to the ground, examining old bottles and jugs along the way. Finally coming upon an empty wine bottle with a screw-on lid, he took it and waddled slowly away. I thought about my sick companion, about the aging Treetop, about thin Lonny, and about the men in the mission and realized that, even though I was no bruiser, I was in much better shape than most of the tramps I had met. Though sobering, the observation was, from the point of view of my personal security, also comforting.

Next into view were a young man and a woman. Adeptly they climbed over the couplings of trains to cross the corridor and paused at the water pipe. Just then, a brown sedan with a tiny antenna on top and spotlights near the side mirrors zoomed up and braked near them in a swirl of dust. Inside were two bulls. The driver rolled down his window and spoke loudly at the couple; they nodded their heads and quickly dispersed.

"We better get outa here," said my companion. He was already on his feet, the puppy under his arm. Together we strode quickly away, disappearing into the brush just as the car slowed behind us.

We listened as it crept by, the noise of the radio drifting to us through the driver's window. Finally he accelerated, apparently tired of hassling poor hoboes. We made our way back to where we had seen the couple, presently finding ourselves in a small clearing in the trackside brush.

"Fuckin' bulls," said my companion gruffly to the couple, who were seated around a small fire. It seemed as good a greeting as any, for the man replied, "He ran you, too, huh?"

"Would've if he coulda caught us," said my companion.

"We're boilin' up some coffee water here—you want any?"

My companion shook his head, and I replied that I didn't have a cup—a casualty of my arrest.

"Hell, we prob'ly got one here for ya. I got all kindsa shit. Honey, check the pack, willya?"

The woman, an Indian several inches taller than the man, and with long dark hair, obliged. She wore sneakers, clean jeans, and an embroidered blouse. They apparently shared between them one large backpack, like my companion's. From it she extracted four cups, two enameled and chipped, one tin, and one plastic. She handed me the tin one.

"Um, well, guess I'll take y'up on that after all," grumbled my companion, reaching for the plastic cup. He pulled up a stump to sit on, and I took a seat on my pack. The man put on a work glove, took the can of water from the fire, and filled our cups. He was short but heavily muscled, and expert in his movements. He wore a faded green short-sleeved sweatshirt and jeans. His hair was short and blond, his face, neck, and arms either well tanned or quite dirty. Dirty, I decided as we sat, sipping the hot drinks.

The silence grew long.

"I'm Ted, by the way," I started, immediately wishing I hadn't. The introductions habit was foreign here, but I found it very hard to break.

Oddly, the short fellow was predisposed to social niceties.

"I'm Buddy," he said. "And this here's Sam." The Indian woman eyed me placidly. Sam?

There was more silence, and then all three of us, having committed ourselves, looked over at the tramp with the dog.

"Thomas," he said, grudgingly.

"And what about the puppy?" asked Sam.

"Him? That's Scamp." Scamp lay dwarfed between Thomas's boots, panting in the midday heat.

Presently Buddy produced a gallon can of sliced beets from next to his pack.

"Where'd those come from?" I asked.

"Found 'em in a restaurant dumpster over there," replied Buddy, pointing vaguely over his shoulder, preoccupied with opening the can. He worked his pocketknife can opener around the edge, slowly exposing the crimson contents. He spooned some out and into his mouth, pronouncing them fine after a moment's rumination—you never were really sure about dumpster fare. "Anybody want some?"

Hungry, I was about to scoop out a coffee-cupful when the sound of an approaching car caught my attention. The camp area was visible from the dirt road, and the bulls in the brown sedan had again caught sight of us. The sedan, off the road, braked to a fast stop a scant fifteen feet away from us, engulfing us in dust. Nobody moved.

Two bulls climbed out, slamming the car doors hard. The younger and taller of the two approached us and drew his revolver, trying to look tough. Instead, I thought, he looked as scared as I probably did. Guns on television are one thing; a real one, brandished by a nervous bull, is quite another. He addressed Buddy, whose back was to him.

"I told you a few minutes ago to get the hell out of here! Now I see you got a fire going, and you're still here. Now, *get movin'!* This is the last time I'm gonna say it. You hear me?"

Buddy remained motionless, nodding his head slightly. "Yessir."

There was no need for the bull to say more, but he did anyway. "There's plenty a' empty jungles up at Twentieth Street, so why don't you go up there? My ass is dirt if they see you around here. Understand? Put out that fire, and move along!" His face was red.

"Yessir."

The bull spun around, reholstered the revolver, and stormed back to the car with his partner. They backed up recklessly, and drove away.

Buddy unfroze and started muttering under his breath. Avoiding everyone's eyes, he got up and started putting the coffee cups back into the pack. We would be leaving, then. It was one of the little defeats tramps are dealt, sometimes several times a day, and you had to live with it. It was reassuring, though, to see that Buddy was angry. His comments soon showed his "yessirs" to be phony, the requisite nods to authority.

"If I had my way," he announced, tying up the pack, "I'd lease a big field here right next to the railroad tracks"—he gestured toward an adjoining vacant lot—"and get about two thousand tramps in it, and then call up the bulls. I'd like to see 'em try and move us all *then!*" We murmured our agreement. It would be nice not to be outgunned.

Barely a minute after the bulls had left, the four of us were gone. We walked up the tracks, stopping in the shade of warehouses to rest and curse the bulls some more. Scamp trotted gamely behind. Buddy and Thomas had walked the stretch before, and checked out a number of possible jungle sites in the shrubs along the edge, only to find them already occupied. Finally we happened upon a campsite with possibilities: backing up on one of the six-foot chain-link fences topped with barbed wire that formed the sides of the tracks corridor, it had a fire area, a fair-sized tree, and tall weeds to help keep it invisible to the tracks and road. But it was also scattered with trash, old clothing, and, worse, numerous piles of shit, which I hoped were from a dog. Buddy took the lead in cleaning it up, using a piece of cardboard to whisk the crap off the ground and into the weeds. When he finished, the place looked better, but still distasteful for all the residues. In disgust, Buddy remarked, "The person who was here don't deserve to call hisself a tramp!"

More remained to be done before dusk. Buddy and Sam set off for the supermarket to get something for dinner. Thomas and I, on Buddy's suggestion, walked a short distance back down the tracks to retrieve some large pieces of cardboard to be used as mattresses, though Thomas's condition left most of the carrying to me.

Soon Sam was chopping onions and potatoes back at the jungle; I volunteered to help Buddy find some water and wood for the fire. He slung the gallon water jug over his shoulder by using a belt he had looped through its handle, carrying it in a very professional-looking manner, like a soldier with a cubical white rifle. It was now after hours, and so we scouted a number of warehouses and small buildings for a spigot. Finally Buddy discovered one. Besides filling up the jug, he rinsed off his hands and face, using his sweatshirt afterward as a towel. "Sam's been after me for bein' so dirty," he explained.

I had no idea where to find wood. For my camping, I was used to taking water from streams and wood from deadfall in a forest. But Buddy could have taught the Outward Bound course on urban survival. Approaching a loading dock closed down for the day, he pointed to some broken wooden pallets stacked near a wall. They were heavy; furtively he climbed onto the dock and passed me two. We stole away with them over our shoulders.

Back at camp, Sam filled a can with the water we had brought to start the soup, then noticed Buddy's clean face.

"He washed it!" she said. "I don't believe it." She was so pleased, she stepped up and gave him a big kiss. Seeing my smile, Buddy reddened. "Now cut that out!" he stammered, prompting giggles and another hug from Sam.

"Don't complain, man," I advised him. "I washed mine, too, but you don't see anybody comin' up and givin' me a hug."

Buddy made the soup hot with garlic and pepper, and soon we ate large helpings, with bread. The whole meal cost $2.10.

"Ahhhh," said Buddy contentedly when finished, leaning back on his piece of cardboard. "I feel like I could go a thousand miles." Judging by the well-worn soles and heels of his cowboy boots, he just had.

"How long you been on the road?" I asked him.

"Oh, since about spring, I guess. How 'bout you? You look kinda young to be on the rails."

"Only about a month. Before that I was in school, out East. But I got sick of that, and was lookin' for something new. I'd heard there were guys still doin' this, so I thought I'd give it a shot."

"Yup, some still do, all right."

"You do it a lot?"

Buddy sat still for a moment, chewing on a twig. To ask two successive questions about his background, I knew, was really pressing my luck. Finally he spoke.

"Ten years ago's the last time. Oh, and back when I was a kid like you, I did it then, too. But this time—I don't know. I didn't think it'd go this long."

Buddy seemed in a good mood; it was a good time of day for talking. As tactfully as possible, I asked him why he thought it had "gone this long."

"Illinois," he answered.

"Illinois?"

"Yeah, see, I was a *ce*-ment pourer there for a while, worked at one of them nucular power plants they're building in Byron. But shit, that place? I couldn't stay there more'n a month. Though I did stay five months on that job. But that was enough. Goddamn Illinois."

I was emboldened by my luck. "But what is it about Illinois?"

Buddy stared at me—either puzzled or in warning—then said "bah" under his breath and waved off the question, turning to the fire. Illinois was trouble, that was all—probably with the law, maybe with a woman, maybe something else. That was enough information. It was enough because the rails, I had begun to see, were a place a lot like the Old West used to be, a place where a man for whom things had gone poorly could start afresh, without the burden of the past. He could be anonymous—even pick a new name, if he liked—and not be reminded of past failures by people who "knew him when." Asking too much about a fellow's past was simply not done.

In coming days I would learn that Buddy's ten-year hiatus from railriding included a stint in the Navy, marked by promotion to chief petty officer, and then successive demotions for striking superiors, until he was given a dishonorable discharge; a couple of factory jobs ("I don't seem to do too good in places that's got a lotta rules," he said, more to himself than me); a marriage and divorce; and a stay in at least one state penitentiary. But the information was offered randomly, in haphazard remarks that Buddy would throw out now and then. If he brought up the Navy, I could usually get away with asking more about it; if I brought up the subject, Buddy would dodge my questions. Months later, I heard a friend of mine telling an acquaintance that I had spent several months "interviewing hoboes." Nothing, I had to explain, could be further from the truth.

Twenty or thirty minutes went by around the campfire without anyone saying a thing—the remedy for too much talk. Finally, small chatter started up between Buddy and Thomas. Sensing the bad feeling had gone, I asked on a hunch if either of them had ever heard of the National Hobo Convention.

"Sure, that's in Ohio, right?" said Buddy. "Yeah, I went one year. There's thousands of hoboes go to that thing. Problem is, so many of 'em's niggers. I never seen so many niggers in my life, 'cept maybe for in California. There's another state for you. Whole place is niggers. What they oughta do is put a fence around it and put all the niggers in and have free season four or five times a year!"

He laughed and Thomas smirked. Sam just looked into the fire. I almost said something, but then checked myself. A good anthropologist, perhaps, would have laughed along with them, in order to be better accepted. But appearing to agree was far too great a price to pay. I sat quietly and uncomfortably. Things didn't get any better.

"Hey, Buddy," croaked Thomas. "Where's the mission in this town? I couldn't find it."

"Shit, a mission? I stay outa those. All you get at missions is a sermon and the shits. Go to a mission if you wanta get treated like a kid." Missions were an easy but demeaning way out of the business of urban survival at which Buddy was so adept. "I can think of ten ways to get a meal without checkin' into a Sally," he said, and proceeded to name them: trash hoppers, "free grocery" places like the Bishop's Warehouse, pizzerias (walk in, sit down, wait for somebody to leave, finish their pizza), church handouts, the Volunteers of America, food stamps, money from blood, money you find, money from welfare, money from day labor, money from "hitting"—panhandling, in tramp language. He elaborated on this last, with a twist.

"The best way is to ask them niggers—they're always good for some bucks. One day, I earned twenty bucks in a hour at a shopping center, just asking them niggers—"

"—I can't believe you did that!" interjected Sam in mild dismay, almost her first words of the evening.

"Hell, why not? Makes 'em poorer. They like to do it, too, 'cause it makes 'em feel superior to white folks."

I had been wanting to get Sam to talk, and her spontaneous remark made me think now was a good time to try. I asked the question that had been bugging me since our introduction.

"Why do they call you Sam, anyway?" I said, catching her eye. She looked at Buddy self-consciously and giggled.

"Well, it was in summer . . ." began Buddy, the usual spokesman for the couple. But Sam interrupted.

"I was playing pool in a bar up in Pasco," she said. I recognized the name from Portland Gray's list of jungle towns. It was in eastern Washington state. "This other guy kept comin' on to me, givin' me a hard time. He wanted to know my name.

"Anyway, Buddy was watchin' all of this. I think he was gettin' ready to save me or somethin' "—she cut off, giggling and squeezing Buddy's arm—"but I just told this guy, 'You want to know my name? Okay, it's Sam!' " The response had angered the man, and he had left the bar. But it had tickled Buddy.

"He got pissed 'cause he knew she was makin' fun of him. That's when I moved in," said Buddy, with a sly smile. Sam hugged him tighter.

"So what's your real name?"

"Dorothy."

She moved closer to Buddy, though she had been right next to him all night. She plainly adored him—if she wasn't squeezing his arm, her head was on his shoulder, or her hand rested on his forearm. Though it was getting dark, I was somewhat startled to notice, in the light of the campfire, that she and her clothing had remained very clean throughout the afternoon, an almost impossible feat on the rails. One reason was that Buddy let her do almost no work—she had sliced the onion and potatoes, but he had done the dishes and most of the chores, including cleanup. He also carried all their gear, in the large red-frame pack.

Sam busied herself with the pack now, untying the large bundle of blankets and fashioning them into an inviting double bed atop two pieces of cardboard. Buddy and I watched Thomas play with Scamp—they were battling over an old sock.

"Scimpy, Scampy, Scampy-oo, how are you-ooo?" Thomas crooned to his pet. He finally let Scamp win, and, triumphant, the puppy pranced away with the wet and dirty sock, tripping over it, and deposited it near Sam.

"Oooh, he's so cute!" she exclaimed, reaching down to pet him.

"Don't do that!" sputtered Thomas, a little too sharply. Sam looked in alarm at Buddy.

"What I mean is, I want him to be a one-man dog. I don't want other folks bein' nice to him 'cause then he might go away with them. He's gotta stick by me."

"Okay," said Sam defensively. Later, as Thomas rearranged his pack, I noticed a hand-lettered cardboard sign that said, DON'T TOUCH THE DOG.

"Cute as Scamp is, though, you must have a hard time of it," I observed to Thomas.

"Cute, cute, cute, everybody says he's cute," complained Thomas. "Why don't they ever tell me *I'm* cute? Sometimes I wish I was the dog."

But at two hundred fifty pounds, whiskery and with a sandpaper larynx, Thomas could not have been less like the dog in size, liveliness, or appeal. Buddy and I watched them play until the fire died.

Buddy and Sam's big alarm clock sounded at dawn; by the time I got up he was gone in search of a job. Sam and I kindled the fire again, heating coffee water and warming our hands. Thomas's muffled snores came from his sleeping bag. Scamp, out of sight, apparently was in there with him. "If he can stand the smell of my ass, I guess I can stand the smell of his," Thomas had said the night before.

It was the first time I had been alone with Sam. I still was amazed to have found her on the rails, with a man or otherwise. Whenever I had asked tramps before about women on the rails, I had gotten the impression that what few there were were pistol-packing roller derby queens, more dangerous than most of the men. One tramp said that the last woman he saw was followed from her boxcar by a contingent of seven male tramps, "her guys," her harem. Sam was a large woman, but didn't seem tough. Her quiet-ness, in fact, led me to think that if I prodded her with too many questions I would scare her away. Yet I had a hundred.

"Do you see many other women on the road, Sam?"

"Oh, three or four since we've been at it."

"Were they alone?"

"One was, but mostly they were with black guys. Why—do you miss girls?"

I confessed that I did. I had entertained thoughts of finding my own Boxcar Bertha.

"Well, I don't know," she said. "I don't think this is the best place to look for 'em."

"Doesn't it ever get lonely for you?" On my mind was the macho atmosphere around the jungles, and the tramps' frequent telling of dirty jokes. Just the night before, Buddy and Thomas had exchanged information on their favorite ways of performing cun-nilingus. Buddy preferred it with peanut butter; Thomas main-tained he always had luck using a Lifesaver. "Drives 'em wild," was his claim.

In answer to my question, Sam just gave a little shrug.

Buddy returned, to Sam's relief, saving her from a long day with a busybody and a hairy weirdo.

"Did you get the job, honey?" she asked.

"He said he can't take me till Monday—just wanted me to fill out forms today," he said bitterly. "I want a *job,* not an application!"

He made himself some coffee, changed the radio from one country-and-western station to another, and tended a fire that didn't need tending.

"A job," he repeated several times, half to himself, "not an application."

But Buddy was a man of action, and also Sam's provider, and before his coffee was gone he had convinced us this hot, arid day could be better spent inside the Mormon Bishop's Warehouse. I had heard of the Bishop's Warehouse from almost everyone I had met on the road. In exchange for a day's work, a transient received an all-you-can-eat lunch and a big box of groceries.

Buddy stashed the leftover firewood in the weeds, we shouldered our respective gear, and the group of four, plus Scamp, set off down the tracks for the Bishop's Warehouse.

Buddy and Thomas both knew the way: two miles toward downtown, then out the right-of-way through a hole in the fence, over guardrails and across both directions of interstate highway, then over a six-foot chain-link fence—Thomas barely made it— into a small plaza called Welfare Square. Outside of the building with the Bishop's Warehouse sign, Thomas tied Scamp to a tree. We walked through swinging glass doors and into a reception room.

Buddy, it had been agreed, would do the talking for him and Sam; Thomas, being more seasoned than me, would be our spokesman.

Buddy addressed the receptionist. "Ma'am," he began dolefully, "I'm awfully sorry to bother you, but we're just into town, we're broke, and—"

She cut him off. "Through those doors, second left. You'll have to talk to the bishop."

Buddy was undaunted. "Straight to the top," he said, with a smile for Sam as we left the room.

We waited uncertainly in a large room where about fifteen middle-aged white people were bustling to and fro, stacking shelves with canned goods for use in the welfare programs of the Mormon Church. Directing them was a tall man in a suit. Eventually someone tapped his elbow and gestured in our direction. Irritated, he looked up at us: another interruption. A few minutes later, he found his way over to our side of the room. Buddy and Sam were interrogated first.

"You're married, I assume?"

"Oh, yes, newlyweds," said Buddy.

"Got any cash?"

"No, sir. We're flat broke. We just got into town last night—"

"You plan to seek full-time employment?" the bishop interrupted.

"Oh, yessir. Why, just this mornin' I went out askin' about this *ce*-ment-pourin' job . . ."

"Sign here." He proffered a registration card. Buddy and Sam did and were ushered away.

The bishop then approached Thomas and me. Though Thomas was the spokesman, he had asked me during our walk over to come up with a hard-luck story. Before the bishop said a word, Thomas began reciting the first few lines of it: "Our house burned down in Pittsburgh, and my brother was killed. I lost my job so I headed west. Met my friend here in Denver and—"

"You ever been here before?" asked the bishop, looking past Thomas to some imaginary object behind me.

"No, sir." Actually, Thomas confided to me later, it was his fourth time that year.

"Well, make sure this time's the last. We have had enough of your type around here." Thomas was silent. There was no need for that remark, I thought. The Bishop's Warehouse was charitable only in taking you the day you showed up; certainly, the value of eight hours of labor had to be worth more than the groceries and the cafeteria lunch we were going to receive. The bishop was no dummy. We signed his registration card.

Sam and Buddy spent the day doing inventory in a stockroom. Thomas and I moved pieces of sheet metal around for an elderly welder, swept out some garages, and loaded hundred-pound burlap sacks of wheat chaff onto pallets. This last job was hard for Thomas, with his rupture. Why didn't he tell the Mormons about it, I asked, and get assigned to something easier?

"Naaah, they'd probably just come up with some stupid light labor, like sweepin' or somethin' "—which, I guessed, would not do justice to his pride or manhood.

We started hefting the bags together, so that Thomas could stand the pain. A grain trucker walked by, holding up a dollar. "Anybody got change?" he asked.

"Man, I ain't seen that much money in six or seven days," said Thomas. The trucker looked at him for an instant, then tossed him the bill.

Thomas was ecstatic. As the man walked away, Thomas expounded to me on how a guy can make it in this world if he just knows the tricks. Receiving the dollar was proof of his savvy. "Didja see the way he just tossed it at me? Didja? Man, I got to him."

We retired to a bench in the shade beside a building to enjoy a celebratory smoke of roll-your-owns. Thomas was just putting away his pouch of Bull Durham when the trucker happened around the building. We exchanged nods with him as he walked by, but then he froze. He looked back at Thomas.

"Tobacco," he said. "Mister, you got tobacco in your pocket. You've seen money lately!" It was an accusation.

Thomas made a gesture toward his shirt pocket. "You need it back?"

The trucker softened. "Naaah." He walked away.

There was no sign of our supervisor, an extremely clean-cut, overhelpful Mormon youth, so Thomas and I indulged in a bit more shade. Pleased that he had retained the dollar, he started telling jokes.

"Know what?" he said, spreading out his arms. "I caught a

trout *this big!*" The arm closest to me thumped me in the chest, and Thomas laughed and laughed. It was a gag I remembered from elementary school.

"Hey, what's that on your shirt?" he asked, pointing at a spot on my hole-y sweatshirt. When I looked down, he flipped his hand up, catching the brim of my cap and knocking it off.

"Heh heh heh heh!" rang Thomas's thin laugh. The only other time I had seen him this way was when he was playing with Scamp. His mood now changed precipitously. "Go get me my matches," he ordered abruptly, pointing at the steps. That too reminded me of Thomas with Scamp, giving a command to the one-man dog. Unlike Scamp, I could refuse.

"Forget it."

"But I thought we were friends!" protested Thomas angrily.

"That has nothing to do with it," I said. I returned to the more desirable company of the burlap sacks.

A couple of hours later, we each received a box containing our day's wage. I looked into mine and was stunned: inside were oranges, loaves of bread, cans of pork and beans, chili con carne and soup, peanut butter, jam, cheese, hot dogs, sandwich meat, and even a roll of toilet paper. My back was feeling like Lonny's had even before I got the box outside. And there were two miles to go!

Thomas followed me a few minutes later, in a very bad temper. He was already tired from work, and now he had this box to carry. Scamp was thrilled to see him, but in his excitement in greeting his master, wrapped his rope around Thomas's leg and made him trip. Thomas hollered, grabbed the puppy, and began to paddle him. Scamp squealed, screamed, got one too many spanks, and peed on Thomas. Then, in a desperate escape, he ran under a large bush, which just made Thomas madder. *"Get out here!"* he cried. *"Get out here or I'm gonna whoop your ass!"*

"Hey, man, let's go, it's getting dark," I urged Thomas, anxious to stop the scene.

"Just a minute, just a minute," said Thomas. "I gotta take care of him."

"Why don't you give the puppy a break and get goin'?" I said.

"What are you complainin' about? What are you cryin' for? Huh, crybaby?"

"Christ, Thomas, you're the one who gets bent outa shape because your dog's glad to see you," I said.

"Yeah, well what business is it of yours?" he asked.

"I wanta get goin'," I said, picking up my bags, sick of Thomas. But the prospect of my actually leaving brought another personality change over him. Suddenly he was plaintive, helpless, childlike, as on the first day when I had met him under the bridge.

"So how'm I gonna carry all this?" he whimpered, gesturing at his frame pack, box of food, and Scamp. Even without his rupture, it was a problem. "Will you help me?" His tone now was the one he had used on the first day I met him, when he asked me to buy groceries. But now that we were, well, "acquainted" and jungled up together, it was harder to say no. I helped him figure out a way we could carry it all.

When we reached the interstate, Thomas had to make two trips across, one with his gear and one with Scamp. I held the puppy while Thomas crossed the first time, and despite his recent treatment, Scamp squealed and struggled and nipped me in an effort to follow his master. I had to hold him very tight. Thomas's "one-man dog" strategy really worked.

When we were almost at the jungle we ran into Buddy and Sam, and finished the walk with them. They had received even bigger boxes of groceries than us—the reward, it seemed, for being married, or saying you were. We all started musing over whether our camp would have been ransacked.

"Ten years ago, you could leave all your stuff at your camp, come back a week later, and it'd still be there," said Thomas. "Right or wrong, Buddy?"

"Right."

"Man, if those tramps down the line came and took our cardboard, I'm gonna bash their heads in."

The cardboard was still there, and mayhem was averted.

Dawn found me dull-headed and baggy-eyed, and I was grateful for the absence of a bathroom mirror. As Sam rolled up their bed, Buddy began going over the resources Salt Lake City still had to offer us. Food stamps were "hard" here, he said, taking about a week to receive after application, and he and Sam had given blood too recently to do it again. There was a temporary labor agency, though, and he had heard from men in the next jungle about some churches that offered relief of various sorts.

Thomas opted out of the expedition but assured us he would stay at the jungle all day. Just the same, we decided to stash our gear at the jungle of the tramps with the information on churches. Buddy had met two of its three occupants the night before, and felt they would be more trustworthy overseers of our property.

We approached the jungle. Ensconced in shrubbery and situated in a small hollow next to the tracks, it was invisible until we were almost on top of it. Their two tied-up dogs started barking crazily. Behind the bushes a figure rose to his feet.

"Mornin', how y'all doin' today?" said Buddy, trying to put him at ease.

"Hey? Who's that?" A thin middle-aged man with long gray hair, a beautiful beard, and quick, lively blue eyes, rounded a bush. Recognition crossed his face. "Oh, hi there."

"Last night the other fellow said maybe we could leave our gear here for the day," said Buddy, at his charming best.

"Sure, come on in."

It was a remarkable setup. Not just a campsite, it didn't really qualify as a shack, either. Three walls of sheet metal, about five feet high, formed its main boundaries. Within these were a couch, sheltered by a tarpaper roof, a small fireplace about one foot tall made of unmortared bricks, with a grill—an old refrigerator shelf—laid across the top, a card table with two chairs, a night table, and an easy chair in the process of becoming unstuffed. Everyone's eyes except, it seemed, the tramp's watered from acrid smoke from the smoldering fire, which gathered under the tarpaper awning and hung in the air. Next to the wall nearest the tracks, and an important part of the jungle, were the mouths of two huge culvert pipes that stretched under the tracks. The two dogs ("Females," explained the tramp, "the only kind you can have on the road") lived in one pipe; at least one of the three men slept in the other, judging by the pillow and blankets spread out there. The pipes provided a private underpass, an alternate entrance and exit to the jungle. Light was visible at the far end, about sixty feet away.

I could not believe I was in America, in the 1980s. The man sat in the easy chair and fiddled with the AM-FM radio, connected to a green-and-white Burlington Northern brakeman's battery. Two of the tramps, I had learned the night before from the crook-necked, clean-shaven one that visited Buddy, were "on the lam from alimony payments in Illinois" (perhaps a common hatred of Illinois underlay their friendship?); this one said he used to play guitar at some hotel in Las Vegas. He talked expressively, revealing a row of big white teeth on top, but only two rotten, lonely ones on the bottom.

The three of them, he said, had been in the jungle three years, which made them much less "transient" than many of my friends from the normal world. Occasionally one would take a little trip—say, down to Grand Junction to get food stamps or some work—but another was always left behind to guard the camp and care for the dogs. Such was the position of this tramp that morning, and it displeased him: the other two had gone off to play pool.

On his instruction, Buddy, Sam, and I packed our gear into the far end of the tunnel and sealed the entrance with cardboard. The dogs heard everything, he said, so the gear should be safe. We agreed to pick him up a package of rolling tobacco.

The three of us began a brisk walk toward the tall buildings downtown, Buddy and Sam holding hands. Buddy, I noticed, was always careful to place himself between me and Sam. The sidewalks were dusty and hot. Buddy's eyes swept them, spotting first a quarter, then a nickel, then a couple of whole cigarettes—unlike Lonny, he left the half-smoked ones behind. When he was picking oranges in Orlando, Florida, he said, he found lots of money: he lived on a dark street full of hookers. In the process of making their transactions, the bills of both hookers and johns would sometimes drift to the pavement unnoticed. The fives, tens, and twenties had made up a big part of his income.

Our first stop was S.O.S. Temporaries. Though it was no later than eight A.M., the benches and plastic chairs that filled the bare and dreary storefront office were empty; a distracted fat man behind a desk told us, without looking up, that the jobs were gone by six—"but come back tomorrow."

Buddy was undaunted, and his attitude paced ours. Churches, he explained, were the next resort. "Look for the ones with the tallest steeples," he said. "They're the richest." What Buddy sought was some kind of shelter, preferably an apartment where Sam could stay during the day while he looked for work. But three miles and four churches later, he had failed to exact any relief. One place wanted to see their marriage certificate, one wanted them to spend some time in the church shelter first ("No way!" Buddy had sputtered, striding quickly back toward us across the church lawn), and at the other two the pastor was not in. Only slightly fazed, Buddy suggested we get some coffee.

The first coffee shop we passed was at a downtown hotel. Sam hesitated at the steps. "I think they might kick us out," she said.

"Aaaah, come on," said Buddy, on his way in.

I looked at us. Sam looked fine. Buddy's face, though, somehow dirty again, and the soiled sweatshirt he wore set him apart from the others we passed in the hotel lobby. I, having not combed my hair that morning, and with dust on my baseball cap and almost everywhere else, looked worse.

We sat in a booth with a white tablecloth. Sam and I were uncomfortable, but Buddy was defiant. A petulant waitress took our orders; Buddy tried killing her with kindness. "Yes, ma'am, just coffee. We need a little pick-me-up." She strutted away. "I'd ·like to buy her for what she's worth, then sell her for what she thinks she's worth," he said, a little too loudly.

She brought the coffee quickly. Buddy glanced at the bill. "Fifty cents a cup!" he exclaimed. "Jesus!" At this point the cook, who had been glaring at us from the window where the waitresses left their orders, stalked out and approached our table.

"Folks," he said grittily, "behave like you're in the nice place you're in, or get out." He spun on his heel, not waiting for a response.

"I knew this would happen," said Sam.

"No, it's fine," whispered Buddy. "Quick," he said, pointing at our cups of coffee, "drink it."

We downed them, rose on Buddy's cue, and headed for the door.

"But—the check—" I started to say. Buddy hushed me. Once we were in the lobby, he explained.

"He told us to get out, right? So we got out!" Suddenly he changed his course, bent down to the carpet near the front desk, and discreetly snatched up an errant one-dollar bill. We exited into the overcast day.

"That," said Buddy triumphantly, "was the first time I ever been paid to drink coffee!" He beamed. The morning had been redeemed.

We left downtown on a long walk to a large Catholic school to which Buddy and Sam had been referred. The walk took longer than expected, and when we arrived, Buddy learned the place they really had to go was the Catholic charities office, a mile and a half away. I decided to return to the yards.

First I passed by the three-year jungle, to pick up my gear and give the tramp his tobacco. From a distance I heard dogs barking hoarsely; as I approached, Thomas came puffing out from around some shrubs.

"What's going on?"

"You missed some excitement," he said. "There was six or seven Mexican kids, up on that bridge"—he pointed to the viaduct spanning the tracks. The aerial view it provided of the jungle was probably the best vantage available. "They started throwin' rocks at these guys. One of 'em got hurt real bad in the leg. He went to the hospital."

"How's the guy with the gray beard?"

"Oh, he's still in there."

I entered the jungle. It was in disarray: the radio was off the table, torn from the green battery; the grill had been knocked from the fireplace; utensils were scattered in the dust. The place was littered with stones, many bigger than a fist.

"Them bastards," said the tramp. I noticed one of his arms was skinned and sore. "They started throwin' rocks. Second time this week. 'Course I tried to throw 'em back, but by the time they get up there"—he gestured upward at the bridge—"they ain't got no force to 'em."

"Your friend got hurt?"

"Yeah, well, Neal went down and so there wasn't nothin' I could do. Nothin' the dogs could do either, since those kids were up on the bridge. I couldn't leave him here and run for help. Then this guy come and helped out." He pointed to Thomas.

Thomas began an improbable description of his assistance. "I heard 'em yelling so I came right over. Caught a bunch of them rocks in midair—just like this—and tossed 'em back, harder than they came. Nailed one of them Mexicans," he said proudly, placing an index finger on his forehead, "right between the eyes."

"Anyway, when he came," Graybeard continued, "I tore over to the NAPA factory and called the cops."

"Wait a minute—the cops help you out?"

"Sure, times like this. So, they come pretty quick but by then most of the kids was gone. Anyway, then they found 'em. Cops said a lot of them kids work out at that gym run by the Police Athletic League. So they knew 'em. And they came back and told us they're gonna have a talk with those kids' folks."

The tramp spoke righteously, obviously satisfied by this result. Thomas filled his pipe and smoked a bowl while I helped the tramp straighten up the jungle, gave him his tobacco, and then reclaimed my gear.

I returned to camp and, very tired, sprawled out on my cardboard. Probably suspicious of me alone with his gear, Thomas followed shortly. The episode had excited him and had left him talkative. He wanted me to talk with him—about Mexicans, about why kids don't give him shit, about "things you can throw" that do the most damage, about Buddy and Sam, about leaving soon to finish his trip to Arizona. Would I want to come with him, by the way?

"No, Thomas," I replied curtly. "We've been over this. I'm headed north and want to see what it's like up there before it gets too cold. I won't be traveling with you."

Then I raised a different, more personal issue: "Besides, you don't even know my name, do you?"

Thomas paused. "No. Well, so what? What is it?"

"Ted."

"Don't make no difference to me."

He was quiet for a mercifully long time. Then he began gabbing some more and started rekindling the campfire. Wanting badly to nap, I got pissed off.

"Hey, Thomas," I said meanly. "Have you collected any more wood yet?"

"No. What of it?" If he had been Scamp, I think the hair on his back would have risen.

"Well, it's just with you burning it all night, there's almost none left. I think if you want to stay friends with Buddy, you better get some more."

"Whaddya mean?"

"Well, just that he mentioned it to me this morning, you using all that wood he brought in."

"You want to fight?"

"What?"

"I said you want to fight? A guy gives me shit like that, and I figure he wants to fight."

I sat up. "Hell, no, I don't want to fight." I had not expected this.

"You want to fight? Go ahead, come on, I'll fight you."

He made fists, and assumed a boxer's posture.

"*Thomas.* I just said it for *you,* man, so *you* could stay friends with Buddy and Sam. If you don't want to get wood, then forget it. I really couldn't care less. I just thought you might be interested."

Thomas put down his dukes and grumbled. What I had said was true. Yet also, maybe *he* was right—maybe I *did* want to fight. Lately my patience had been wearing thin, and I didn't much feel like tolerating his inconsiderateness.

The sight of his fists, though, brought home the reality of a fight. Unless I could take advantage of his disability, he would probably slaughter me. Both possibilities were unpleasant.

"Say, Thomas," I said, trying to effect a friendlier tone. "When are you thinkin' of leaving?"

"I don't never know when I'm gonna leave," he replied, with slight irritation. "When I do it, I do it, that's all. I can't say in advance. Don't ask me like I know."

As bad for a hobo, it seemed, as having someone else impose a schedule on you was imposing one on yourself. "Do you want your fortune told?" an old gypsy woman had asked Buddy that morning, as we walked by her parlor. "No thanks," he replied. "I want it to sneak up on me!"

No more was said between Thomas and me. As the sun began to go down, I slowly drifted off. I was startled awake an unknown length of time later when Thomas came running into the jungle. He had the Bowie knife in his hand. In a daze, I watched him stash it in the weeds, and then do the same with the sheath, which was strung on his belt. Then he jumped over and shook me.

"Hey! Hey! I been in a fight! There's cops comin' over—if they ask you, tell 'em you known me for a long time. Tell 'em I been here all afternoon!"

Blinking, I said, "Shit, Thomas, what happened?"

"I'll tell you later. Here he comes," he said in a low voice, and started pacing around the jungle with a forced nonchalance.

The police car, lights flashing, zoomed up the dirt road on the far side of the tracks, then turned and crossed them. It stopped ten feet from where I lay. The policeman and a Chicano in his twenties climbed out.

"That's him," said the Chicano.

The cop approached Thomas. Involvement in this dispute clearly was not going to be the highlight of his day. "May I see some I.D., please? Thanks. Now I want each person to tell me what happened. You first." He gestured toward the Chicano.

"He pulled a knife on me!" he said.

"He's a liar!" returned Thomas.

"Shuddup!" yelled the cop at Thomas. "Let him finish!"

"We were waiting on the corner for the light. I bent down to pet his dog, and he says, 'Keep your fuckin' hands off that dog.' So I said, 'All right man, be cool, I ain't gonna touch your dog.' And then he pulled the knife on me."

Thomas denied it. "Look for yourself, officer. I don't even have a knife."

"Yeah, of course he don't now," said the Chicano. "But hey, look! Look at his belt! The knife was hangin' on a sheath on his belt, see?"

Stupid Thomas had forgotten to refasten his belt. He buckled it quickly. "Aah, that don't mean nothin', officer. That ain't shit for evidence."

The cop refused to make a judgment. "One thing I can tell you, though, buddy," he warned Thomas, climbing back into his car. "I hear another thing about you, and I'm runnin' you in." Thomas shrugged. The car left.

I was fast losing whatever faith I had in Thomas. The actions the Chicano described sounded totally in character. Thomas probably had no plans to use his knife, he just wanted to underscore his point. And he was sore about Mexicans that afternoon. The number of ways he had of finding trouble seemed as great as the number of places he had told me he grew up, as great as the number of jails he had been in for stupid crimes—like defrauding one-armed bandits in Las Vegas by using pesos or yen instead of quarters. Certainly, he must have received psychological treatment at some time for his very apparent personality disorders. The problem perhaps, was that Thomas was always turned back out into the same crazy world, to meet up with the same kinds of people that had given him difficulties before, to try, as he had with me, to make friends, but then to find himself unable to keep them. He was on the road, he once told me, in order to "get away from the assholes." Yet somehow, he seemed to keep finding them. There was not enough love in his world to make any cure stick.

Buddy and Sam, who had found their own kind of love, returned, winded but smiling. They finally had met with success—Catholic Charities was giving them a motel room for the night and had promised an apartment for several days after that. When I helped Buddy retrieve his gear from the pipe, he suggested I join him in Orlando in a few months to pick oranges. I promised him I'd consider it.

Realizing the end of our acquaintance was near, we traded food—Buddy and Sam hardboiled their eggs for me, and I gave them items that would be hard for me to travel with.

Just as we were finishing dinner, I heard a train approaching from down the corridor. It was a work train, chugging along at five or ten miles an hour; catching it would save me the three-mile walk to the U.P. yards, from which trains left for the north. I wolfed down the last of my chili-smothered wieners and said a quick round of good-byes. Buddy, Sam, and Thomas stood up to watch as I landed the work train. By the time I had a chance to look back, the jungle had shrunk to a spot in the distance, peopled by three tiny specks . . . and I felt a regret stronger than the twinge I had expected.

9

The main corridor forked after a couple of miles; the work train, to my chagrin, angled left, away from the Union Pacific yards and toward the Western Pacific. I leaped off, landing harder on the gravel than ever before because of all the surplus booty from the Bishop's Warehouse. Trudging up the line toward the Union Pacific, I was glad to see a home guard sitting near some shrubs, watching me. Happily he accepted most of my groceries, and happily I continued on my way, having been warned once again of all the cops around the U.P. yard.

Darkness fell, and I thought I was there. The track had divided, divided, and divided again, until I found myself in the middle of a wide stretch of railroad tracks, some occupied by aging boxcars. But there was nothing going on. The cars were all still: no air hissed out from underneath, none shuddered or banged from the push or pull of a faraway yard unit. In fact, there were no units around at all. The utter darkness was even stranger. The yard obviously was not in use. This was a ghost yard.

The deadness unsettled me. Bordering the yard were empty apartment buildings of dark red brick, many with windows knocked out, exposing a greater darkness. Shouts echoed faintly down the streets which ran between them, but I could see nobody. Abandoned railroad buildings dotted the right-of-way between the tracks and the tenements, sinister in their emptiness.

I walked another mile, the gravel under my boots making the only sound I heard. Some of the tracks converged, but the unused yard showed no signs of ending. I worried about whom I might run into. An old Ann Landers column I remembered had quoted a physicist who claimed, in order to settle a reader's bet, that a person who walked through a rainstorm would get wetter than one who stood still. Maybe, I thought, muggers were like rain, and the same principle would apply. If I stood still I would run into fewer of them. Certainly I would get less tired. I made a trip across the yard, inspecting each pair of rails to see which carried the trains, that is, if any passed through here. It was an easy distinction: one pair of rails reflected the beam from my penlight like a mirror. Trains *did* come through, and the best thing to do would be to wait for one. I stacked some trash next to the track as a marker, then climbed onto an abandoned loading dock at the edge of the yard to stretch out and wait.

A few uneventful hours passed. Then I noticed a glow enveloping the trash and the track I had marked, slowly becoming brighter, and heard the deep thrumming of an engine. I jumped off the loading dock. The engine emerged from behind a row of cars, fiercely bright, and I retreated into a shadow until it passed. It was pulling piggybacks, like the train out of Lincoln. As there was only one unit, it had to be a work train going toward the real U.P. yards. My usual fear of approaching the monster was tempered by my happiness at seeing something alive in this railroad graveyard. I couldn't wait to climb aboard, and leaped onto the first car I could reach. As I struggled to climb over the edge of the flat car, a metal burr caught my too-short Cub Scout pants, leaving a five-inch rip over my thigh. But I was on, and out.

The work train trundled on up the line, passing through the sporadic light of intersections, overpasses, and storage lots. The air was cool, but not yet cold. In the distance, from underneath the semi-trailer, I could make out a huge glow from tall clusters of mercury lamps. I began to worry about my arrival there, about remaining unseen in the legendary nest of bulls that was a U.P. yard. Should I get off before entering and circle around? Should I have a story ready? Should I try to escape if they spotted me?

The thoughts were interrupted by a new set of lights a few hundred yards ahead. At first I thought they were the headlights of cars at a crossing, but there were too many lights for that, and they were more focused. Then I had another idea: as part of the increasing automation of freight yards, all cars now carried individual identification in the form of a small row of colored bars somewhere on their frame. Electric eyes could "read" these legends on slow-moving trains as they entered the yard, confirming the arrival of certain cars. But on second thought, these lights were too bright for that, and they were on both sides of the train. As I drew closer, I saw these lights were spotlights, attached to automobiles and aimed to shine directly across the tops of the flat cars. The lights were going to shine on me. They were looking for hoboes.

Almost as fast as the adrenaline shot into my blood, I scrambled with my gear toward the wheels of the trailer. There were only seconds to spare. I stashed my gear up into the suspension above the two axles, as Lonny had showed me in Lincoln. The car ahead of mine was now bathed in a white glare. Scooting as close to one of the big wheels as possible, I curled around an axle and tried to match my body to the shape of the wheel. The light arrived, like a ten-second flash bulb. I saw it hit my pants leg. Oh, don't let them see me, I prayed. The glare passed on, and I saw the cops standing beside the cars, guns on their hips. One was making a fine adjustment to the spotlight. It reminded me of World War II movies of a government agent infiltrating enemy territory. I had just passed the border checkpoint.

I stayed hidden as the train rolled into the yard proper, past an illuminated roundhouse the size of an aircraft hangar. When the train stopped, my car was at the yard's far end, away from the brightest lights. Spotting the lantern of a brakeman walking my train, I stayed put until he came near. I cleared my throat before he got too close, so as not to startle him, and asked if the train would be stopping in Ogden. Yes, he said, it was bound for Los Angeles but it would stop in Ogden on the way. And it was leaving soon.

He lingered, playing his lantern light over my gear and me. "Don't see many of your type in here," he said finally.

"You gonna turn me in?"

"Naw . . . That's the gumshoes' job, not mine. Long as you keep your hands off the important stuff, I don't care."

"Gumshoes"—there was a faint disdain in the way he pronounced the word. His lantern now hung at his side, throwing light around his own shoes, work boots, sturdy and thick-soled. The railroad detectives, the gumshoes, wore street shoes with gum soles. They were a different kind of working man: their hands weren't tough, their clothes weren't dirty, they stayed in their cars. Detecting employee theft was one of their concerns; and I supposed they weren't unionized either. The brakeman, even in this yard, had no greater fondness for them than he did for me.

"Now, you ain't gonna touch anything, are you?"

"No, sir."

"All right, then." He continued his walk down the train.

Piggybacks, since their trailers contain mail and other priority freight, never stay long in a yard; soon we had pulled out and achieved the breakneck speed that only piggybacks are allowed. The train was going so fast it was passing cars on the highway parallel to the track, creating seventy miles per hour of wind and forcing me to put on my jacket. It was going so fast that, despite the brakeman's assurances, it passed the town I judged to be Ogden without so much as the blow of a whistle. I couldn't keep track of where it went then, for thick clouds gathered, obliterating the scenery. Then the black clouds opened, and seventy-mile-per-hour raindrops began to thud against my jacket. I tried pressing closer to the huge trailer wheels, but the wind's eddies brought the drops back into my face. I got out a piece of plastic sheeting that I had been toting—wisely, I thought—for just such an eventuality.

But in this wind it was useless. It rained sporadically, and I went through two or three cycles of being soaked and then quickly, if chillingly, dried out by the wind. I had no idea where I was going, but Los Angeles sounded likely, and that further dampened my spirits. A friend who had lived there had heard I might go down the West Coast, and left me a message at home. Mom read it to me one night over the phone, in a dubious voice: "White boys stay out of skid row, L.A."

"Thanks, Mom. I'll remember that."

"I should hope you do."

At the rate this train was going, skid row, L.A., would be the first stop. I just prayed I would be awake, or at least not frozen, when I pulled in.

But the first stop was a small town with a lot of pine trees, and the moment the train stopped, I was off. Finding nobody around the yard to tell me where I was, I walked into town and found an all-night convenience store.

"Green River," answered the store clerk.

"Green River, Nevada?" I asked. It was logical, assuming I was en route to L.A.

He looked at me as though I were crazy, or on drugs. *"Wyoming."*

"Ahhhhh, okay, thanks."

I bought a little food and, enjoying the warmth of the store, stayed a few moments longer to browse through the magazine rack. Soon two cops came in, staring at me as they walked to the cash register, where they spoke in low voices with the cashier. Now I'm in for it, I thought. My newly torn pants, dirty, strange face, and disoriented behavior had probably been enough for the cashier— gun-shy like most all-night convenience-store clerks (and with good reason)—to call the cops. Yet questioning was the last thing I needed at two A.M. that day. I spotted *U.S. News & World Report,* snatched it up, and walked boldly to the register. Perhaps the cops would be impressed by my taste—after all, wasn't it less reprehensible to be a vagrant interested in current events than one who would spend his cash on wine? Lonny's advice also lingered in my mind: they were more likely to come after you if you looked scared. I casually dropped the magazine on the counter.

"Evenin'," I said to the cops. I couldn't believe my audacity.

" 'Lo," returned one, suspiciously.

"Dollar fifty-seven," said the clerk, punching the register buttons and glancing hesitantly at the cops.

I handed him exact change. "Do you have a bag?"

"Uh, sure," said the clerk, opening one and sliding in the magazine.

"Thanks a lot." I turned on my worn heel and walked out of the store, watching them watch me in the reflection of the front-door glass, but not daring, until I was two blocks away, to smile over my victory over the Green River police.

The city of Ogden looked even grayer than the day. Squat, dusty buildings and dingy frame houses with dirt lawns lined my route around the Union Pacific yards. Late-model cars, fancier than the neighborhood, zoomed past me as I walked down the narrow sidewalk, their drivers probably chagrined that the road took them through this part of town.

I had just jumped out of the car carrier from Green River, and had decided to walk around the yards instead of through them after encountering some fresh graffiti on a support pillar under a bridge:

> *Aqui estubo Raul el gato Villa. Sinaloa Mexico les*
> *adbierto que se cuiden de los policias de la yarda. Los*
> *chicanos son mentiros los que trabajan aqui.*

Watch out for the yard police, Raul "The Cat" Villa advised his fellow Mexicans, confirming my suspicions of the railroad. Also, the Chicanos who worked in the yard were liars. Unfortunately, by this point the Union Pacific was the only way for me to get up to Montana, to visit the jungle at Havre before it got too cold. Northbound trains would leave from the other end of the yard; to avoid the heat, I chose to walk around it.

Abutting the sidewalk ahead of me stood an especially dreary building with a familiar sign: JESUS SAVES, in the form of a cross. The logo was becoming as familiar to me as McDonald's golden arches, and almost as welcome a sight. But the building this one hung on was as cheerless a place as I had ever seen. The dust around it appeared to have settled on and killed every plant; dust and dirt were so thickly deposited on the windows that they might as well have been boarded up—and as I got closer, I noticed that some were. The mission's classic dinginess reminded me of a yellowing photo from the Depression era.

Across the street a car door slammed, and I turned to notice a kindly-looking gentleman in overalls, retirement age, leave his camper truck and cross the street toward me. As he approached he asked a couple of questions: Where had I come from? Was I broke? His truck and benign demeanor reminded me of Sal Broder in St. Joseph, Missouri. Happily I chatted with him, half expecting this fellow, too, to dig into his pocket, produce a bill, and foist it into my pack.

That was not quite what he had in mind.

"Interested in makin' a dollar?" he asked, through his dull white dentures.

"How do you mean?"

His little eyes glanced quickly around. He gestured toward his camper. "Jack me off."

"What?" I asked in surprise, although I had heard it right the first time. Anger welled up inside me. The man obviously hung around here, waiting for a guy down and out enough to debase himself. What was disgusting to realize was that he probably sometimes succeeded.

"No, thanks," I said, walking away from the man and the lifeless gray mission building. I felt sick.

"Hell, I was just askin'!" he protested from behind me. His tone turned to a whisper. "Can't hurt nothin'."

God, I thought: Did I look like a person who would do something like that—for a dollar?

The many tracks of the Ogden U.P. yard converged into just two at its northern end, and these passed almost immediately under a small highway bridge. Still queasy from the mission encounter, I walked there, looking for a place to rest and recover. Rounding a bridge support, I stumbled upon a group of three Mexicans.

I had noticed in my travels that American tramps of whatever color—white, black, or brown—almost never associated with Mexicans. The language barrier was one reason for this, but more important seemed prejudice against their race and country. According to the tramps' own formula, Mexicans on the road should have been tramps of prestige; they were after all workers, not just traveling "for the hell of it." Poor, unskilled, migratory workers, they seemed to me the truest descendants of the original hoboes. But to the modern American hobo, they didn't even qualify as tramps. Instead, they were just "wetbacks" or "Mexicans," words always pronounced with disdain, men who demeaned themselves with illegal farmwork that didn't even pay minimum wage. Mexicans were people the tramps could feel superior to. Just who the Mexicans were able to look down on, I didn't know.

Familiar with the conventions, the Mexicans saw me and then looked away, probably thinking I would do the same. But I wanted company. "Say, do you guys know if this is a good place to catch out?" I asked, forgetful, in my daze, of the language barrier.

"No speak English," one of the two who was awake reminded me, directing his answer distractedly across the tracks.

"Es buen lugar para coger un tren, éste?" I said. The man and his friend now stared at me. White men never spoke Spanish. I knew they had understood me, but this situation called for the help of their friend, who lay fast asleep on the trio's only sleeping bag.

"Espera," said the man to me. Wait.

He bent over the soiled, tattered bag spread out upon the gravel, and roused the sleeper, "Psst. *Guillermo!*"

Most tramps can wake up in a second, but it took Guillermo a good minute. Drawing himself up on his elbows, he looked as though he had not slept in days. "*Qué?*" he asked.

"*Cómo estás?*" I greeted him.

"Oh, hi," he said. Yes, he confirmed, mostly in English, this was where the northbound trains were supposed to pass on their way out of the yard.

"We been here thirteen hours, though, and ain't seen nothin' yet that we could ride."

Guillermo told me to call him Bill. He wore a purple nylon muscle shirt, jeans, and dusty black oxfords. Despite his tired eyes, he was handsome. His friends, similarly dressed, were named Carmelo and Juan. We exchanged nods as I introduced myself.

"*Adónde vas?*" asked Carmelo.

"I'm going to Pocatello, then on up to Montana," I answered in English. "How about you all?"

"Idaho Falls," said Bill with a yawn, "for the potatoes."

"You guys thought about hitchhiking?" I asked, thinking thirteen hours was an awfully long time to wait.

Bill laughed. "Shit, man, ain't you heard? Ain't nobody picks *us* up."

Oh, that's right, I thought to myself: Mexicans. I soon learned that thirteen hours was not such a long time for them to wait for a train. The trip from Los Angeles to Ogden had taken them six days because they had overshot San Francisco and ridden all the way up to Klamath Falls, Oregon.

"How did that happen?" I asked in Spanish.

"*Él estuvo durmiendo,*" said Carmelo wryly, pointing at Bill. Bill reddened. Assuming they were on their way, he had been sleeping and had not thought to ask for directions. But the worst thing about the thirteen hours in Ogden was that they had spent it without a meal. I had a chunk of cheese in my bag and got it out to share with them. At first they refused to take it, but when I insisted, they ate ravenously.

Soon Bill was telling me about himself. He was born in the United States, which explained his English-speaking ability; later his family returned to Mexico. Now he was married to a Mexican woman, Maria, and had two kids. Maria's name had been immortalized in blue cursive writing on his shoulder, underneath a heart. Bill apparently had not spoken to her in months.

"She got bummed out when I got arrested in El Paso," said Bill. His crime was purse-snatching, he said when I asked, again reddening slightly. He had received ten years' probation, the terms of which were surely violated by now. He said he had telegraphed her parents recently to find out where she was; they hadn't responded. Having missed her birthday, he was carrying a package to mail to her as soon as he could afford to. Wrapped in a grocery sack, the package lay next to a water jug and a small, ripped vinyl travel bag emblazoned with BEVERLY HILLS TRAVEL AGENCY— besides the bedroll, the trio's only gear. I wondered if they knew what the logo meant.

Carmelo and Juan also were married, and that was their reason for traveling to the United States: the "nothin' " wages of farmwork were three to four times what they could earn at home. As soon as they were paid, they sent money orders home. I remembered being puzzled by the scores of men lined up outside the Western Union office in Dallas on Friday afternoons. If their wives were careful with the money, Carmelo and Juan would return to Mexico someday, richer than their friends; they were on a kind of business trip.

Apparently they had a small amount of change left. The cheese had awakened their hunger, and speaking rapidly and excitedly in Spanish, they argued over how to spend it. The talk was full of slang—*"Simón"* for *"sí,"* *"pinche"* for "fucking." Would *La Migra,* the immigration police, be in town? they asked me. I didn't know. Did I have a pan for cooking? Yes, I did. Good, then they could buy macaroni and cheese—they would just be able to afford it. Bill and Juan would go, leaving Carmelo behind with the gear. The two of them got up, tucked in their shirts, brushed themselves off, and shared a comb. Soon, dirty but spruced up, they climbed up to the bridge to walk into Ogden, heads held high, degraded but not yet broken, young and full of machismo. It was a pride I had seen only in young Mexicans.

Carmelo and I talked. Juan had been to America before to pick potatoes, he explained, but he never had. Was the world's tallest building really here? Had I ever been to *Nueva York?* Was it true there were some places left in America where land was still given away free to those who would settle it—and did I know exactly where they were? Finally, was there really an influential American group—he knew only its initials, "KKK"—which hated everyone who wasn't white, and sometimes killed them?

I told him the truth.

Bill and Juan returned. They had changed their minds about the macaroni and cheese—later I realized it was because they feared I might have gone, leaving them without a way to prepare it—and had instead bought a small package of vanilla sandwich cookies. Tearing off the cellophane with relish, Bill removed the four cookies. He handed one each to Carmelo and Juan, and then one to me.

"No, no, I'm fine," I protested, remembering uneasily the few dollars in traveler's checks that remained in my hip pocket. But Bill was adamant.

"Una por cada uno," he explained firmly, and the others nodded. "One for each. You gave us the cheese." To keep one's dignity, one had to repay gifts. Feeling terrible, I ate the cookie. I could not remember having received a more valuable present.

At last the train came. The engine, Union Pacific yellow and black with red lettering, nosed its way out of the strings of cars still in the yard, pulling a long line of russet-colored boxcars interspersed with covered grain cars that offered, at each end, a small platform and a tiny cave in the car frame. We were on our feet by the time it reached our bridge, straining to see a place to ride. Finally two covered grain cars in a row passed by. The four of us, at staggered distances along the track, stepped easily up the ladders and swung ourselves around onto the end platforms, facing each other. The train soon achieved twenty-five or thirty miles per hour, and we wove our way through a light forest and then onto the plain. Above us were clouds, but to the left, just over the western horizon where the sun hovered, the sky was clear and the sun shone brightly, its warmth almost neutralizing the chill of the wind. The sunlight glanced off the huge body of water that was the Great Salt Lake, and then lent a luminous green to the lush pastures and alfalfa fields that separated us from the lake. Fat livestock, mostly cattle, filled these fields; amid them ran the narrow line of a super-highway, carrying glittering supercars. To the right, also glowing in this rare light, were the chalky white Utah Rockies, with their bare, eroded lines.

I was on the right-hand side of the train, and as I bent forward to catch the sun I saw the three Mexicans framed in this magnificent, affluent tableau. How hard for them to know that it was not theirs, that they had no chance of owning a piece of it. That they would be arrested and deported if they were found, perceived of as having somehow robbed us—even though they worked harder for American employers than almost anybody, and for lower wages. Somehow, we celebrated the escape of East Germans over the Berlin Wall, but deplored the escape of Mexicans. For the first time, I really wished that I had a camera. The picture of these three young Mexican hoboes, gazing out over that Valhalla . . . it would explain so much.

Late at night, we pulled into Pocatello. I would have stayed with the group, but they were uninterested in leaving the yard. Tired, I wanted a place away from trains to lie down and sleep. I said good-bye and began to cross over the several trains that lay between me and Pocatello. Suddenly I stopped. Why hadn't they come? Didn't they trust me? On a hunch, I bent down and looked back underneath the three trains I had just crossed. Bill jumped down from the car, landing noisily on the gravel. I froze while he retraced my steps over the first two tracks. Apparently satisfied that I really had left, he returned to the car.

Trust does not come easy on the rails.

I walked around town, my search for a place to rest becoming desperate as my eyelids grew so heavy I could hardly keep walking. Finally I came to the county historical society, a sandstone building with a well-kept lawn. The front was well illuminated by a streetlight, but around the side it was darker, and on the edge of the narrow lawn a row of shrubs lined a short chain-link fence. Anyone passing by who looked hard enough would be able to see me lying on the ground between the shrubs and the fence. But I had stopped worrying about cops, muggers, mean dogs, or historical society watchmen; somehow, when you get that tired, nothing is easier than lying down.

10

"You're headed for Havre? And ridin' the freights? Then you must know about Hobo Alley."

No, I admitted to the man driving the van, I did not.

"Oh sure, it's real famous. Kind of grew up alongside the railroad in Havre. Railroad put Havre on the map—don't think they bargained on all those hoboes, though! Actually, I think they used to use 'em for the grain harvest and stuff. But now, with all them combines they got—hell, I don't know what those guys do. Stay in that alley, I s'pose. I'd keep outa there if I were you."

He took a concluding swallow from a can of beer and added the can to the collection swinging in a trash bag under the dash. "You know that place, don't you, honey?" he asked the woman reclining in the swivel chair next to him, turning in his own to look at her. The van began turning with him, onto the shoulder of the road. He corrected it, more slowly than he should have.

"Huh? Oh, you mean Hobo Alley in Havre? Sure, sure," she replied in a voice slurred by the contents of the cans that had been hers. "Ever'body knows 'bout that. Town's famous for it. Hobo Alley. Iss very dangerous."

"You make it sound like the whole town is tramps," I said to the man. But before he could answer, a dog appeared trotting down the edge of the road. He steered left to miss it, swerving almost to the opposite shoulder of the road. Hitchhikers get lots of ride offers from drivers who have been drinking; normally, I didn't accept them. But my luck had been bad that day, and the weather worse, and when the man slid open the van's side door, the sight of the warmth and luxury within had been too much. Damp from rain, I sat gingerly on a soft couch next to a big bubble window and marveled at the floor-to-ceiling carpeting. The woman handed me a can of beer from the well-stocked mini-refrigerator. I wiped the dust from my eyes, leaned back, and listened to the stereo.

Actually, the road had ceased to require much serious attention from the driver. The further I traveled from the Rockies and front-range towns like Helena and Butte, Montana, the flatter it became. Butte was where the trains had failed me. I was headed vertically up the map, but nearly all the trains traveled horizontally, between east and west. At first resigned to wait for the rare northbound trains, I had been persuaded by the chilly nights of impending autumn to take the faster route of the highways.

My brief brushes with "normal people" had set me to thinking about the strange, ambiguous way I was living. My appearance and my modes of travel had pretty well disqualified me from acceptance by "normals." Police stopped to check my I.D. frequently now, and fewer drivers picked me up. Store clerks watched me like eagles, sometimes discreetly and sometimes not. And there was a change in me: places I could go before, I felt funny about going to now. I felt out of place now in almost any restaurant, mostly because of my dirt and because of the problem of having to park my bags—someone was always looking. My clothing and gear were like flags announcing my degraded lifestyle, and where other people could see me, I had no privacy.

By getting into the van, I had offered myself up for close inspection. Its luxury made me feel awkward, clumsy, crude. Secretly, I wondered if the couple regretted picking me up, now that they could see me—and probably smell me—up close. Certainly they would if they knew the details of my life over the past few weeks.

But the driver had started talking about Hobo Alley again, a

place which he made sound like a chunk of darkest Calcutta trans-
planted to the middle of Montana. I was reminded of the reactions
of some acquaintances to the news that I was moving to Dallas to
do VISTA, and had decided to live in the neighborhood where I
would be working. Their descriptions of life in the neighborhood
where I proposed to live—constant street fights, broken windshields, rapes, and robberies—sounded not too different from the
description being offered of Havre. Maybe, just as the poor felt
awkward and out of place in wealthy areas, the wealthy were irra-
tionally frightened by poor areas.

I was open to the possibility that the poor operated under
misconceptions of the rich as well—and in my ambiguous state
between the two groups, one popped into mind: the idea that
wealthier classes were somehow "better" classes, filled with a finer
grade of people. The evidence to the contrary was seated five feet
in front of me. Though the driver of the van had been wealthy
enough to surround himself in mobile luxury, he was endangering
the lives of innocent people, including me, by driving while drunk.
Were hoboes better people for not having the opportunity to do
such harm? Probably not, but they certainly were no worse.

I looked out the van's windshield at the vast expanse ahead.
Space—more of it had been packed into the last few weeks than in
any other period of my life. Lately I had been traveling the region
where the mountains met the plains, where rock met space, often
with striking results. Sometimes the mountains cradled the sky,
holding it between the arms of a wide valley; sometimes they
pushed flat up underneath it, in buttes, mesas, and alluvial fans.
Always they gave the space free rein, holding it not so tightly as to
close in or complicate the landscape. Complementing one ridge
would be another perhaps fifty miles away, lending large, simple
form to the space in between. The scale and configuration were
majestic in ways the Rockies farther south were not. And though
my hitchhiking may have put me under the spell of the Montana
license-plate slogan, BIG SKY COUNTRY, I could have sworn the sky

was bigger, the distance between horizons somehow greater, especially as we drove north toward Havre.

This land and its features were the tramp's road map, and his knowledge of American geography was proving phenomenal. I, too, was learning to live without road signs. It meant paying close attention to the land, and I was awed by the beauty of Montana. The sheer vastness of Montana's spaces was more than something to see; it was something to feel. The feeling was the opposite of "cramped in," the feeling I often had in New York City and much of the East. Yet strangely, I could think of no word that described it. Something inside me just became more free and expansive— "opened out," I guess I could say.

At first blush Havre was a typical-looking northwestern small town, unusual only in the enormous size of its railroad yards. They were on one side of the highway, and town was on the other. After the couple dropped me off, I searched for a mission, tired from not having slept during the previous chilly nights, and feeling a cold coming on. Finding none, I squandered twenty dollars on two nights at the well-named Shanty Motel. I spent the days mostly in bed, arising on the third day refreshed but a bit wary. A few casual walks around town had failed to reveal to me the location of Hobo Alley, and I was not entirely secure in my belief that the driver of the van had been overestimating its dangers. Also, it had been several days since I left the Mexicans, and even longer since I left the "real" hoboes in the Salt Lake City jungle. How difficult would be the transition back to jungle life?

After I checked out, I returned to the office of the Shanty Motel. The desk clerk there, I hoped, would not consider my request for directions to Hobo Alley too strange.

"You mean the jungle? I ain't never heard of no Hobo Alley, but the jungle's over there on the other side of the tracks," she said, raising an eyebrow and pointing out the window.

I tried to get a bearing on the area indicated. The location made sense: on the other side of the tracks *and* the highway. The question I really wanted answered, though, was harder to phrase. "Well," I started, "can you tell me . . . do you know what it's *like?*" I envisioned dark streets and trash cans and the scattered wreckage of buildings and humans.

"Well, it's rough, that's what it's like," she said. "There was a shootin' there a couple weeks back, local kid got roughed up a couple weeks afore that. Smart folks stay away." She eyeballed me: was I smart folk or dumb folk? "You mind my askin'—" she started.

"Oh, I'm, uh, just meeting a friend—"

"Over *there?*"

"Yeah. Uh, thanks for your help," I said, registering the foreboding and disapproval on her face.

Soon I was across the main highway and atop Havre's only viaduct, which afforded a good view of the expansive yards. The jungle remained hidden. Off the viaduct, I followed a disused dirt road between the tracks and the Milk River, a cloudy body of water that had been disciplined by the Army Corps of Engineers into a straight, bulldozer-banked, flood-controlled canal through town. Lining the Milk were gigantic cottonwood trees, rivaling the grain elevators as the tallest things in the wheatfield-bound town. I knew from the desk clerk's instructions that I must be close to the jungle, but the scenery was so beautiful that I was having trouble believing it. The gold and yellow leaves of the cottonwoods flickered above me as I walked the dusty road, afraid but trying not to look it, on guard against my first attacker.

Spotting tramps is an acquired skill. Their dirty clothes are a natural camouflage in both industrial and wooded landscapes, and it's to their advantage to keep a low profile. And I was rusty.

At first I found nothing. Then, from the railyard on my left, I heard a faint banging noise, growing louder as I continued. Expecting a railroad section crew working on a stretch of track, I was surprised when I came upon a lone tramp, young and white like me, standing on top of a flat car. He was hacking away with a hatchet at some heavy wooden bracing around the edge of the car.

Apparently, it had been erected there to keep a load, no longer present, from falling off. Though the bracing would probably have been removed by the railroad at some point, I was dismayed to see the tramp destroying it, for no discernible purpose. I stopped and stared at him. So intent was he at his work that it was several minutes before he paused and noticed me.

"Hey," I said when he did.

"What's happenin'?" he returned. He wore a red handkerchief Aunt Jemima-style over his shortly cropped hair.

"Where's the jungle, do you know?" I asked.

"You're lookin' at it," he said, gesturing over my head to the brush and woods behind.

"You're kidding."

"You just ain't lookin' hard enough. There's jungles back there. Keep goin'." He returned to his work, now taking up a chunk of wood he had separated from the car and tossing it into a pile scattered next to the tracks.

"By the way, what're you doin' that for?" I asked. "Railroad pay you?"

The tramp laughed. "Hell, no, man. I'm usin' it for firewood. They're done with it, so why not?" He looked at me more carefully this time. "Hey," he asked. "You a tramp?"

"What?"

"I said, 'Are you a tramp?' "

Few questions could have caught me so off guard. I was prepared to answer almost any question a tramp might ask of me as though I were a tramp, but this struck right at the heart of the matter. I gulped and looked back at him as though he were crazy—a good way, I figured, to defend the length of my pause.

"Yeah," I answered, too defensively. "I guess I am." Just saying the words was unexpectedly empowering; if I claimed to be a tramp, who was going to argue? "What about you?"

"Oh, sure."

I continued along the road, pondering that exchange. I was certainly closer to being a tramp than when I began. But as far as actually *being* one—that was stretching things. I still thought about my family, about my friends, about girls I missed at school. My professors would still accept collect calls. I had still been more nervous than a tramp should have been entering the Havre jungle.

Yet a change had occurred. In part because my own desire was so strong, the jungles were becoming my home. For weeks I had been concerned with appearances: Did I look like a tramp? When tramps looked at me, would they see themselves? Those seemed the most important things. But now I saw that I had neglected what was going on inside. Sloughing off that *feeling* of being an outsider, a stranger that did not belong, was essential to achieving the ease of mind and manners that would make tramps see me as one of them. "Yeah, I guess I am," I had said, and it struck me that, to a degree, saying it made it so. Emboldened, I hefted my load, kicked a stone from my path, and continued down the dusty road.

"Sonny, open this up for me, wouldya?" asked the old cowboy, handing me a new jar of instant coffee.

"Sure, Pete." I bent forward from my seat on an old couch with a cardboard canopy and met his outstretched hand halfway. It was the right hand, swathed in gauze now dirty with campfire dust and pus.

Pistol Pete settled back onto the long automobile seat suspended between two large cans next to the campfire, where he had spent the morning. It sagged but was still the best seat in the house. The ground wasn't too far away, after all.

"Can't twist with it no more," he said, looking at the swollen hand. It was an explanation, not a complaint.

The top came loose easily for me, and I passed the jar back. "So why don't you get it fixed up?" I asked. "You said the migrant office gave you a check for drugs, right?"

"Yes, dammit, and I also said I spent it! Don't you remember that?" asked Pete, annoyed. It was the kind of admission you don't want to make someone repeat.

Pete took a pair of pliers and removed a can black with soot from the fire. He poured some boiling water into a smaller can for coffee. Then he took a dog-eared Western novel from his hip pocket, put on his glasses, squinted shut one eye to compensate for the missing lens, and resumed reading.

It was the scene I had walked in on two days before. Pete, evidently absorbed, had started when his partner's dog announced my presence. Then his rumpled cowboy hat tilted back, revealing light-blue eyes and several day's growth of white whiskers. His round, wrinkled face might have been cherubic fifty years ago. Though it was a warm day, he wore an old down parka, dotted with tape where it had ripped. His pants, double-knit slacks instead of the cowboy jeans I would have expected from a ranch hand, were extra long. This, Pete assured me later, was so that he could tie the bottoms shut around his boots when driving a tractor, to keep out insects.

I would also learn the hand had been injured a week earlier in Sandpoint, in the Idaho panhandle, where Pete had offered to help a motorist with engine trouble. The driver had turned on the ignition at the wrong time, catching Pete's hand in the fan belt. Pete's nonchalance about the episode amazed me; back in civilization such an injury would have required immediate treatment and daily care, and perhaps provoked a lawsuit. To Pete, it was simply an annoyance. He just wished it would go away.

" 'Lo, BB," said Pete.

"Hiya, BB," I said, raising my eyes to watch the tall, dark tramp, a plastic bag full of crushed aluminum cans over his shoulder, drop down along the path from the road to the jungle. He was dark, partly because of his dirty clothes: old brown jeans, soiled sneakers, and an insulated denim jacket with slits cut in the front for pockets. And he was dark because of the shade cast over his face by the visor on his cap. And dark because his hair, roughly cropped at collar length and bristly on his chin, was black. But mostly he was dark by virtue of being the dirtiest man I had ever seen. His hands and face and neck, his only exposed skin, were covered with a film of black dirt, heaviest where it had filled the pores, making black dots. Even his eyes were dark.

"Hiya, Pete," said BB, who had yet to get in the habit of returning my greetings. Most noticeable about his speech was the thick backwoods Mississippi accent, and the fact that he formed his words without benefit of teeth, although he looked only about 35. Wiry and lithe, he had the build of someone ten years younger. Few tramps were both so young and so powerful; it was one reason BB set me on edge.

"Much luck?" asked Pete.

"Oh, thar's prob'ly 'leven, twelve pound thar. What'd that be?"

Pete figured for a second. "'Bout two-fifty."

"Enough for a bottle or two. Or it will be, anyway, when we cash in that wire, too." He motioned at the lengths of copper wire coiled near the fire. Some BB had found on his "canning" expedition of the day before, he said, much of it in the form of a transformer coil inside a television set. Since the wire was insulated, Pete had set the thing on fire, melting and burning off the insulation in a cloud of acrid smoke. Tramps, I was about to conclude, were the human biosystem's most reliable recyclers, reclaiming discarded materials not because of altruism but out of need.

"Saw them other guys, too," added BB to Pete.

"What guys? Oh, you mean Tiny and that—"

"Yeah, them two. They wanta sleep back here tonight, which means they'll want their house back. Which means, son," he said to me, not sounding too sad, "that you're gonna find yourself somewhere else."

"Hmm, where d'you think?" I asked, uncertain of just what was being suggested here.

"Ah, we'll build somethin' later," said Pete. "I'll help ya."

"Oh, well, thanks, Pete."

BB dropped the bag of cans noisily and walked over to the tawny mongrel that had announced my arrival. She wagged her tail as he drew near.

"How's Daddy's little girl, Brandy Lee?"

Brandy Lee had been lying on a woolen shirt of BB's; he unchained her from his front "tent pole," picked up the shirt, and shook it off. Placing it back on the ground, he sat down, tuned a transistor radio at his side to a popular music station, and lay back in the dog's place in the shade. Canning was not easy work.

Brandy Lee, meanwhile, took a smelling tour of the jungle. Like most, it had a fireplace in the geometric center; next to this was a cable-spool table topped with food supplies. After lingering near the two, Brandy sniffed out the three wood-and-cardboard shelters. The one I sat upon, the couch-with-a-roof, was Pete's "canopy bed"; another, no more than a crude lean-to offering shelter to a king-sized boxspring underneath, was where I had been sleeping; and the last, a simulated pup tent made with a plastic rainfly draped over a cord strung between wooden two-by-fours, was BB and Brandy Lee's.

The dog's next stop was the jungle periphery. This area, mostly trampled brush, served as the hoboes' toilet and garbage dump, and it looked it. Brandy Lee rooted around intently. Beyond the polluted zone, though, was lush green shrubbery, which served as a kind of thick fence between jungles on either side, keeping the hoboes good neighbors, and just above towered the cotton-woods, leaves flickering as before. It was such a paradox. Back East, poor people—wealthier than these men—lived in tiny apartments in huge, dangerous cities, where you could walk for blocks seeing only people as hopeless and destitute as you, and no plants, and trash everywhere. Tall buildings kept sunlight off the street and out of most windows except for a few hours of the day. Maybe the tramps had a less secure roof over their heads, but if I were really poor, I thought to myself, this is the place I'd want to be.

Back issues of men's magazines were a feature of many jungles. I picked up one of the two old copies of *Penthouse* that circulated around ours, with the centerfolds missing and some pages stuck together, and looked at the pictures. If nature was in short supply around the tenements, women were almost nonexistent in these rural ghettos.

My daydreams were interrupted by Brandy Lee barking. "Good girl," said Pistol Pete. Brandy Lee, he had explained to me earlier, was their doorbell. In that and other ways, dogs were more than just pets to tramps. We turned to watch two figures descend the path from the road.

"Hi ho!" cried the one in the lead, bearing a bedroll under one arm and a paper bag containing a large bottle. He wore a dark cowboy hat with a large plume in the headband, an old nylon parka, jeans, and glasses. Also young and also wearing glasses was the fellow behind him, but most striking about the second tramp was his size: easily six feet tall, he had a massive, fleshy body encased in a too-tight black raincoat, his fat folds putting extra strain on the seams around the waist. The coat, and his whiskers and long hair, made him look seedier than his friend.

"Still got this bra, huh?" said the first tramp, reaching over to examine the mammoth-sized bra tied to one of the lean-to poles in the manner of a flag.

"Yeah, we're still waitin' for somebody to fill it," mused Pistol Pete. "Things ain't been the same since that Injun girl ran away."

"Say, Tiny," piped up BB, a momentary sparkle in his dark eyes, addressing the fat tramp. "You got tits, why don't you try it on?" He cracked up.

"Ha, ha, very funny," said Tiny, who, after a fashion, did have tits.

The first tramp, Roger, came to his partner's rescue. "Hey, I saw your girlfriend in town," he said to BB.

"Huh? Who's that?"

"Oh, you know, that little girl you hang around with in the hopper at the Safeway." Laughter rippled around the circle, though it was hard to tell if what passed over BB's lips was a smile or a sneer. The day before, while rummaging through the mammoth dumpster, BB had pushed aside a carton and suddenly came upon an old woman doing the same thing. After the initial fright, they had apparently had a good conversation.

"At least he's got girlfriends," said Pete. "Tiny, you wouldn't know how to pet a pussy if you had one."

"Would too, better'n you," answered Tiny.

"How?"

"Hell, I known girlfriends."

"Yeah, you got girls every night, you take 'em home and squash 'em!"

"Oh, here they come—the Fat Jokes."

"Who said fat?"

"You did."

The jesting continued, helped along by Roger's jug of wine, and so went the days in Havre, filled with talk and drink. Tiny and Roger were waiting for their food stamps to come through, so that they could return to Idaho, to pick up the ones they had just applied for there. Meanwhile, they were living off Pistol Pete, BB, and me; they promised to pay us back as soon as they could. When the wine ran low, two people—usually Tiny and I, the two youngest—would make a trip into town to "change stamps" and buy some more. Because certain products, such as alcohol and tobacco, could not be bought legally with food stamps, we would visit all three of Havre's food stores, buying something small, like a candy bar, at each, and paying for the purchase with a $1 food stamp. The change was given in cash, and this could be used to buy the next jug. The process was relatively easy, though some checkout clerks would make a scene if they recognized you and it was your third or fourth candy-bar purchase of the day. Late one day, in jest, Pistol Pete plunked his cowboy hat on my head as I was leaving to go change more stamps. "Now they won't know it's you again," he said. Everyone laughed but BB, and I sensed a sort of sibling envy growing in him. I hoped it wouldn't grow too large.

We drank Thunderbird wine, Mogen David 20/20, Night Train, and various brands of white port. Once, on a wine run by myself, I noticed that even cheaper than what we had been drinking were the fruit-flavored wines that I knew from weekend nights in high school. Pleased by my discovery, I returned to the jungle with nearly twice as much wine for the money as usual. I was immediately berated.

"Soda pop!" cried Pete. "What'd you get that for? Sure, it's cheaper, but did you take the time to read this?" He pointed at the label, even taking the pains to put on his one-lensed glasses. He looked very professorial.

"See? 'Alcohol content not less than seven per cent.' Now look at this Thunderbird label"—he resurrected a bottle floating nearby in a shallow ditch that formed one of the jungle's edges; I wondered how many hundreds of bottles had been laid to rest in that canal, fodder for anthropologists of the next millennium. "See? Eighteen percent! You get what you pay for? Didn't you say you went to college? What did they teach you there, anyway?" Wine was for getting loaded, and the stronger it was, the better.

The only acceptable alternative to the standard wines was something Pete and BB claimed to have invented. Called Phantom Punch, after BB's road name, "The Phantom" (THE PHANTOM STRIKES AGAIN, he wrote on boxcar walls), you made it by mixing flavor extracts with Kool-Aid or soft drinks. Mint extract and 7-Up, according to BB, was "just like a mint julep"; but lemon extract mixed with Tropical-Punch-flavor Kool-Aid was the favorite. The flavor of Phantom Punch left something to be desired, but the advantage of it was that you didn't need to change stamps to buy soft drinks or the extracts, which typically were forty percent alcohol.

I drank when the tramps drank, but tried never to drink so much that I couldn't defend myself. In contrast to when I went out drinking with college friends, nobody seemed to mind if I drank less than the others: it just left more for them.

Normally, the difficulty of buying wine kept the supply small, the buzzes moderate, and the conversation civil. But one afternoon, when a concerted effort resulted in more wine to go around, things changed between the tramps. Roger, for one, started prying.

"You look young, man," he said to me. "How old are you?"

The tramps guessed, on my suggestion: 27, 25, 23. Twenty-two was the real age, I answered. Roger persisted, his line of questioning rude for a tramp. What was I doing on the road? What was the work situation like in Denver? ("Great!" I answered. "Energy businesses are moving in, buildings are going up—" "No, no, man, not that," he interrupted. "Spot labor, I mean the spot labor, man. What's that like?" I had to confess I had no idea.) Where was I going next? Why didn't I get a steady job?

Suddenly Pete launched into Roger. "Why are *you* on the road?"

" 'Cause I wanted to fuckin' cross the country," said Roger, now very drunk. " 'Cause I got nobody in South Carolina."

"Well, whatta you got here?" asked Pete.

"Nothin'."

"Whaddaya got in the next town you go to?"

"Whatever I find. I'm goin' to Texas."

"Whattaya gonna do in Texas?"

"I'm gonna work if I can."

"Work at what?"

"Anything I can get to get a start. Then I'll look for somethin' better. What I had in mind was a fuckin' labor pool."

"You ain't gonna make a fuckin' thing at a labor pool. Enough for a room, maybe. Eighteen bucks a day."

The future wasn't bright, Roger conceded, and he spilled his story. He had been living in South Carolina, his home state, working in a textile mill. After his divorce he had moved to Portland, to stay with his sister Sue and make a new start. Unable to find work, he had been supported by her. Finally, as he explained it, he became disgusted.

"I says, 'Hey, Suzy. I need a pack of cigarettes!'—like that, man, you know. Well, fuck, I ain't gonna live like that, spongin' my own sister for cigarettes. I mean, if you can't even take care of yourself, what's the point of livin'? So I said, well, fuck, I'm gonna get out, I'm gonna make it on my own. Fuck that shit. So I got me a fuckin' job washin' fuckin' dishes in a fuckin' restaurant. I met

Tiny and got me enough money to buy me a backpack and a sleepin' bag, and we took off." Pete seemed satisfied. Had Roger been more sober, he might not have missed the chance to ask Pete the same question.

"Why, you can talk to every tramp you want to, he's got a different story," said BB. "I didn't have no old lady behind it, like you. I couldn't stand my old step-dad, so I run away when I was fourteen years old. Went and joined the goddamn Army; couldn't stand it so I joined the Navy. Couldn't stand that either, so I got outa both of 'em. When I come out, it was 1966, and I been on this goddamn rail ever since." Among BB's other employers, I would learn later, were a tugboat operator on the Gulf coast, the Masonite Corporation in Mississippi, a carnival, and a Georgia textile plant.

The afternoon drew late, and still the wine flowed. On the next bottle of Thunderbird, Roger decided to "go deadman." In other words, he threw away the screw-on top, which meant the wine would lose its sparkle and get dirty if it weren't finished in one sitting. Tired of the whole scene, I volunteered to make a grocery-store run for dinner supplies. As I stood to leave, Roger, barely able to speak, said, "Wait a minute. Here—you goin' t'town? Buy me some cig'rets, wouldja?—Marlbros." He reached in his shirt pocket and drew out a five-dollar bill.

"Hey, I thought you said you guys was broke," BB accused Roger.

"Well, uh, umm, I just found that—" stammered Roger. He was cut off in mid-sentence as BB leaped to his feet, took two big steps, swung his long arm, and landed a fist in Roger's face. Roger, on the car seat, tumbled backwards into the dirt, legs in the air. Kicking furiously, one of his feet caught the pursuing BB in the face. But BB was undaunted and fell on him, punching. The two rolled about the jungle, the blood on their faces forming a dark red mud as it mingled with the fine dirt. With Tiny and Pete on the edge of their chairs, I wondered if the fight would spread.

Roger finally eluded BB's grasp for a moment, long enough to get to his feet and sprint out of the jungle, grabbing his blanket along the way. BB, now upright and breathing hard, let him go. He devoted the next half hour to describing Roger in the worst terms he knew. "That two-faced motherfucker," he summed up. "He's only been on the road a coupla months, he don't deserve to call hisself a tramp."

Then he turned to me. "There's a lesson to be learned here, son," said BB. "On the rails, you don't trust nobody. Ain't that right, fellers?" Pete and Tiny nodded in agreement.

Tiny inexplicably remained at the jungle that day. He had not joined in the fight ("I'm a born coward," he told me later), and had somehow remained unimplicated in the money fiasco. "I didn't know he had it, either," he said to us. "Honest." But BB knew he'd see Roger again, and had some words for Tiny: "When you see that no-good partner of yours, you tell him I got somethin' for him. You tell him I'm gonna give him a stain that soap and water won't wash out."

I shuddered. For a moment it seemed to me that the driver of the van and the motel clerk were right: these hoboes were very dangerous men, crude, lawless, and violence-prone. They were men following mean, bestial instincts in a world not far from what Thomas Hobbes called the state of nature. In comparison to the tramps, I felt saintly, civilized, and in control. Repulsion mingled with my fear.

Later that night, I slid into the small lean-to Pete had helped me build—actually an addition to Tiny and Roger's old shelter. Tiny was snoring a few feet away, but that wasn't the only reason I couldn't sleep. I played over the scene in my mind: Roger sitting drunkenly on the car seat, mouthing inanities and drinking our wine. Roger hassling me. He was something of a con man and a jerk. How many times, in my life before the rails, had I encountered people as repellent to me as he had been to BB—bosses, professors, bad drivers—and dealt with their rudeness, arrogance, or duplicity simply by turning the other cheek, by walking away, by *not* dealing with them? It was the gracious, big-hearted, morally superior thing to do, the Christian response I had been trained in.

But how many times had that been what I most *wanted* to do? How good would it have felt, if no one had been watching, to land my fist in the face of such an asshole, as BB had? My pacifist friends at school would have been dismayed by such a thought; until a few hours before, so would I. What BB did frightened me, partly because I could imagine myself on the receiving end of the punch, but also because I could imagine myself on the delivering end. It awoke in me an impulse I was not sure I wanted to admit was there.

The world of the jungles was like polite society with its mask off. Hoboes seemed to say what they felt and do what they felt like doing. People seemed to have quite an appetite for the violence which is part of such an attitude when they saw it in the movies or on television; but when they looked for it in themselves, many like me seemed not to see it at all.

How much like the hoboes was I?

Outside the tent, I heard Pete fall, hard. He had been drinking heavily since the incident that afternoon, and I found him face down in the dirt near the fire, nearly passed out. I helped him up and onto his couch, then noticed blood trickling down through his gray beard—he had landed on a rock. I took out my handkerchief and helped him wipe it off.

"Do you know where *your* money is?" barked the announcer on a radio advertisement for a bank, later in the week.

"Sure," answered Pete aloud. "It's spent."

Tiny, finally, had left to join Roger where he had taken refuge, under the loading dock of a disused warehouse in town. Their loan, of course, had not been repaid, and our funds were low. To make things gloomier, the local police had made a visit to the jungle that morning, checking all of our I.D.s: word was out in the jungle that a girl had been raped the day before, near the tracks. We had until the weekend—one day—to leave town, the cops warned. Nothing much had happened in the past few days at our jungle, and I, for one, was bored stiff. The monotony seemed to be catching up with BB and Pete, as well. A radio ad for a local airline suggested a course of action: "First-class legroom at coach prices to Fargo! Discounts with a two-week advance reservation!"

"Fuck that shit," said BB. "Hell, we can get there free, in our own private car, with all the fuckin' legroom we want!" They decided to leave that evening. Plans for their next destination had been made and changed all week—head to Great Falls to try and get sleeping bags from the migrant worker office there; to Wyoming, to find work on a ranch Pete knew; to Kansas City, to work in the stockyards. Today plans had changed again.

"Beets," said Pete. "Now's the beet harvest in Minot, and we'll find work there." When BB had gone to cash in his last remaining cans, Pete said to me, "Son, BB and me been talkin'. I like you. We're leavin' this afternoon. You can come with us if you want."

I had been wondering about this moment, and was glad for the offer. But I told Pete I was worried about BB's hot temper. "I don't want what happened to Roger to happen to me. I'm straight with you about stuff, but I don't know if that's any guarantee that nothin'll happen."

"Oh, BB," said Pete. "You know, one night he hit me too? Right in the jaw."

"You're kidding."

"Nope. But the next mornin', he was cryin' like a baby. Tell you what: you don't order Brandy Lee around, and help out with stuff, and I think it'll be okay. And here's another thing. If you come with us, it'll be like partners: all for one, and one for all. We'll all look out for each other. Whaddaya say?"

I couldn't resist.

A long mixed freight pulled in on the eastbound main at dusk. Two minutes before we saw it, though, Pete said it had arrived. The sound of the road units pulling it, he told me, was how he knew: they had a deep rumble, and ran at low rpm's. The modernistic silver Amtrak engines, in contrast, had a high whine and ran at high rpm's, as though they were about to take off. Yard units were somewhere in between, but you could tell them by their distinctive whistles and by the way the engines were always speeding up and slowing down, pushing and pulling cars about the yard.

The three of us hurried down the dirt road adjoining the track, toward a series of empties that had passed us by as the train slowed. The food and gear that BB and Pistol Pete had accumulated during the Havre stay, however, slowed them down, especially Pete. He cursed his load as he hobbled along. I realized this was the first time I had ever seen him walk any distance, and was struck by his feebleness.

BB reached the chosen car first. Flashlight in hand, he scanned the dark interior: there were no other riders, and there was cardboard to lie on, he announced.

"Wood floor?" asked Pete. "I don't want no metal floor. It's gonna be cold tonight." Metal boxcar floors, I knew from experience, stole the warmth from under your body and lost it to the nighttime air. Old wooden floors, on the other hand, preserved body heat.

"Yeah, it's wood," said BB. He had already tossed his gear aboard and now helped Pete do the same with his. Brandy Lee was hefted up next, and then I jumped in—no mean feat, as the elevated main line put the boxcar floor at about chest level. Pete couldn't make it, so BB gave him a boost. I wondered what the old man would do in this situation if he were alone. His need, I guessed, was a strong reason for his tighter-than-usual bond with BB.

Next began a series of actions that could best be described as tramp ritual. The three of us lugged the packs to the front end of the car, where they would be well hidden should a bull pass by before we left. Next BB, with my help, gathered up loose cardboard and laid it in three stacks across the front half of the car. I knew we were in front because in the back it was windy, but I didn't understand why the mattresses had to be placed sideways. The shaking train, I mentioned to BB, would rock us head to toe if we lay like this; wouldn't it be more comfortable to be rocked side to side?

"Well, mebbe," he said. "But tramps do it this way 'cause of a derail or a crash. If you're lyin' the long way and he crashes it, you'll probably break your neck. But sideways, your body'll hit the end all at once. You might even live through a derail this way."

I gulped. "Have you ever seen one, BB? A derail?"

"Seen one? Hell, yes. I been *in* one. Actually, I was on the back end of a grain car, right in front of the empty that jumped the track and started the rest of that train off. It was a stretch of bad track before Minot—we'll go over it—and that engineer shoulda slowed down, but instead he highballed it. Man, I saw that empty a-jumpin' and a-shakin'—saw them front wheels lift right up once, too—'course nothin' happened that time, 'cause they came straight down. Well, later they didn't. And that train . . . well, all I can say is, be glad you weren't there. Them cars went off into a stream. They looked . . . they looked just like those cans I had, remember? Aluminum cans, after they're squashed?"

I remembered. BB's vivid metaphor made me think he was telling the truth; if so, he was one of probably very few authorities on train derailments. It was like what Scott, my mountaineering friend, said about avalanche experts: almost all the experienced ones are dead.

We then unrolled upon the mattresses. Pete sat down on his bed and sipped from the jug of Phantom Punch, while BB showed me how to jam the boxcar door open by wedging a piece of wood into its track. This would prevent it from slamming shut like a guillotine if the train made a sudden stop. Finally, at Pete's request, BB jumped back outside, unlatched the door on the opposite side of the boxcar and, with my help from the inside, succeeded in sliding it open part way. This improved our view and, more important, provided an escape route should trouble appear at the other door or should the other door wedge fail.

Moments later, a succession of small booms rang out, starting at the front of the train, probably fifty cars ahead, and proceeding domino-style through our boxcar to the rear: the engine was picking up the slack between cars. The floor jerked, and we were off.

There was little to be seen once the train left, but much to be heard and felt. The doors banged on their tracks, and the wheels of the empty squealed on the rails. Wind rushed in the doorways, and Pete cautioned me against standing too close: one random jolt of the car could send me flying out into the blur. BB took a bedtime pee, this one not out into the rush of wind, which always managed to send some of it flying back at you, but in the far back corner of the car. Then all three of us stood for a moment, watching the prairie dash by in day's last light, getting our train legs back. Now, finally, we were going somewhere. Exactly where, and to what, we didn't know: the destination, perhaps, was less important than the movement itself. We felt it, in our feet and on our faces, and we saw it, through the twelve-by-twenty-foot window of the big dark room in which we were encapsulated. The train was moving for a reason; by climbing inside, we came to share that reason: getting to the next place. After all those directionless days in the Havre jungle, I felt back on a purposeful course, a straight line down the middle of the huge, chaotic Montana plains.

Darkness fell, and we lay down.

11

Light flashed across my face, and I couldn't see.

"Awright, bums, up and at 'em, outa the train."

Pete's supine figure was illuminated, then BB's and Brandy Lee's. The dog growled, and BB hopped to his feet.

"Who is it?" he demanded.

"Special agent," came the gruff reply from the end of the flashlight beam.

"Yeah, uh, all right," said BB. "Say, where are we?"

"Williston."

"Yeah, thought so. Come on, Pete." Pete rose stiffly to his feet, the light trained on him. "All right, all right, we're movin'," he said.

"Just while the train's in the yard," said the voice of the man, still invisible. "You know the rule."

We hopped out, and the figure retreated to his car. There he turned his spotlight on us. "Take off your hat!" he yelled to BB.

"What?"

"I said your hat!"

BB doffed it. To my surprise, he was almost completely bald on top.

"You wanted for any crimes?"

"Nope."

The spotlight turned to me. "How about you? Have you ever committed a felony?"

"Never even been charged with a crime," I bragged. I heard a small laugh from near the car. The bull slammed the door and drove away.

"You ever heard of that rule, Pete? Gettin' out while the train's in the yard?" said BB.

"He's just lookin' for somethin' to do—just blowin' smoke out his own asshole," said Pete. "Give those guys a tin badge and they think they own the world."

He climbed back in.

The train was rolling, and the track was getting rough. Every few seconds, huge vibrations shook the car and it bounced up and down on the rail. The floor, of course, followed this motion, raising my body up and then letting it drop, sometimes in rapid-fire succession. Sleep was impossible. I lay on my back and held my head up, trying to predict the next shock waves, trying not to get the breath knocked out of me. *Boom boom boom boom boom.* Sometimes my head hit anyway. Lacking a helmet, I bunched my sweater under my head, which helped some.

Between bounces, the car shifted violently from side to side. I felt like a kernel of popcorn in a rectangular pan. Contact with the floor was seldom lost during these sideways motions, but that was a mixed blessing: my skin stayed put, while the rest of my body rolled back and forth inside it. When the car lurched toward the side nearest my head, I felt my scalp pull back and my eyes open a little wider. On the swing back, skin from my shoulders bunched around my neck. I speculated on the folds of extra skin that would probably result. Elephant Boy—now, there was a monicker for you!

Often the booms and lurches were rhythmic, and songs and ditties would come to mind to match the beat. One I had heard on an old Woody Guthrie record before leaving:

I've been a-riding them fast rattlers,
I thought you knowed,

I've been a-riding them flat wheelers way down the road,
I've been a-riding them blind passengers, dead enders,
kicking up cinders,
I've been a-having some hard traveling, Lord. ©

Fast rattler, that was the kind of train we were on. Probably a flat wheeler, too, to judge by the ride. But the names must have been out of date, for I heard BB mutter under his breath as he turned over, simply, "Noisy, bumpy, fuckin' sumbitch."

I began to discern a more regular beat in the noise the wheels made when passing over a joint where sections of rails were connected. It was a subtle clicking, and to it I hummed a verse of one of the earliest tramp songs, "Jay Gould's Daughter":

Jay Gould's daughter said before she died,
"Daddy, fix the blinds so the bums can't ride.
If ride they must let them ride the rods,
And they put their trust in the hands of God.
The hands of God,
The hands of God,
Let them put their trust in the hands of God."

The "rods" were brake and suspension rods found underneath the boxcars of old, where tramps could always find a dirty and risky ride. The "blinds" were relatively protected platforms behind the wood or coal car on a steamtrain, out of sight of the fireman. Jay Gould was a robber baron and railroad kingpin.

Later another song occurred to me that seemed written from a Jay Gould perspective:

Engine, engine, number nine,
Roaring down Chicago Line,
If the train should jump the track,
Do you want your money back?

It was a schoolyard chant, one I had sung many times. Never before, however, had it seemed intended for investors. Suddenly in the position of one who had much more to lose than his money if the train jumped the track, I felt demoralized and left out. I leaned back and closed my eyes, but the tune wouldn't leave my mind. It took on a sinister feel. . . . If the train should jump the track . . .

. . . If the train should jump the track. . . . I was standing near the door, absorbing the shocks with my knees, when suddenly I saw the cars in front of me caroming off at an odd angle, and I could see their gleaming wheels, plunging downward instead of ahead. The light was suddenly red, as though the sun, too, were falling, or like the glow of hell. The cars ahead would drag off mine, I knew they would, the moment was just seconds away, and nearing, nearing, oh God. The floor had begun to tilt, and I leaned against the boxcar wall . . . we were tilting, toppling . . . I screamed and nothing came out. Harder, harder, I strained until, at the last moment, it burst through: "BB! BB! Help, help me!!"

I woke up, heart pounding, and sat up. The train was still rolling. Pete and BB, on either side of me, were both asleep. Neither, apparently, had heard my cry over the noise. Of all the names to call out! How the hell would BB be able to help me? I hoped he hadn't heard me call. Quietly this time, I spoke his name—if he were awake, I would explain to him that I had had a nightmare. But he rocked loosely back and forth with the motion of the train, unresponsive. Shaky, I got up and walked around.

Sunrise, and my companions were not about to let the train, which had robbed them of a sound night's sleep, rob them of morning's sublime pleasure, coffee. From his pack Pistol Pete removed a gunboat—or cooking can—brought along from Havre, and filled it up halfway with water from his jug; BB lit one of the several flares he had "borrowed" from a caboose in Havre. He aimed the flame at the bottom of the can; the metal was soon so hot that it faintly glowed. "Works real good for startin' up wet wood, too," Pete remarked. Steam began rising from the gunboat, but the most visible by-product of the process was the clouds of smoke put off by the flare. Pete noticed the wind whisking the smoke out the doorway, and he cautioned BB to hurry up. "If they see that smoke from the crummy," he explained to me, "they might think the car's on fire, or that they got a hotbox. Then they'll stop the train, and we'll get the boot." A hotbox was what they called one of the old-style wheel-bearing boxes when it ran out of lubricant. First the box got hot and smoked; then, if it wasn't repaired, the wheel could seize. Such a wheel would soon get a flat spot from rubbing the track, one genesis of the bad ride on Guthrie's "flat-wheelers."

Two cubes from Pete's box of sugar made my cup of coffee ideal, and we stood in the sun, sipping. Never before had I enjoyed coffee, but now mornings seemed incomplete without it. It wasn't just the flavor or caffeine lift I liked, either; it was the idea of something scheduled, regular, and counted on in a world where almost nothing was that way.

Mealtimes were a prime example of something fixed gone random in the tramp world. Most often, everyone ate according to his hunger, or when someone else got out meal fixings. For an early lunch, I produced apples, bread, meat, mayonnaise, and some of my accumulated candy bars for all of us. "Guess somebody around here still got teeth," noted Pete, eyeing the apples. I apologized for the oversight and made Pete a sandwich, and then one for BB, so he wouldn't feel excluded. "No begging, Brandy Lee!" declared BB, the master scrounge, as the dog crept near.

BB never reciprocated my sandwich-making. Including me in the partnership clearly had not been his idea; one way he made this plain was by making aerosol cheese with crackers for him and Pete, but not for me. "Make your own!" he snapped at me, the first time I pointed out the oversight. I decided to keep quiet.

The sun was high in the sky when the train pulled off the main track and into a hole, to let another train pass. This had happened several times already on this trip. What made this stop unusual, though, and unfortunate, in the eyes of Pete and BB, was that our car came to rest directly in the middle of a crossing over a county highway. The racket of the crossing bells was bad, but what bothered them was the public exposure. Several cars lined up behind the crossing gates to await the passing of the train. And, despite Pete and BB's best efforts, the fellow in the first car spotted us, climbed out of his, and peeked in the boxcar door to say hello.

Pete and BB looked away, as though they had not heard him. I was intrigued with the man and his curiosity, though, and got up from the back of the boxcar.

Perhaps he had expected to find in the hoboes kindred souls. He told me he was a traveling salesman, on the road as often as he was off. I explained our journey in the sketchiest possible terms, following the convention, and it seemed to satisfy him. Like so many people on the road, he just wanted to chat. When our conversation flagged, he mentioned that he had a hot Thermosful of coffee in his car. This got Pete and BB out of the back of the boxcar right away. On BB's mind was whether we were getting close yet to Minot, North Dakota, our destination.

"Oh, you're way past there," said the man. "I'd guess you're closer to Fargo."

BB took the pronouncement as an insult to his navigating abilities, and argued with the man. Our rapport dwindled quickly, and the train pulled away none too soon. "Shit, he don't know what he's talkin' about," said BB. "I bet he was a railroad inspector, anyway, just fuckin' with us."

Most of the afternoon I stationed myself in the boxcar doorway, watching the miles go by. There was something about all that space squeezed into the fixed time of day that was like all travel, and, though the tramps mistrusted him, it seemed to me we did have a lot in common with the traveling salesman.

But there was an important difference, I thought, that afternoon as we flew across the limitless Dakota plains. Traveling salesmen, airline pilots, and tourists covered a lot of ground, but they didn't come to understand the geography in the same way tramps did. Tiny expressed it well to me: "Riding in a boxcar is being there," he said. "You look out the door and there's America. It's all in front of you, with no windshields or billboards in between." The wind hits the tramp in the face, bringing with it flies and mosquitoes, warmth and coolness, and the diesel fumes of the locomotive—as well as the distinctive smells of different places: the grim industrial side of St. Louis, the sweet Colorado mountain forests, the Utah desert in the morning, and, today, the lush, fresh scents of soy and sorghum in place of yesterday's wheat. The differences were subtle, but you could tell if you tried. For the tramp, the spatial relationships between places were more than mileage figures on a map. He gauged distance in terms of hours or days of train travel, time colored by all he had seen or smelled on the way.

And it seemed to me that the tramp understood the *size* of the West in a way unknown to virtually anybody else. Most tramps had ridden freights not only across it but around its perimeter, from Everett, Washington, to St. Paul, Minnesota; through Galesburg, Illinois, to Fort Worth, Texas; Yuma, Arizona; and back up the coast to Washington. Over the course of hundreds or thousands of train rides the tramp got to know his country. Somehow, American geography *meant more* to the railroad tramp.

Pete got to his feet and joined me near the doorway. I knew spending so much time there probably betrayed me as a novice, but it was so damn beautiful. We stood for a long time, staring out. Finally he said to me, loudly in order to be heard over the noise, "You know what I said about you needin' a camera?"

"Yeah?"

"Well, I was wrong. You could take a picture of all this, but you'd lose the pictures. You look at it with your eyes instead, and it's in your head forever. There's not many people can understand that."

I looked hard out the door and began my mental album.

"Yeah, I'm an Injun, too," said BB, finishing the story of his ex-girlfriend, Nancy, who, he had claimed in utter seriousness, was "one-half Cherokee, one-half Sioux, and one-half white."

"No kiddin'?" I said.

"Yup, and as a matter of fact, you are, too. It's the Fuckawee Tribe—a bunch of Injuns in the Northwest. They roll into town and the first thing they say is, "Where the Fuckawee?' "

I laughed. The train had stopped, and that was exactly the question on everyone's mind. "I still think it's Minot," said BB, clinging to his prediction like a stubborn astrologer. Pete scanned the yard, but would not hazard a guess. A crusty old tramp from several boxcars down who passed ours on a search for water shed no further light on the question.

"I'm just headed to Minionapolis," he said, "and I reckon I'll know it when I see it. This ain't it."

BB disparaged him as he left. "He's just a bum. He don't know his ass from his elbow on these rails. He don't know where he's at and he don't know where he's headed." He spat; Pete nodded.

Pete thought we should unload, and we did. The sun would be setting soon, he noted, and nighttime was no time to search for a spot in an unknown jungle. Besides that, we were starving. Camp was set up under the only viaduct, a huge bridge supported by nearly eighty tall concrete pillars set in rows of four. Some of the pillars were blackened at the bottom, where fires had been built against them; Pete chose one of these, which came complete with a grill, sitting-can, and windscreen, to start his own, for a chill wind blew. Then he put on a second pair of pants. BB and I started toward town on a food run. Just before we left the shelter of the viaduct, I cast a glance back at Pete. The setting sun flashed through the forest of concrete columns; the grassy carpet shone luminously. The figure of Pete, dwarfed by the pillars, sat hunched on a can in front of a small flicker of fire. In this improbably spectacular scene, he looked obeisant, a sorry hobo in a great cathedral.

Of course, the viaduct was never intended to give the impression of a church; nor was it constructed as shelter to homeless men. But neither could it have been anyone's intention that this worn-out, used-up old man, once somebody's little boy, would depend on bridges for a roof.

I noticed a contractor's oval stamp on a square of sidewalk as we went on: E.J. KUNICK, FARGO, N.D., but BB argued that perhaps we were in a town close to Fargo, and Kunick had driven in to do the work. Not until a collegiate-looking fellow on the porch of a fraternity-looking house confirmed that this was Fargo did BB capitulate, and then only to the dog.

"Well, how 'bout that, Brandy Lee?" he said. "Your daddy made a mistake." Actually, I was glad he had. It was comforting to know that old hands could lose their way too.

The fellow also told me that the college was North Dakota State University, a statement borne out by the number of people my age we started passing on the sidewalk. We passed a block of sorority houses and started panting. BB was much more vocal than I: whistles, catcalls, and bold stares at any girl that walked by announced his lust. "*Whoo*-oo, lookie there!" he said a bit too loudly as one buxom girl jogged by in shorts and T-shirt. I was embarrassed. He was articulating my feelings, but the style was all wrong.

Another way of looking at the situation was that BB simply was from the wrong fraternity. Most sorority houses had a favorite fraternity, a house full of compatible guys, and vice versa. But for BB's fraternity, the nonselective brotherhood of the rails, there was no female counterpart. A few women rode the rails, but only about one for every hundred men I had seen. Many more homeless women live in cities; but in cities or out, the female homeless are a minority.

Certainly, men make the road a dangerous place for a woman to be, and this could partly account for female tramps' smaller numbers. "Wanderlust," traditionally a male trait, could be another reason. But it occurred to me that perhaps there are more male tramps for the same reasons that men, on the average, die several years younger than women, and that more men than women kill themselves. The greater level of stress experienced by men in our culture is the vague, general reason researchers give for these phenomena—men's responsibility as providers for their family, as soldiers for their country; the competitive pressures to succeed. Male homeless, perhaps, are an evidence that not all men can succeed, that there are not enough jobs to go around, that wars take their toll.

Anyway, BB was out in the cold, but that didn't stop him from pretending.

"Say," he said as we sat behind a grocery store, waiting for it to close to see what might be thrown away at day's end, "you know, one night me and some fellas went into one of them—whaddaya call 'em?—sororisy houses."

"Oh, yeah? Where was this?" I smelled another one of BB's fanciful stories brewing.

"Oh, it was down South. It was at night, and we climbed up the fire escape, way up to the sixteenth floor."

"They didn't know you were comin'?"

"Well, no, 'cept they couldn't help but hear us. 'Specially when we got up to that door up there, and it was locked. Well, I was the only one with a claw hammer, and I had to pull them nails outa the hinges. It was a quiet night, and them damn things went *squeeeak squeeeeak.*"

"So they called the cops."

"No, man! When we got that door open they were all lined up in the hall, you know, in their nighties. You wouldn't believe how excited they were. They all wanted us at once, but, of course, we had to take turns. I worked my way through every room on the floor before I was done. Then that head lady—what do they call 'em?"

"Matron?"

"Yeah, one of them, she shows up, and at first she was pissed off, but then, shit, I told her I'd fuck her, too, and that was that."

The story, like others of BB's, could have come straight out of the *Penthouse* Forum. BB's imagination made them interesting to listen to, and I understood his need: when there are no women around, you make them up. You make them do exciting, erotic things, and you make them crave you. When I was just becoming a teenager, and hormones were pouring into my bloodstream, my head had been filled with similar stories. Later, real girls had come along, mostly displacing the imagined ones. But not, it seemed, for BB. If the girls had come, they had not stayed . . . or perhaps BB was the one who left.

At the dumpster, I held the bag while BB dug in. It was a reasonably good haul. Some of it we ate and some we reserved for camp; then we stopped at another food store. BB headed back but I lingered in town for a while.

A girl I knew in Dallas had been contemplating going to school up here. I ached for her companionship; also, she would provide the only conceivable "in" I had to this familiar yet frustratingly inaccessible college atmosphere. I tried the operator; Joan did go to school here. But when I reached her home, a roommate told me she had gone for the weekend. Dejected, I sat for a while in a park, marveling at how well-scrubbed and comfortable everybody looked.

Wind whistled through the darkened pillars of the viaduct as I walked back to the jungle. Pete and BB had gathered some large pieces of cardboard together as windbreaks. One was left over for me, my only consolation of the sad, lonely night. The kids in town weren't really my people; they wouldn't have believed it if I told them I was sleeping in the railroad yards. The hoboes were only sort of my people. If I said the right things. If I could continue to stand this life . . .

The next morning was Sunday. Pete and BB were reading the morning paper I bought. Since we had come to find work in the beet harvest, I expected them to turn immediately to the Help Wanted section. Instead, Pete scanned the sports section, and BB turned directly to *Parade* magazine. The cover story was "The Worst Penitentiary: Marion, Illinois."

"That's right—it *is* the worst," said BB. I was disturbed

because for once, BB did not seem to be trying to impress me. He looked at the pictures inside, naming several of the faces he found there. He had discussed a number of county jails with Roger and Tiny, and had even mentioned a state prison. But this was the big league: a federal pen.

"See this guy here, Pete?" he said. "He's one mean motherfucker. They called him 'The Ox.' " BB went on, describing conditions in the pen before even looking at the story. I read it later, and the descriptions jibed; BB evidently had been there. This was no *Penthouse* magazine fantasy.

"You don't *never* want to go there, son," he said to me. I nodded, in equal earnest.

Pete meanwhile had moved on to the comics, then the front section, and then the insurance-company inserts. BB followed him through each; they then discussed the penitentiary article some more. Finally, when all else was finished, BB picked up the classified ads. His perusal of the Help Wanted section took all of three minutes.

"Well, there's only one job, Pete," he reported. "Truck driver for beets. And none of us got a license."

"Nope, and we need jobs for all three of us, too," said Pete, considerately. They did not seem too disappointed.

"So what do you think?" I said. "Employment office tomorrow?"

"Employment office is seven miles down the road!" said BB to me, as though I were crazy.

"No, son," said Pete to me. "BB and I was thinking. Cold weather's settin' in, and my bedroll ain't good enough for the kind of cold we had last night. So we been thinkin' of California."

"You're kidding!" I couldn't believe we had traveled a thousand miles just to turn around.

"Hey, if you wanta stay here in this piss-ass town, go ahead," offered BB.

"No, it's not that. It's just that we've come all this way, and California's in the other direction."

They just shrugged, and it was decided: we would leave on the next train west.

On the way to the departure point, we passed again by a tall heap of junk that Pete and BB had stopped to examine the day before. They had come upon large pieces of aluminum siding and more copper wire. "I'm gonna cash some of this in while we're here," BB had said. "And if they won't take it, I'll load it in an empty and take it back to the center in Havre." Thinking he had forgotten, I reminded him of the plan.

"Naah, 'tain't worth it."

"Well, what about those copper rods you were carryin' when we left Havre? You still got those, don't you?"

"Naah, too heavy. Shit, I ain't gonna be carryin' all that shit around! I left them in Williston!"

"Oh." I sat in some grass next to the main line. Pete rolled himself a smoke. BB took a piece of chalk from his pocket, walked over to some empty boxcars on a switching track, and began signing them with his monicker: THE PHANTOM STRIKES AGAIN. The tramps understood plans in a way I did not. Plans, to me, were something you made and then carried out. But to tramps, plans were simply possibilities. Not one of them I had been party to had been carried out—at least, nothing more forward-looking than applying for food stamps in the afternoon. I remembered a line of George Orwell's, written when he was living "on the bum" in Paris: "Poverty," he wrote, "obliterates the future."

On the trip back, relations between BB and me worsened. His storytelling continued: Had he told me about the time his partner of five years jumped a train pulling out of the yards with all of BB's stuff? BB was able to grab the caboose, travel the tops of the cars until he was directly over the thief's empty, and then swing down through the doorway, nailing the guy between the eyes with a kick of his steel-toed boot. Or had I heard of the stream we would be crossing soon? It was Rock Creek, so named because there were so many rocks in it there wasn't room for the water to flow. I began to be annoyed that he actually thought I was dumb enough to believe these, and started calling his bluffs.

One night, we stopped in Havre to restock our food supplies with a midnight raid on the Kentucky Fried Chicken store. They had just closed, and in the trash hopper behind the store BB found a plastic garbage bag full of still-warm chicken. Also in there was corn on the cob, wrapped in foil, and mashed potatoes with gravy. "They start fresh every day," explained BB. "What ain't sold, we get." We were living off the fat of the city.

Back in the train, BB explained that usually the authorities didn't mind such scavenging, but sometimes they did. Once in El Paso, he was sitting in a boxcar minding his own business when "about five" Mexicans burst through the doorway, one carrying a bag of dumpster chicken. Unluckily for BB, two cops were hot on their trail, and arrested the boxcarful.

"Reason I was arrested," BB claimed, "was that you can't be found with them wetbacks. If you are, they'll say you helped 'em, and you'll get automatic five years for aiding and abetting a foreign alien. You don't even get a trial."

"Oh, man, that's not right," I said. "I been with Mexicans lots of times—even had Immigration check my I.D. when they were around—and I never had any trouble. What gets you in trouble is if you help bring 'em over the border. Those 'coyotes' always fuck with those Mexicans, rip 'em off. Those guys deserve to go to jail. But even they get a trial."

"Boy, watch your mouth," said BB, suddenly menacing. "I know it's right 'cause I done the time—in Huntsville, Texas. Five goddamn years, and I done all of it. Now, how 'bout you?"

I just shook my head and was silent. BB backed down.

"Fuck, man, those Mexicans—they get on my train anymore, I just wait till it's rollin' and throw 'em back off," he said. "That's the onliest way t'stay outa trouble.

"And you know what else?" he added presently. "Them hawks and vultures, they won't touch them motherfuckers when they find 'em lying dead on the desert. They're too hot—ate too many of them peppers. Birds won't touch 'em."

I looked at him, incredulous. I hoped he was making a joke. He was not. There was not an iota of humor in his entire tense body, in the eyes that glared at me from under the brim of the dirty hat, in the fists suddenly clenched at his side. I had seen him this way before, right before he landed one of those big fists in Roger's face. There would be no verbal threats, no more cross words. He was baiting me; it was the only warning I'd get. I swallowed my protest, and answered the outrageous claim with silence. The vultures, I thought, *would* enjoy me.

Towns flew by. Pete followed our progress on a road map of the Northwest he kept folded in his hip pocket. "This here's Shelby, comin' up," he would announce, mentioning only the familiar names, towns that had something to do with the railroads. Most of them, I discovered, he had memorized. Glasgow, Shelby, Sandpoint: he had been to all of them at one time or another. So that's how they do it, I thought to myself. Regular maps jogged the memory, but mostly tramps knew their way around simply by having been there before. I had withheld from Pete and BB the information that I was carrying a book of official railroad maps so that I could find out how tramps, in the absence of such expensive reference guides, found their way around.

We unloaded in the western Montana mountain town of Whitefish, to change more stamps and buy some wine and a little food. Returning to the yard, we got directions to the next westbound train, and found an empty. But just before we climbed in, Pete looked in the door and paused.

I noticed it, too. "Hey," I began, "isn't this the same empty—" Pete interrupted me. With displeasure, he said in a whisper, as though the truth were almost too terrible to speak, "Fellers, I don't think we want this one. There's been *tramps* in there!"

It was the first time I could remember BB really laughing.

The day was hot in the mountain town, and as we sat in the boxcar doorway, making our sandwiches, moods became more subdued. Pete took a swig from the bottle of cheap wine and made a face. "This ain't what we should be drinkin' with lunch," he said seriously. "Y'know, when we find some work and ain't so goddamn broke, you know what I'm gonna do? I'm gonna buy me a big, tall, cold milkshake. I dream about it. Chocolate fuckin' milkshake."

From the smile on Pete's face, you knew he could almost taste it. I could almost taste it myself.

The wine had ostensibly been traveling wine, wine to warm us on the long impending trip "over the hump." But it was almost finished before the train even left. Assured by a brakeman who stopped by "to make sure all our passengers are comfortable" that the train wouldn't leave for an hour yet, BB returned to town to hustle up another half gallon. Pete, slightly drunk, was talkative, and I, also tipsy, was, too. The two of us had been getting along quite well lately, and as we talked, it struck me that I knew almost nothing about the background of this man whom I now considered a friend. I tried redirecting the conversation toward the experiences which preceded his long trip on the rails.

He was born in 1930, said Pete, which made him barely 50 years old. This news amazed me, for I had taken him to be at least 65 or 70. Much, probably too much, must have happened in those fifty years.

He ran away from home for the first time at age 12. "My momma was dead and my sister was too bossy . . . she was trying to run the house." He ran away a total of seventeen times "before they stopped lookin' for me.

"I been cowboyin' all my life. Got my first ranch job right when I turned into a teenager," he continued. "And once you asked me where I got my nickname. Well, it was on Don Hicks's place near Colville, Washington. That ranch foreman and me never could see eye-to-eye on things, and one day after we had an argument I picked up my pistol and blew out his windshield. Then he walked over and knocked me out. We became beautiful friends.

And ever since, they been callin' me 'Pistol Pete.'" I liked the name a lot; it reminded me of the hoboes of old: One-Eyed Willy, Hood River Blackie, Whitey Malloy.

He had gone to England in World War II, he said, and afterward stayed to attend "bake school." "But then I came back and went back to ranchin'. Just seemed right for me, that's all."

He never finished high school. He had been married once, and divorced. "She couldn't stand ranch life, and I couldn't stand city life. It's nobody's fault. We just didn't see eye to eye." Two children came out of the marriage. "My boy's a doctor in Aurora, Colorado," said Pete—a suburb of Denver that I knew well—"and my daughter dances with the San Diego Ballet." They were impressive claims, and I expressed my respect. Later I would try to find Pete's son, the doctor, but to my great disappointment, nobody by his name worked or practiced in Aurora or any other part of Denver.

Mostly, though, I believed Pete. He didn't seem inclined, as many hoboes did, to make his life sound any more glamorous than it had been. BB, for example, told me he first hit the road during a coffee break at a weaving plant down South. He was standing on the loading dock, he said, having a smoke, "when that train come by and I was standin' there wavin' at the tramps. Well, I decided I wanted to be on that fuckin' sumbitch. It was payday, so I said to the guy, 'Can I get my paycheck in cash?' And he said sure. And I took out on that motherfucker."

Pete took to the rails most recently, he said, a little more than a year before, after being fired from the Matador Cattle Company in Wyoming. "They fired all the old guys and brought in kids. Mostly college kids, but they even had some niggers!" Pete's voice was full of hurt and outrage. "And that's why I'm on the road— been on the road ever since. Somebody to hire an old man. But experience don't count for a thing no more—I got one strike against me on that." I wondered how big a strike against him was his heavy drinking, and if it had caused or been caused by his firing. But that I could not ask.

We left the doorway and sat against the wall in the shade at the back of the boxcar. Discovering we had a little Phantom Punch left in one of the jugs, Pete and I, but mostly Pete, drank it. He lay down then on his piece of cardboard. I was thinking hard about our conversation. Apparently he was, too, for presently he rolled over to face me, and, very drunk, said, "I've had a hard life, a tough life. I'm not complainin' or nothin', but I don't want to live it over again. My nephew said, 'Uncle Pete, I want to be just like you'—he's wanted to be a cowboy all his life. I said, 'Kid, no you don't.' I don't want to wish hardship on nobody."

We almost kept going when we reached Spokane. Often I have wondered what might have turned out differently if we had.

The idea of stopping in Spokane to work a day or two had been discussed since Fargo. The St. Vincent de Paul charity store there employed transients, paying them partly in cash and partly in the necessities of life: food, clothing, showers. Sleeping bags, in particular, were the currency Pete and BB hoped to receive, for though they each slept in two, one inserted inside the other, often wearing all their clothes, the bags were too old and thin for the autumn nights ahead.

But just a few steps off the train, BB stopped. "Wait a minute," he said. "It's Friday night. Tomorrow's the weekend, and St. Vinnie's ain't open on the weekend. We'd have to wait till Monday."

"Forget it, then," said Pete. "Let's keep on going."

They had already turned around when I spoke up. It was Thursday night, I asserted, and tried to prove it to them by counting back the days since the last weekend. But both of them refused to listen. Just then, however, a brakeman swung out from between two cars, not far from us, and I posed the question to him.

" 'Course it's Thursday," he said, laughing. BB and Pete were humorless. Silently they changed directions again, and we arrived at a weedpatch not far from where they had jungled up just a few weeks before. The tramps had been traveling so much that they were the victims of their own kind of if-it's-Tuesday-this-must-be-Belgium syndrome.

I was up at dawn. Arrive at St. Vinnie's much later than that, BB said, and they might already have all the guys they needed. Because of his ever-worsening wound, Pete would not work; instead, I would donate the bedroll I earned to him, since I already had the best bedroll of the three, and BB would keep the one he earned. We were, after all, partners, and among partners, as Pete had said, it was "all for one and one for all."

But BB, strangely, lingered over his coffee, and then spent a lot of time helping Pete wrap his hand in a clean bandage "borrowed" from the first-aid kit of a caboose. "You better get goin'," he said. "I'll finish this and be right over."

The work involved a lot of loading trucks and moving furniture. I was somewhat annoyed as the day progressed and BB failed to show, but other things kept my mind off it. One was the arrival of a police car and paramedics at the loading dock of a plant across the street. "Old Willy's been hurt," I heard one of the workers tell another. It seemed that Willy, a well-known personage around the yards, often slept under the dock. Apparently, the night before an eight-by-eight-inch wooden beam had fallen on him while he slept, pinning him and fracturing his ankle. It was midday now, and he had just been discovered. After learning Willy was still alive, though, nobody seemed worried: "He's got it good, now. Two or three weeks in the hospital, with clean sheets, a real roof over his head, new clothes, free food, nurses . . . I want to go there, too! Only there's no wine. Poor Willy!"

My salary, at day's end, was a small pouch of Bull Durham tobacco, rolling papers, two dollars, and the bedroll for Pete, consisting of a green blanket, comforter, and a length of twine.

Back at the jungle, BB and Pete were packed and ready to continue west, this time to Wenatchee, in central Washington. Pete grunted his thanks for the bedroll and then sat silently. After rekindling the fire, I reached for my knapsack to get out a can of chili I knew I had there. But . . . one of two straps on the knapsack had been left undone, and not by me. Odd. Maybe Pete or BB had needed some little cooking item, I thought, and had taken a quick look to see if I had it. It was a violation of etiquette—you *never* went in another tramp's pack without permission—but probably not serious.

Yet the chili was not where I had put it. And where were the old cotton gloves I used as hot pads when cooking? And my knit hat—that was gone, too. Suddenly I became alarmed. I looked over toward the campfire—BB was sitting there, chewing on a match and staring into the flames and Pete was gone. My railroad maps—the maps I had not told them about, which had been so hard for me to find, had been hidden at the bottom of the pack. Now they were gone, too. Apprehension grew in my stomach. To mention this or not to . . .

"Hey, uh, BB," I said, deciding. "Were both you and Pete around all day?"

"Well, yeah, I believe we were," said BB, closing the only route of escape from the impending conflict.

"That's funny. Stuff is missing from my pack."

"Oh, yeah? Like what?"

I recited the list, including the train maps.

"I didn't know you had no train maps."

"Well, I did."

BB chewed silently on the match, not looking at me. "So, you want to search my pack, right?"

"No, I don't want to, but I don't know any other way to go about this." The offer had caught me off guard.

"Well, there it is. Go ahead. I got nothin' to hide." He gestured toward his small carry bag. I looked at his bedroll, too, to which he had tied Brandy Lee. If he had offered to let me search his little bag, the stuff was probably in his bedroll.

"Okay if I look at your bedroll after that?"

"Sure."

I approached his pack, on the ground next to BB, my anger growing. I knew I had to ask this of them—if I didn't press it, what would be taken next? How far behind the loss of respect for my property would be the loss of respect for my person? Yet, as I reached into BB's bag, I was scared. BB, clench-fisted, hovered above.

"Careful—my knife's in there," said BB. It was an oblique threat.

My missing gear was not in the bag. I stood up. BB straightened, too, raising himself to his full height, a head above me. I gestured toward the bedroll.

"What should I do with Brandy Lee?" I asked.

"You'll leave her right fuckin' where she is, you son of a bitch!" snarled BB.

I stepped back. "You said I could look in your bedroll."

"Sure, you can look in it," he said, "but if you don't find your map I'm gonna bash your motherfuckin' head in."

It was just like with Roger. Everything fine one second, and then the next—bam. Complete changeover. But I was not drunk, and I had a dispute to resolve with BB.

BB advanced. I took another couple of steps backwards, out of the range of his fists, and put my hand in my pocket. "I don't want no trouble, BB—just my stuff back."

He wasn't even listening. BB, prison-trained, was sizing up the fight. He stopped walking toward me.

"I see you got your piece," he said, eyes on my pocket. "Well, I got mine, too."

He thought I had a gun, a mistake that would work in my favor. He claimed to have a gun, but I was almost certain he did not: few tramps did, because of a gun's high pawn value. Also, BB almost certainly would have told me about it before, in his own menacing way, if he did have it. But things were moving too fast. All I knew was that BB had stopped moving toward me. And his knife, in the pack, was closer to me than to him.

"Look, man, all I want is for us to be fair and square with each other. You don't want your ass whipped by me, and I don't want mine whipped by you. So play it straight with me."

"I tell you what, if I didn't have no faith in the sumbitches I was travelin' with, I wouldn't be travelin' with the motherfuckers," said BB, drawling at triple speed. "And if I lost somethin', I wouldn't go lookin' through your shit, I'd say, 'Yeah, I take your word for it, man,' and all that. And then I'd just go lookin' for the shit."

"If I didn't find it," I returned, "I'd owe you an apology, and I'd give it."

"I don't accept fuckin' apologies, I sure as fuck don't," said BB heatedly. "They ain't worth the fuckin' paper it's wrote on."

Pete, I noticed, had quietly returned to pick up his gear, and was starting to leave. BB, still hollering, started to do the same. Along with his own bedroll, he picked up the one I'd gotten for Pete. I moved suddenly toward him as he did, my only offensive move of the night.

"You'll leave that," I said.

He drew back from the blankets, cursing me. He and Pete, with Brandy Lee trailing, began crossing the yard toward the tracks.

Pete's neutrality infuriated me. "Hey, Pete," I cried after him. "What ever happened to 'all for one and one for all'? Here we are, friends one minute and the next you split without a word. What happened, did you lose your voice?"

"You shut the fuck up, man," said BB, turning around and shaking a fist at me. "You ain't been straight with us."

"What the hell do you mean by that?" I said. But they disappeared into the strings of trains. I stood alone in the field, desolated and stunned. More than two weeks of round-the-clock companionship had just unraveled in about three minutes.

Gradually my heart slowed, and replacing the anger and adrenaline was fear. The field seemed suffused with BB's malice. I was afraid that he might circle around, trying to catch me unawares while I slept. I couldn't bring myself to eat anything at all. I repacked my gear and walked away, disposing of Pete's bedroll in a ditch as I headed toward the main road. I didn't want any tramp to have it.

To my disgust, two tramps walking in the opposite direction

approached me to ask about the jungle conditions. I answered curtly, but they kept talking, filling me in on life at the Spokane rescue mission, though I hadn't asked. Slowly, I began to listen; it sounded like a good destination. Then, to my surprise, I told them why I was leaving the jungle. They seemed genuinely sympathetic. "Town's about five miles from here," said one. "You oughta take the bus. Got change?"

I did not.

"Here," he said, and handed me a quarter, dime, and nickel. "That's handicapped fare, so just make sure you look it. And if that mission's full, you just come back and jungle up with us, okay?"

"Okay," I said. The moment I turned, my eyes flooded with tears. I waved them good-bye without looking.

The moonless night was so dark that I could not tell where the sky ended and the land began. Occasional clues to the horizon's location were provided by solitary points of light an indeterminate distance away—isolated farm settlements, shining like stars. Every half hour or so, the train would burst briefly through a cluster of the lights, a high plains hamlet, and then rumble back into darkness.

I thought about the people in those towns. They would be in bed now. Family, friends, and people they loved would be next to them, or in the next room, or on the next block. In the morning they would go to work with those people, making plans and getting things done. For the most part, their lives would be steady, predictable, organized. The friends were people they could count on, people they had known a long time. That was what I envied the most.

I had been puzzling over the split with Pistol Pete and BB for the past few days, at the Spokane mission and now, back on the rails en route to Klamath Falls, Oregon. BB probably needed a reason to justify taking my book of railroad maps. His "you ain't been straight with us" was a clue to his justification, as I understood it. Like Roger, I had withheld from the group something that might have benefited everybody; I had violated the Rule of Disclosure. By stealing the book, BB probably felt he was setting the accounts straight.

My book was worth more to them than my friendship, as it turned out. Yet they probably had hoped to keep both, and had counted on my not noticing the loss of the book, or not mentioning it. Otherwise, they could have ditched me during the day, getting away with the book, my sleeping bag, and all the rest of my gear. Possibly Pete had not known of the theft. I hoped that was true, though if it were, it would be hard to explain his quick and timely exit from the jungle. Regardless, he could have stuck up for me when the conflict began to heat up. But, as in BB's and my sandwich wars, he did not, and I saw his inaction as a betrayal. They had both betrayed me, and that stung.

Yet I had been forewarned, back in Havre: "Don't trust nobody." I never dreamed they meant themselves.

Most devastating to me was the speed with which the relationship self-destructed. The sociologist whose book I had read at school called tramp society "a world of strangers who are friends." The sociologist had never really lived with tramps, though, and I now thought he was off the mark. We weren't friends, we were "partners," acquaintances who had found it convenient for a while to share food stamps, fires, and conversation. The dictionary defines "friend" as "one who maintains for another such sentiments of esteem, respect, and affection that he seeks his society and welfare; a well-wisher; an intimate associate." That wasn't tramps at all. "Well-wishing" was foreign to tramps; "respect" meant keeping one's distance, "affection," though it did seem to exist between BB and Pete, was rarely acknowledged and appeared more a cause for embarrassment; "intimacy," for reasons I had yet to fathom, seemed something tramps resisted at all costs. The whole episode left me confused and shaky, uncertain of whom or what, if anything, I could count on.

The old freight train slowed and pulled off into a hole. When it screeched to a stop, sudden silence fell, broken only by the intermittent rumblings of the idling units, many cars ahead. I listened hard for the train we were letting pass. Finally I identified its high, distant whine as an Amtrak, with my Pistol Pete–trained ears. The high-powered beam of the sleek silver locomotive exploded upon the track next to ours, and the train shot by in the other direction. I tried to see through its windows: it was light in there, warm, and not windy. People's hair and clothing were neat. Some were reading newspapers, some were chatting. Some were sleeping with their heads on pillows.

The rapid glimpses of each car were like single frames of a movie, subliminal cuts. Their effect was one of deep, disturbing sadness. A friend of mine who had done much traveling alone suggested that the best antidote to such feelings was to recall pictures of good times in your mind's eye, dwelling on their warmth. But when I tried, it simply emphasized the chill I felt everywhere else.

The freight trundled back onto the main line and picked up speed.

12

The smell of the sea, humid and briny, met me as I awoke from a deep sleep. The sky was dark, with just a touch of pink: was it sunup or sundown? For a long time I peered out through the side panels of the empty car carrier I was riding, trying hard to remember where I might be, or what day it was.

Partly to blame for my disoriented state was a common mistake of unseasoned tramps: not packing enough food. I had not eaten in the last day and a half, and the lack of nourishment was having its strongest effect on my mood; mixed with anger at myself was the worn-out, miserable feeling that hunger brings.

Yet, to my surprise, the sky brightened into dawn. When I saw the sun catch the disk-shaped top of a tall, thin tower, my heart jumped: it was the Space Needle, and this was Seattle! I felt anchored again, firmly located on the map. And, in spite of myself, I thought sunny Seattle looked beckoning. I dropped stiffly off the train as it rolled slowly between downtown and the sea, and climbed up toward the city.

Though the streets looked empty, I was spotted nearly as soon as I stepped into the sun. Two tramps under a highway overpass whistled and waved for me to join them. I seldom turn down friendly company.

They were probably in their early thirties, and had the urban look of mission stiffs. "Just in?" asked the worse-off looking of the two, a man with stringy hair and only a few teeth. I nodded. "Well, then, wanta join us for Sunday breakfast?" They were the tramp version of the Welcome Wagon. I took a seat next to them and shared ravenously in the fare: a bottle of cold white port, a small, dirty Baggie of lettuce, and two brown bananas. The men were so forthcoming that when the same one asked my name, I didn't feel imposed upon.

I decided to try out the monicker inadvertently given me by BB and Pete: "I'm Sonny."

"Sonny, Tony Baloney," he replied, extending his hand. This obviously was no railroad tramp; he wasn't guarded enough. But I was delighted.

We shook. "Pleasure to meet you, Mr. Baloney."

"And this is my brother, Larry," said Tony Baloney.

"Larry Baloney?" I asked, suppressing a laugh. "I'm honored." Larry was Chicano; Tony was white. "You must have had interesting parents," I suggested.

"Oh, yes, they raised us very well," said Larry, in mock seriousness. "Tony, for example, grew up to be a doctor—a brain surgeon."

"No kidding!"

"Show him your surgical tools, Tony," said Larry. Tony dug through the pockets of his old blazer, one arm of which had almost fallen off. Underneath, he wore two pairs of pajama tops. Both men, for some reason, wore orange hard hats, and Tony's had a sticker on the front: ARMOUR COCKTAIL SMOKIES.

"Here it is, man," he said, producing a butter knife, "my scalpel. I do lower lobotomies." He gestured to his forehead. "Just pick up a rock and pound it in. Need one?"

"No thanks, that's the last thing I need."

"You probably need one like you need a hole in the head, huh?" asked Larry. We laughed. Next, they filled me in on the Seattle scene: there was the mission, the Sally (special Sunday breakfast at ten-thirty), and the "Service Center," which, Tony explained, "ain't a gas station, it's this place where they'll give you broth and shit."

"Mmm," I said.

"And then Monday, you can go by the Millionaire's Club, if you're into that sort of thing."

"Just what sort of thing is that?"

"Day labor—it's the day-labor office."

My mood took a turn for the better, and I knew it wasn't just the port. Though tempted to see Seattle, I was also eager to see a friend in the area, and needed a break from hoboes after what had happened in Spokane. I hitchhiked south the next afternoon.

My destination, just down the coast in Olympia, was The Evergreen State College. Lara, a friend from home who studied there, said she'd happily put me up for a few days. I felt I had earned a short vacation, and the prospect was wonderful: at last a rest, and a chance to remember who I was and what I was doing.

The college, an alternative school founded in the sixties, was the perfect place for a rest. Lara and her friends, many of them unconventional in dress and attitude, accepted my appearance and were intrigued by my stories. I stayed in her house off-campus, a former trailer home they had dubbed the "Immobile Hut." In the Hut, and in Evergreen's student union, I typed up and went over my notes, listened to the music I had missed, and made phone calls home and to school. I helped cook meals, went to a party, and played Frisbee. I trimmed my long, jagged nails and scraggly beard. I flirted with girls and exercised and took showers for five heavenly days. Then, with the prospect of departure becoming more difficult with each passing day, I did one of the hardest things a person traveling alone ever has to do: I made a plan to leave my newfound friends before week's end, and I followed it through.

Yet already, resuming the journey involved more than just traveling back to the rail yards. Within the space of a week, emotional barriers had been erected between me and the freights. Certainly the life of a student, carefree and protected in comparison to that of a tramp, was hard to give up. But it wasn't just the easiness I missed; it was something to do with being around friends—not just Lara, a friend of mine, but all of Lara's friends, friends with each other. Some dried-out part of me soaked up their friendliness like a sponge. I worried about how long it would last, how long I could carry water in the desert.

Hitchhiking down the Washington coast eased the passage back to the rails. I began to recover the tough, savvy outlook necessary for survival in the tramp world, a world with its own rules and few second chances. By the time I reached Vancouver, in southwest Washington State, I thought I was ready to ride the rails again.

But already I had become careless.

My plan was to ride a train to Wishram, Washington, one hundred miles east of Vancouver along the Columbia River, and there to change trains and cross the river into Oregon. On the way to Wishram, though, I drowsed, taking little account of the towns the train passed through or otherwise keeping track of its progress. It was late night when the train stopped and I awoke.

I rose from my bedroll and looked out the boxcar door: all was black. I didn't know if this was Wishram. There were no lanterns to indicate a brakeman walking the train, and both the units and the caboose were many cars away. As Wishram was supposed to have a large jungle, I knew it would be unwise to leave my gear while I searched for information; the car might have visitors while I was gone. I had just decided to roll up and take a little walk when I heard footsteps on the gravel. I tensed up. A short man stuck his head in the boxcar door.

"Johnny?" asked the tramp.

"No." He ducked back out.

"Hey, wait a minute," I called. "Is this Wishram?"

"Ayup, that's right," he said.

At that very moment the train lurched ahead. It was on its way, probably to Spokane! I associated that destination with Pete and BB, and, in a panic, I hurriedly began tossing my gear out the door. By the time I had found everything and thrown it out, the train was going so fast that the gravel was a blur. The exact speed was hard to judge in the dark, but I really didn't have any choice: my worldly possessions were scattered alongside the last quarter-mile of track. Remembering Lonny's advice, I leaned way back as I jumped, my legs already in running motion, trying to compensate for the momentum of the train.

I might as well have dived head first. The instant my feet hit the gravel my torso was propelled forward over them. My hands hit the gravel second, followed by my chest and a thigh. I skidded to a stop on my stomach, feeling skin and clothing tear, and didn't try to move until the caboose passed me by, just a few seconds later.

Slowly, I rose and assessed the damage: skinned palms, cuts on my chest, a bruise on one thigh, a slightly twisted ankle, and missing buttons. Gingerly, I made sure nothing was broken. If my wits hadn't been about me on the ride into Wishram, they certainly were now. *Never get on or off a train rolling faster than you can run.* How had I forgotten? I limped my way back along the long, scattered trail of my belongings, feeling stupid.

I found the railroad office and station, and walked in to see if there was a place I might clean up. Already there, to my surprise, was another tramp, a very out-of-it-looking fellow, older than Pete. I greeted him but was horrified, as he turned, to see blood trickling down his forehead, around one eye and onto a cheek; blood dark and sticky in the thin hair above his left ear, where there appeared to be another wound; and blood on his right sleeve, near where he held it with his left hand. He looked at me, unblinking and alarmed.

Sympathy tempered my fear. Another casualty of this unlucky night, I thought—he had probably fallen off the same train. "You too, huh?" I said.

"You, too?" he said. "The kids got you, too?" Very upset and slightly drunk, he was hard to understand.

"What? What kids?"

"Out in the park, the kids in the park, the kids with the stones when I was sleepin' . . ." He looked around agitatedly. "The kids that . . . *those* kids!" he yelled, as two young girls dashed through the door to the station and into the ladies' room, giggling. "They throwed stones at me! And they hit me!"

The restroom door opened an inch, enough for two pairs of eyes to peer out. Was it possible?

"I come in here to get some help," said the old tramp, pointing at the railroad personnel inside a glass-enclosed office across the room. "I'm gonna go talk to 'em."

He made his way painfully across the floor and apologetically opened the door to the railroad office. The people inside looked at him for the first and last time. Through the office window I saw him go complaining from person to person, gesturing with blood-covered hands at his wounds. But to the office workers he was a grotesque ghost. Incongruous in his big, dirty overcoat, he whirled around to try to engage someone else each time he discovered the person he addressed wasn't listening.

"What's the old bastard saying now?" I heard from the ladies' room. I turned. The girls, who looked about twelve years old, stared at me.

Finally the old man gave up and left the room, some of the flame gone from his eyes. The girls opened the bathroom door a little wider to get a better look at what they'd done. He noticed them.

"You!" he said. "Why can't you leave me alone? Where's your parents? What'd I ever do to—"

"Keep away from me, you old bastard!" spat the older and bolder of the two girls, a Chicana, leading the way out of the bathroom. The two of them ran back outside, laughing another laugh, this one too cruel to be called a giggle. I watched through the door as they skipped down a path, picking up rocks and tossing them into the air. There was no doubting the old tramp now. They had hurt the only kind of adult a child can get away with hurting.

The old man knew enough not to follow. "Them guys told me

to get the hell out," he said of the railroad workers. "They won't do nothin'." He looked out the doorway, into the darkness outside. "Now I'm scared."

Suddenly my scrapes didn't hurt very badly. We walked together to the men's room to clean up.

I wanted out of Wishram, and so I continued south to the next big tramp town, Klamath Falls, Oregon, on the California border. But "K-Falls" looked cold and empty, a town of dry, empty fields with few trees to jungle under, and those few already taken by unfriendly tramps. From my book of train maps, I remembered that a Southern Pacific line extended from Klamath Falls back north across the Cascade Mountains to Eugene and Salem. A sucker for mountain train rides, I decided to take it.

At dusk I ventured into the S.P. yards. Steam, illuminated by the stark light of the mercury lamps, rose from hopper cars full of moist wood chips brought down from the north, testifying to the warmth of the day. Unfortunately, there were no empty boxcars in the next train to Eugene. The covered grain cars, with their little platforms front and rear, were my second choice, but there were only three, and all had brake equipment on their back platforms. Indecisive, I spoke with a conductor, who said there would not be another train out for twenty-four hours. But it was the warm, piney smell of the wood chips that finally made up my mind. Soon I was seated on the windward side of a covered grain car, mountain bound.

Shortly out of K-Falls, pusher units were added to the end of the train for the impending climb. We wound our way up into the hills, the units chugging hard and slow. Large valleys opened beneath the three-quarter moon, misty and luminous with snow. The railroad bed was the only route through the mountains: no headlights could be seen, no towns. Now and then, when the train negotiated a sharp turn, I could see the powerful headlight beams of the front unit lighting up the rocks on the mountainside and the entrances to a succession of small tunnels. As the moon was obscured by clouds, the woods grew deep and dark. Though the wind began to feel brisk, I was glad to be on the train, a string of ordered energy safe from the wilderness.

The train pulled into a hole. Uphill trains usually yield to downhill trains, since the latter are so hard to stop. In the headlight of the oncoming downhill train I was surprised to see snow drifting down. It was falling heavily by the time the train had passed, and, perhaps to enjoy it himself, the engineer of my train waited several minutes before heading back out on the main line. In the darkness, with snow falling and the train motionless, I could not remember a greater quiet. The moon reemerged, making faintly visible the silent flurry.

Finally the train reached the end of its climb. It began picking up speed as the units joined forces with gravity, and soon the wind whistling over the metal grain car platform became much colder. Quickly I put on an extra pair of socks, but with the loss of my gloves and hat to BB, I had no protection for my hands and head. My scalp soon felt numb and my face stiff. I began to shiver violently. Sweets, I knew from mountain trips, help warm cold bodies, but the only food I had required cooking. Then my feet, despite the socks, began to grow numb—and at that point, I remembered Lonny telling me that on his winter trip to Lincoln, he had built a cardboard shelter under a piggyback trailer, his "piggybank house." Up from beneath me came one of the two pieces of cardboard that separated my butt from the metal floor. I tied one side of it to a ladder in front of me, and supported the other side with my foot. The windblock offered some protection, but not enough to keep from my mind Lonny's description of his own feet after the "piggybank house" trip—"they felt like ol' wooden stumps"—all the way down to Eugene.

There, with just the front halves of my feet and my hands benumbed, I sat at the counter of an early-morning cafe, sipping cup after cup of hot coffee amid a crowd of overalled railroaders. I hoped my shaking would stop soon. I wished I had made my way up to the units when the train was in the hole. And it occurred to me that a November hobo crossing of the Cascade Mountains probably was not the brightest thing in the world to do.

It sure had been pretty, though.

13

"No, I ain't seen no other empties," said the heavy, affable-looking tramp. "And this yard is hot, man. Bull's been drivin' up and down that road all mornin'—just nabbed four wetbacks a little while ago. I'd lowline it if I was you and get out of sight, quick."

I lingered at the doorway to the man's boxcar. Behind him his partner, a short, slight man with a red handlebar mustache, wavy red hair combed back, and cowboy boots, sat on his pack rolling a smoke. He looked interesting.

I was feeling more confident around tramps these days. The naïveté of two fellows my age I had met in Eugene who were trying to catch a freight for the thrill made me feel like a real veteran. And after the challenges presented me by the rails since Havre, I felt like a road-hardened survivor. The scrapes from my spill in Wishram, the split with Pete and BB were like Purple Hearts.

"Well, you know, I didn't see no empties down the line, either," I remarked, fishing for an invitation.

"No, there might not be any left," replied the tramp presently, not offering one.

It was the bull who solved the impasse, his car suddenly appearing again on the road at the end of the Southern Pacific outbound yard where we stood, trailing a cloud of dust.

"Quick, get in so he don't see us!" said the tramp, reaching for my gear. Moments later, the train left Salem for Portland.

. . .

Riding with the tramps was like coming in on the middle of somebody's long conversation and not being offered the background information that would let you understand it. Gradually, I had to work my way in.

"So how much are we gonna need to fix up that truck, Bill?" asked the mustachioed tramp.

"Christ, Forrest, how many times do I have to tell you?" he said, laughing and giving me a look that said, "You see what I've got to put up with?" "Four hundred bucks, like I said before. If we work a month, we'll be able to save four hundred for the car, and four hundred for gas and stuff. And that'll be our grubstake."

"Gonna do some prospecting?" I asked Bill.

"Yeah, man, we're gonna strike it rich. I figure it's about my turn!" he laughed. The laugh was odd. On meeting him in the yard, I had taken Bill's laugh as a sign of good humor, of friendliness. Now it seemed affected, high and tittery, even effeminate. Later it would sound sinister to me.

From the conversation, I picked up that the truck was resting next to Bill's sister's house in Albuquerque, where they had gotten their deep tans. It had been in a wreck, but Bill, who had spent most of his working life in body shops, felt he could fix it. Their ultimate destination was the Yukon, which was still scarcely explored and where staking a claim was supposed to be easy.

Forrest nodded. He was not calling the shots in this partnership, but that didn't seem to trouble him. He seemed, as I got to know him better, like a modern American Sancho Panza, following the quixotic plans of his buddy Bill partly because he didn't have any of his own, and partly because following suited him. It seemed he would go along with anything, though that was not to say he had a bland personality.

"Ooohh," he moaned as the afternoon wore on. "Nothing to eat! And no goodies in the fields, like in California. Just grass, lots of grass." We passed a herd of cows, and Forrest pursed his lips and mooed at them. "All that grass, always enough to eat," he mused to himself. "You know, I wish I was a cow."

"You would!" said Bill, rolling his eyes at me. "Hey, I got an idea, Forrest! Wanta go join 'em?" He feigned pushing Forrest out the door, and laughed a long, weird laugh. Forrest, who took the laugh differently than I did, thought it was funny.

"So where are you headed?" Bill asked me, when the train stopped for a moment and conversation was easier.

"Portland, I think," I replied. "I got an old buddy there. I think I'll drop in."

"Portland!" exclaimed Bill. "Man, I wouldn't stay there. All they got in Portland is tramps! Tramps and bums, but in Portland you can't tell 'em apart. They'll all stick a knife in your back. Why, in Portland, a tramp'll hit up another tramp for a quarter, and then when he crosses the street another tramp'll hit *him* up for a dime. Shit. And niggers and wetbacks everywhere. No, man—Portland sucks."

I marveled at the way entire cities acquired personalities, good or bad, for tramps. Being on the bum in Portland apparently was like trying to start a medical practice in Aspen: there were too many others trying to do the same thing.

"Well, then where are you guys goin'?"

"Everett, man, north of Seattle. Food stamps take two days, plus you can get seventy dollars' welfare in a week. Now, that's a good town for a tramp. And we're gonna get jobs, too—get an apartment with the welfare money, and make us some dough. Right, Forrest?"

Forrest smiled. "Yeah, Bill, that's right. That's right, all right!"

"Hmm," I said, plotting. "You know, Portland doesn't sound so good. What would you think if I came with you guys?"

"Okay by me," said Bill, apparently answering for Forrest as well. Forrest was preoccupied by two pigeons that had entered the stopped car to take advantage of oats scattered around the floor, remnants of a previous load. "You know," said Forrest absently, "pigeons can be real good. Taste kind of like chickens."

"Oh, for chrissake, Forrest."

Preoccupied, Forrest didn't hear. He got down on his hands and knees, one hand extended and full of grain. "Here, pidge-y, pidge-y," he coaxed. "Here, little pidge-y."

The pigeons looked interested, in their stupid sort of way. Just as they neared Forrest's grasp, however, the train jolted forward, and they fluttered away.

"Darn!" said Forrest.

The train spent most of the night in Portland. Before falling asleep, Forrest satisfied the rumblings of his stomach and ours by raiding the dumpster of a seafood restaurant on the river. Bill tried to satisfy his desire for an after-dinner smoke, but found he was out of rolling papers.

"Oh, well," he said. "Guess it's time for the Good Book."

"You're gonna read the Bible in *this* light?"

Bill laughed. "Well, no, not really. Forrest, you still got the little Bible from the Stockton mission I told you to keep?"

"Yeah, somewheres," said Forrest, rummaging through the burlap potato sack in which he carried his belongings. "Here it is, Bill." Forrest handed him a miniature Bible which contained some small chunk of the New Testament in microscopic print.

Bill opened it and tore out a leaf. To my surprise, it was shaped almost exactly like a rolling paper, and was even close to the same weight.

"Burns a little fast, and don't taste too good—it's the ink, I think," explained Bill. "But it'll do in a pinch!"

He got out his pouch of Prince Albert, folded the Bible page in half, and sprinkled in a line of tobacco. Though not a very religious person, I was a little shocked.

"Yeah, whenever they'll give ya a Bible, take it," said Bill. "Why, I once knew a guy saved up all kinds of Bibles, then packed 'em up in a suitcase and went door-to-door, sellin' 'em. He'd probably be a rich man today, 'cept for one night—the night I met him—it got real cold, and he couldn't find any firewood. . . ."

"And he froze to death."

"Hell, no! He wasn't no fool! He got out them Bibles, and pretty quick that fire was roarin'!"

When we awoke the next morning, the train was again on its way. I vaguely remembered its departure, partway through the night. As the train slowed and entered a yard, Bill, who was nearsighted, told me to be on the lookout for signs.

"Shit, I hope it ain't Bellingham," he said, "If it's Bellingham, I'm gonna be pissed." Bellingham, Washington, was on the border with Canada, way beyond Everett. Soon, though, I picked out a sign identifying the yard as that of Auburn, Washington, and Bill was relieved. We were still south of Seattle, and had a few hours to go.

"You oughta get some glasses," I told Bill.

"Yeah, well, I had some, once," said Bill, "till I lost 'em in Albuquerque. Lost some teeth, too." He showed me the empty space on one side. Then he laughed. "Remember that, Forrest?"

Forrest looked rueful. "Oh, yeah. Sure, I remember that."

"So what happened?"

"I told three niggers in a Mercedes that niggers shouldn't be driving a thirty-thousand-dollar car." He smiled again, but didn't look as rueful as Forrest.

"Was it worth it?" I asked Bill.

"Hell, yes, it was worth it. At least now they *know* niggers shouldn't have that car!" He laughed by himself.

"I got bad eyes, too," confessed Forrest, "but these help." He removed from the burlap potato sack an old, bent pair of eyeglasses he had gotten off a shelf at a Salvation Army, and related his story. Out hitchhiking, he had been caught in a snowstorm in a remote part of the Nevada desert. He sought refuge in a tiny building with a collapsed roof, and built himself a fire. He stayed there more than twenty-four hours, he said, with the snow swirling around him, staring into the fire. Suddenly his eyes became extremely dry and sore and his head started to throb horribly. For a long time, he couldn't see. Eventually his vision returned, but it was impaired, and had been ever since. Forrest shrugged. "It's just one of those things you have to learn to live with."

In Seattle, we passed a Boeing aircraft plant and spotted two 747s on a runway. Bill offered us the first of a series of violent speculations. "Can you imagine what'd happen if two of them things plowed into each other?" Actually, I said, I could: I remembered photos taken after such a crash in the Canary Islands not too long before. They were horrible.

"Oh, yeah," said Bill, "with people on 'em—that'd really be somethin'!"

The train followed the coast of Puget Sound the rest of the way to Everett. Once, when we crossed a bridge over a small part of the Sound, Bill speculated on what would happen if the train were to derail and plunge us into the water. "I say we'd land upside down," he mused, "maybe with enough air for half an hour or so—*if* we could breathe. We'd probably be knocked out, bleedin' all over. No—if we go off this bridge, fellers, forget it." How creepy, I thought, while Forrest disputed his conclusions.

The town of Everett perched on a heavily wooded hill overlooking Puget Sound. Most of its industry lined the water's edge, with easy access to the timber it processed in various ways. Just offshore, tugboats pulled along huge floating masses of logs bound together with thick cables. Bill told me he had for a time worked on one of the log-pulling crews. Occasionally one of the logs escaped its tethers, he said, and floated loose around the sound. At first such a log would be visible to boaters, but later it would start to sink, until it hung just under the level of the surface. Such logs, extremely dangerous, were called "deadheads." In lurid detail he imagined what would happen if a fast-traveling boat did smash into one. I decided to stop providing an audience for that kind of talk, and looked away. Behind Bill's affable demeanor, something seemed twisted.

A clue to its nature was offered me that afternoon. We

dropped off the train as it made its slow approach to Everett, and jungled up on a piece of beach littered with washed-up "deadheads" just south of the factories. Bill started a fire underneath a large can full of sea water—the only water that was convenient—while I added a big package of beans, and Forrest carved a long-handled spoon from an old plank to stir our dinner with. As it boiled, Bill carved his road name, THE BONDO KING, in one of the deadheads. I knew from my uncle back in New Jersey that Bondo was a putty used to fill in car dents. Bill, of course, had spent a lot of time working in body shops—and, I soon learned, in another place as well.

A big military helicopter passed us overhead. After a hard look, Bill commented, "Sikorsky CH/HH-53B—the 'Super Jolly.' "

"How did you know that?" I asked.

"Vietnam," said Bill. "I sat in the doorway of one of them things. Was a gunner. Blat-a-tat-tat-tat-tat . . ."

"Were you drafted?"

"Nope, volunteered. It just sounded like the place to be."

Bill had spent five years in Vietnam. After the third, he said, he had decided he didn't like it, but they wouldn't let him leave. A buddy and he had hatched a plan: they would convince their commanders they were alcoholics, and get a medical discharge. After they had some "amazing" binges and wrecked a Jeep, the commander was convinced, but they were sent to a treatment center, not home. Later, said Bill, he became addicted to "horse" ("Heroin's so goddamned cheap over there"), and then morphine.

"But now," he said, with a laugh, "I'm too poor to buy any of that shit." His marriage had broken up soon after his return, and after a couple of disappointing years in body shops, he hit the road.

"But for a while there, I was rich," Bill told me. He owned fifteen cars one year, he said, including an MG, a Blazer, and a Triumph. He had more guns in his collection than the mayor and police chief of Central City, Colorado, combined. He had a little house in town, and "an outhouse with a view."

His father was a geophysicist with a Denver oil company; he had grown up in a nice Denver subdivision that I was familiar with. Was Vietnam the experience responsible for sending Bill to the rails? He thought so. "I had some fun over there, but man, it fucked me up."

Still, he had a plan for getting out of it all and into a better situation. The next day was a textbook lesson in "taking a town for what it's worth," to use Forrest's words. Welfare and food-stamp applications could be filled out in the same office, so we went there first. It was in a squat brick building; the reception room, even at the early hour we had arrived, was crowded with dejected people seated in plastic chairs. I felt them watching us as we came in and stacked our bags and bedrolls next to the others, but when I turned around, nobody would look at me. It was a place of shame, but fortunately my companions were undaunted.

"I need some assistance, please, ma'am," said Forrest, preceding me to the desk so that I could see how it was done. Getting welfare was not simply a process of filling out forms. It involved strategy, wits, and acting.

"Next available appointment time's in two days," she said, not looking at him. She shoved a large sheaf of papers in his direction. "Please fill out these."

Forrest ignored the papers. "Two days!" he said, sounding shocked. "Ma'am," he implored her, "if you don't help me quick one of you gals is gonna have to take me home or somethin', because I'm broke. Just flat out." The prospect of Forrest in her living room seemed to alarm the woman. She looked back down at the appointment book.

"Tomorrow morning," she conceded, "but late." She handed him an appointment card.

"Oh, I do thank you, ma'am," said Forrest, a vision of gratitude.

Bill and I got the same treatment, and soon we sat down to fill out the forms. The first question read:

1. I am *now* or a person for whom I am applying is receiving or has *in the past* received financial or medical assistance, or food stamps from a public assistance office of this state (including this office) or some other state.

_____ Yes _____ No

"What the fuck?" said Forrest, barely under his breath.

I read it closely, three times. "I think what they're asking is, 'Have you ever gotten welfare?' "

"Then why don't they say so?" complained Forrest. "Of course I have. Hasn't everybody?" Annoyed, he checked "Yes."

Later, we were confronted by a sheet demanding to know what we had done during every three-month period of the last four years.

"How are you supposed to remember that?" I asked.

"Bill, how do I handle this situation?" said Forrest. "Put 'Nothing,' " said Bill. "Make 'em think you don't have nothin', and you don't expect nothin'. Don't make it any more complicated than that. Believe me, *they* don't want you to."

We returned the forms forty-five minutes later. "Where's your address?" demanded the receptionist. "We have to see some addresses."

"Ninety-nine Railroad Lane," Forrest deadpanned.

"Where's that?"

"Here, I'll draw you a map." In the margin, Forrest drew arrows to our beachfront property. The woman stared at the map.

"Nobody lives there."

"We do," countered Forrest.

"What are you—camped out?" We all nodded.

She breathed a sigh of exasperation. Everett, we knew, had no residency requirement.

"See you tomorrow?" said Bill.

"Yes," she said, resigned.

We set off, gear-laden, for the employment office. I admired Bill and Forrest's facile manipulation of the bureaucracy, but was bothered by what we had done. In line at the welfare office with us had been a crippled old man and a Vietnamese family with five children, being assisted by an interpreter. Given that welfare resources were limited, I was ashamed that able-bodied single men like ourselves were taking welfare. As tactfully as possible, I asked Bill and Forrest if it didn't bother them.

"Shit, no!" said Bill. "You saw who else was in there—gooks and niggers! Somedays there's spics, too. If we don't get it, they will." As Bill saw it, by applying for welfare we were saving a piece of the pie for white people, who deserved it.

Forrest's reasoning was more sophisticated. "We ain't rippin' off the government—the government's rippin' us off," he said to me. "It's like the Boston Tea Party. . . . What'd they call that?"

"Taxation without representation?"

"Yeah, that's it. I pay taxes—shit, every time I get a paycheck, every time I buy somethin', I pay taxes. But do they let me vote? Not on your life."

"But do you register?"

"Man, it don't make any difference! If you're livin' like us, you can't register. You gotta 'stablish residence! And we can't.

"And one more thing—the government spends all kinds of money on shit like this: studyin' the sex habits of African beetles. And there's guys out here *starvin'!*"

Forrest did have a point. My mind was still on the matter when we reached the unemployment office. Its sign said, euphemistically, JOB SERVICE. It was packed with men, very few of them tramps.

"So when you get a job, are you going to vote, Forrest?" I asked.

"Well, maybe," said Forrest, "*if* I get a job. Christ, look at all the guys in here!"

Our moods plunged. Getting jobs was integral to Bill and Forrest's plan, but the situation looked bad. Men were milling around a bulletin board covered with tiny notices of job openings; periodically a worker would come by and pull one off: one less possibility. Bill had the first interview with a job counselor, leaving Forrest and me on a bench to survey the whole scene. One of the job counselors was interviewing a downhearted-looking man, talking loudly at him.

"Well, look, do you intend to get a permanent job or what?" she demanded. He mumbled something we couldn't hear. Forrest fidgeted. The unpleasant way she spoke reaffirmed that unemployed was a shameful way to be in America. The men had come here to rid themselves of the stigma.

Forrest couldn't sit still. "This is a real hassle," he said to me, on the edge of the bench. "I hate goin' through this fuckin' crap." For once he swore with conviction and sounded truly upset. I asked him why.

"It ain't the fuckin' work I don't like, it's the gettin' started," he said. By this he meant the apartment renting and outfitting, the clothes buying, the pavement pounding, the filling out of applications. Working off the street might be possible, he said, but you would have to stash your gear during the day, probably sleep in your clothes, and show up at the job unwashed and unshaven.

Even if he had the money to start, it seemed Forrest dreaded the prospect. Work was a web of entangling obligations and expectations which he had no desire to get caught up in. His attitude toward work reminded me of mine toward school when I was younger—especially after a period of vacation, the prospect of entering system and schedule again was mildly terrifying.

"Forrest Wise!" called out the receptionist. It was his turn for the interview. "I'm gonna bullshit 'em," he decided as he left. The plan with Bill became a thing of the past.

Bullshitting would be my strategy, too. The idea, explained to me by other tramps, was to profess a job skill for which there could be no conceivable labor demand in the area. That way, if your interest in getting a job seemed sincere, the counselor would give you a white registration card—often useful when applying for food stamps or other welfare—without also giving you work. I still had much of the West to visit, and didn't want to be tied to a job for several weeks. Maybe I'd be able to stick with Bill and Forrest for a while, anyway.

Forrest and I reconvened on the bench. We showed each other our cards and smiled. "What'd you tell 'em?" I asked Forrest.

"Oil fields," said Forrest. "I'm oil field trash. How 'bout you?"

"Cattle. I'm a ranchhand from way back."

"Man," said Forrest wryly, "this is all bullshit. 'Job Service,' my ass." Forrest's view was that the system was set up less to serve employees than employers. He recalled a session with one unemployment counselor who asked him a barrage of questions he felt had nothing to do with his qualifications for a particular job—"personal-type" questions.

"I asked her why the fuck I had to answer all those, and she said, 'It's for the employer, to see if he likes you.' 'Well, how 'bout me?' I asked. 'How'm I gonna know if I like the employer?'

"And here's the other thing," Forrest continued heatedly. "They act like there's no unemployment, like any guy could find a job if he just wasn't too picky or too lazy. But that ain't true! What's unemployment about, anyway? They say there's nine percent fewer jobs than there is guys lookin' for work. And you know what? They don't even count the guys that give up, that ain't lookin' anymore. And how many guys do you know like that?"

I thought of Pistol Pete, laid off and so discouraged he no longer made it past the Sunday Help Wanted ads, and then only sometimes.

"At least one," I said.

"Well, listen: there's more."

Of the many explanations I had heard of why men don't work, my mind skipped back to Jack London's. He saw tramps as a floating army of surplus labor. Among them were both those

> less fit and efficient, switchmen who wrecked trains and blacksmiths who lamed horses . . . [and] good men, splendidly skilled and efficient, but thrust out of the employment of dying or disaster-smitten industries. . . . While it is not nice that these men should

die, it is ordained that they must die, and we should not quarrel with them if they cumber our highways and kitchen stoops with their perambulating carcasses. This is a form of elimination we not only countenance but compel. Therefore let us be cheerful and honest about it. . . . For goodness' sake, let us refrain from telling the tramp to go to work. We know there is no work for him. . . . Let us be just.

Forrest and Bill were no "perambulating carcasses," at least not yet, and in contemporary life more than simply the lack of a job led men to become tramps. But London's ideas about jobs sounded awfully similar to Forrest's, and awfully right to me.

Bill finally emerged with a line on a gutter-installing job that he thought he might be good at, and reassured Forrest that new jobs came in all the time. Forrest smiled weakly.

That afternoon we completed our tour of the Everett free resources circuit. A storefront help center run by the Volunteers of America was good for a small bag lunch. Bertha Sulborski at the front counter was all business, wanting only our names, Social Security numbers, and silence. But as she walked into a back room to get our bags, Forrest heard her mention to another worker something about a man coming in shortly to pick up "that big bag of food" for his family.

"Ooooh, you give to families, too?" piped up Forrest. His face assumed a mournful look. "My little girl's over on the other side of town, and she'd sure appreciate—"

Bertha cut him off. "Single men get one lunch, and that's it," she said sharply. "We hear it all day long. Everybody's got their story."

"I just thought I might have some new wrinkle you haven't heard of yet," joshed Forrest, a twinkle in his eye. He could be very charming; I swore that, for just an instant, the hint of a smile crossed Bertha's lips. Bill and I got our lunches, but Forrest lingered at the counter, engaging Bertha in conversation. His goal was no longer another lunch, but simply dessert: a bowl of chocolate dinner mints sat on the counter, and whenever Bertha was distracted for a moment, Forrest reached up and grabbed a big handful. Twice she almost caught him. Finally the phone rang, and when Bertha turned to answer it, Forrest, lightning-fast, emptied the entire bowl of mints into his pocket. We strode out the door.

The lunch was really breakfast for us and, still hungry, we decided to hit up a nearby church that a tramp at the food stamp office had told us was good for a meal voucher at a local café. Bill introduced us to the head pastor, and said we'd be glad to work for a meal. It seemed to me a fair deal, perhaps better conceived than the VOA form of charity. We were shown out to a large brick patio, where a wizened gardener was pulling weeds out from between the cracks. He greeted us, relinquished his gardening tools with a smile, and took a cigarette break in the shade, watching us work with great interest.

"Say, what's in these bags?" he asked earnestly, pointing at our gear. "All your worldly possessions, eh?"

"You got it," said Forrest, on his knees.

"And so whenever you go, you take 'em with you?"

"Ayup." The man made some comparison to snails. He was very intrigued with us, and getting more so.

"Oh, I'll bet you guys have a heck of a time, huh? Free spirits and all? Get to travel everywhere?"

"Yeah, to hell and back," Bill muttered under his breath.

But Forrest was indulgent. "Yeah, there's some of that to it," he said, "but then you get to feelin' like you've seen it all. The folks you get to know best are the cops, and you know them too well." The man's interest was undiminished. If he lived in Iowa, it was a sure bet he'd be a regular at the Hobo Convention in Britt.

Shortly afterward, while chowing down $2.59 each of hotcakes and coffee, Forrest told me people were always coming up to him and saying that kind of thing—that old romance of the traveling life. "All the straights want it."

The rescue mission was the day's last stop. I thought the sermon, delivered by a preacher with tattooed arms who claimed to have spent thirty-six years in prison, was better than most, but Forrest disagreed.

"You can't take a guy off the street like that and expect him to teach you stuff," he said. "What did he teach you that you didn't know?"

"Well, nothing, actually."

"There you go."

Besides dinner and new clothing, we also qualified for a bunk, but Bill didn't want to stay. "I keep outa missions because of all them little six-legged passengers in the sheets," he explained. "It's like tramps and freight trains—they say, 'There goes one!' and they hop on!"

"But Bill," protested Forrest, "it's rainin' out. And we ain't washed up since your sister's in Albuquerque!"

"But Forrest!" said Bill, imitating his partner's tone. "I said outside."

Forrest was angered, but he wouldn't press the issue; he seldom pressed any issue. The warmth of the mission seemed inviting to me, too, as we stepped out into the drizzle, but I was loath to intervene. One of the keys to getting along with the tramps was a willingness to do things their way. Physical discomfort, I was finding, was important only when the mood was wrong. Tonight it was right, in part because of the fascinating transformation in Bill and Forrest's appearance since they donned their new clothes.

Bill's grimy old sweatshirt and jeans, I saw as we moved underneath a streetlight, had been replaced by slacks and a blue-and-white pinstriped shirt. Over it was a London Fog overcoat that someone had donated in good condition. With a tooth or two replaced Bill could easily have looked the part of a promising young professional. I suddenly remembered a photo article in *Esquire* magazine, in which a number of derelicts were given shaves and haircuts and new suits and presented as up-and-coming business leaders. The illusion had been totally believable.

I was startled by how well Bill recreated it. He reached in his pockets to see if anything of value had been left there, and brought out a pair of ticket stubs to a symphony performance.

"Well, will you look at that," he exclaimed. "All I need now's that Mercedes."

We looked at Forrest. His new wardrobe did not exactly work the same effect. He had been given a ridiculous square-cut vinyl jacket with no buttons, and had assumed the appearance of a barker at a carnival, a real flimflam man.

"Fuck!" he said indignantly. "What kind of clothes are these to give a guy on the road?" We all laughed, and then they had another laugh, at me. My new shirt was of the silky polyester variety, black with bright strokes of orange and yellow, with a huge collar. With a gold pendant for my chest and trousers a bit tighter than the baggy old slacks I'd been given, I might have been an aspiring disco king. The incongruity of it all was amusing, and as we walked back to the jungle our moods defied the weather. Forrest reconciled himself to sleeping outside and seemed to forgive Bill.

"We mighta had a good sleep in the mission, but just the same out here we *might* find a hundred-dollar bill. You never know what's gonna happen. Tomorrow we might all wake up rich, shit!"

Due to continuing rain and the rats that crept out onto the beach at night, consuming two entire loaves of our bread, we moved camp from the beach to a small park on the edge of town adjoining the Burlington Northern offices. There we slept on cardboard under what Bill dubbed the "Waterproof Tree," a huge, dense pine that stopped most of the rain before it reached us on the ground. As it turned out, the Waterproof Tree was a resting place known to many tramps coming in and out of Everett, and on several mornings we woke up to find others sleeping on the thick bed of needles around its trunk. Seldom were there any territorial conflicts, as the tree was recognized as an important shared resource and there was plenty of room—until late one night when two drunken tramps arrived, one looking for a friend.

"Paul?" he shouted, walking right up to where Bill lay. "Paul, izzat you?" The other tramp came up to join him, and together they examined Bill's supine figure at close range, peering around his head.

"Naaah," concluded the first one. "He's too bald to be Paul."

Bill, who evidently had been hoping they would just go away, sat bolt upright. *"Get the fuck out of here before I punch your fuckin' faces in!"* he yelled, waving his fists, and the tramps scattered.

As the welfare and food-stamp applications took a few days to be processed, we spent many hours wandering around Everett, killing time. Bill and Forrest began bickering, much like a married couple that had been spending too much time together—and indeed they had: twenty-four hours a day, for nearly a month. Overall, though, the three of us got along pretty well. I found I was able to live with Bill's amicable weirdness, and I took a special liking to Forrest. He was doing his best to have a good time living in a way that he conceded had its drawbacks, trying to see things in a positive light, not worrying too much about life's next turn. His comments about the injustices of the unemployment office were as serious as I ever heard him get; letting ideas weigh on him was not Forrest's style. His exuberance and zest for life were not clouded by philosophical considerations. Forrest was expert at seeing the humor in life, or if it was not in evidence, creating some.

His humor was seldom very sophisticated. "Your tire's full! Your tire's full!" he was fond of shouting at drivers waiting at stoplights, pointing with alarm at one of their front wheels. Or, when small pleasure boats passed within earshot of our beachside jungle, Forrest would stand up and rant at them, in fake indignation, "Get out of that boat! That's right, get out of it! Now!"

Or, as he implored two pretty teenaged girls about to walk by us one day, while pointing at an imaginary spot on the sidewalk, "Don't step on it!"

"Oh! Sorry!" they replied, embarrassed, stepping around the spot and smiling at him.

"Thank you," intoned Forrest, going over to the imaginary spot, removing the imaginary something, and placing it in his pocket. He eyed their backsides lustfully as they continued on their way, and expressed his approval.

"Too young," I said.

"You think? Let's ask 'em!"

"Let's not." We continued on our walk.

"Oh, I get in a lot of trouble," said Forrest, "but I have a lot of fun, too. Did I ever tell you that joke about the Englishman?"

An English nobleman came to America, Forrest said. He brought along many peculiar habits, but one of the most interesting was the way he would walk straight up to girls and ask them for a piece of ass. Often a slap in the face was the response he got, and one night somebody said to him, "Don't you get slapped in the face an awful lot?"

"Yes," conceded the Englishman, "but I get an awful lot of pieces of ass!" Forrest and the Englishman had a lot in common.

We stopped at a few stores to change some food stamps, bought a half gallon of wine, and headed home to the jungle. Forrest realized we had enough change to buy a couple of glasses of beer as well, and we chose a bar. Suddenly, Forrest veered off the sidewalk and toward a bank.

"Where are you going?"

"Flower shop," he replied, picking a handful of daffodils from the garden in front.

"Forrest!" I hissed loudly, looking around nervously. "Why'd you do that?"

"They're for the barmaid," he explained patiently.

"You know the barmaid at this place?"

"Well, no," he said. "They're for her, whoever she is."

We arrived at Jake & Betty's bar at six. The barmaid didn't come on until eight, the bartender said icily, and her name was Betty. He was Jake.

But Forrest was undaunted. We sat at the bar, Forrest two stools away from a petite middle-aged woman with a small paunch. She and her stool looked well-acquainted, as though she were there most evenings. After we ordered our drafts, Forrest nudged me with his elbow. "Not bad, huh?"

She was not bad-looking, but I whispered back to Forrest: "Too old!"

"Not for me!" he said, with feigned indignance. He continued his sidelong glances, and when the beers arrived, he cleared his throat, turned toward her, raised his glass, and said, "Here's to you, ma'am!"

She blushed slightly and nodded. Presently Forrest changed stools and began to chat with her. She smiled as he talked; he really was a charmer. Slowly, reluctantly, she accepted the bouquet Forrest had offered. I tried to watch discreetly.

Ten minutes later Forrest returned. We paid for our beers with the large number of pennies and nickels that had been making our pants hang low.

"So," I said, not sure if this would be taken as a joke or not. "Is she coming back to the jungle? Do I need to find another tree tonight?"

"Naah, her old man's at home, an invalid," Forrest sighed. "She'll be goin' back there." There was quiet for a while. Then Forrest said to me, "Tell you what, you should be havin' fun now, before they all get married. Get out there and find somebody." The thought had been occurring to me lately.

"Were you ever married, Forrest?"

"Yeah, once. For five years. When I came back from the Army, though, things weren't the same. We got divorced two months later. I got no hard feelings, though—I'm just the kind of guy it wouldn't work for. Marriage, and the old nine-to-five . . . they ain't for me."

We left the bar. The air outside was sweet and warm, and as we walked a warm presence came to mind: nobody in particular, just a composite of girls I had known and girls I wished to know.

I didn't dwell on it though, because lately I had been having a pretty good time. Much of it had to do with my company. Forrest was a person unlike any you could meet in another sector of society, a person whose attitude could survive only out here on the edge, and tenuously even so. The wine tasted sweet and good; I was losing my aversion to hitting dumpsters; I was finding what was good in my company, and feeling confident enough to show them some of me.

Behind a hot building the day before, for example, where the three of us had stopped to rest in the shade, Bill had discovered a pile of large beets and begun tossing them around. I noticed a pile of two-by-fours. "Hey, anybody up for some baseball?" I asked, brandishing a two-by-four as a bat. The idea caught on, and we played a few innings, alternating as batter, pitcher and outfielder. The incident made me feel I had a place here, and that made me proud, for making that place had been a difficult process. In Olympia, I had been reading *Black Like Me,* an account of how white novelist John Howard Griffin dyed his skin and hair in order to take a look at the South from a black perspective. According to him, he *had* fit in—"I had become a Negro," were his words at one point—and I felt a happy similarity to my situation. I had become closer to hoboes than I had ever dreamed possible. My appearance had changed, and then slowly my attitude had, too. I almost dared to say: "I have become a tramp."

But as my familiarity with Bill and Forrest increased, problems began to creep in. In Olympia I had been given a small Instamatic camera. I told Bill and Forrest about it one hot day in downtown Everett, and asked if they would mind if somebody took a picture of us. Bill was reluctant until I offered to buy the next quart of beer; Forrest didn't mind. After a boy at a bus stop took the picture, we retreated to an alley, already filled with other tramps doing the same thing, to sit in the shade and drink the beer. Suddenly, a window opened up above us. "Alcoholics!" a kid yelled down, slamming the window. When the kid did it again, Bill yelled, "Shut up!" and tossed a rock back up at the window.

We joked about the incident, but the three of us were a little less jolly afterwards. It was only ten A.M., after all. By the end of the day we would have drunk up all of the money left between us, save for my few secret traveler's checks. I wondered: Did we drink too much? Did *I* drink too much?

I had the same concern about cigarettes. Slowly, I was becoming addicted: after two and a half months around tramps, I was smoking up to a pack a day of cigarettes, or the equivalent of roll-your-owns. The way I used to dislike the company of smokers, and look down on heavy drinkers, was a dissonant memory. It didn't fit in with the way I was acting now.

We picked up another Volunteers of America sack lunch and walked to a place where we'd be out of sight and left alone, under a small bridge that crossed over a railroad track not far from the Everett yards. Once it had been a cool, pretty spot, according to Bill, but now it was, in his words, "a slum." Every slob in the world appeared to have jungled there, and most had left behind trash, old vegetables, grungy clothing, or shit. We poked around just the same, hoping to find something of value another tramp had left behind. But having no luck, we cleared a spot for ourselves on the small bank running down to the tracks and were about to begin lunch when two more men appeared on the scene.

They were winos, with the staggers and the bottle to prove it. One looked about 50, one about 65; both wore visor caps and were having a hard time standing up. The younger, less deteriorated of the two offered us a drink from the bottle, and Bill took him up on it. His friend, meanwhile, collapsed on the hill, and the first wino, in a voice loud, repetitive, and nasty, sat down and began to talk. But it was not a conversation.

"Hey! Been to the mission yet?" Bill answered that we had.

"Hey! I tell you what else you can do—hey—they got a detox center—hey—take the white cab out there—hey—they got a TV room—hey—they'll bring you back—hey—"

At this point the older drunk tried to say something, but he had a very hoarse, weak voice and a bad cough and couldn't get it out. He began drooling profusely.

"—Shuddup! shuddup, you!—eh—they me—hey—they

feed you not a hell of a lot—hey—are you listening are you fol-
lowin' me—hey—first thing they do is they make you take off your
clothes—hey—they're fuckin' clean when you come out—stay
seventy-two hours, they'll drive you back . . ." He paused, having
lost his train of thought. The "hey's" made me think his average
audience had an attention span of two or three seconds.

"Hey," he continued, less robustly now. "Hey, that goddamn
alcolhol—no, alcol—no, whatever they call it . . . Hey. Make sure
you take your own tobacco."

Forrest looked away, and Bill, after first trying to pay back the
sip of wine by being an audience, stopped listening. But though I
looked away whenever the drunk turned his unsteady gaze toward
me, I was transfixed by the man. He repeated the information on
the detox center twice, several times drowning out the efforts of his
gurgling friend to talk. "Aaa, go stick the bottle up your ass, even
if you did buy it, cocksucker," he told him. His fierce temper did
not seem to interrupt the passing of the bottle between the two of
them, however.

Finally, the first wino took a long draught and tossed the bottle into the weeds. Protesting, his companion got up from his stomach and pursued the bottle on hands and knees, at last finding it
and holding it up to the sun to see if there was a little more. He
unscrewed the top and poured down the dregs. His friend then
announced it was time to go, but the older wino had opened his fly
and was attempting to pee while lying on his side. A few drops
came out.

"Come on, come on, stand up, let's go!" The older tramp could
not quite manage it. He struggled to his hands and knees, and then
hands and feet, swaying back and forth for a good minute, telling
his companion not to help him, he'd make it. His face got very red,
and it looked as though he would vomit. Finally, wondrously, he
stood. I had never seen a human being in such horrible shape.

But the worst was yet to come. As the old wino stumbled off,
the loud, nasty man turned back to us. He whispered harshly,

"He's got a big check comin'. He's got a big check comin' tomorra, and I'm fuckin' gonna get it from him. . . . Oh, yeah, I been with him long enough, I know it's in the mail. Gonna knock that mother-fucker on the head—do you believe me? You think I'm kiddin? I'm gonna kill 'im, that's what. Come back, you'll see." He cackled.

Forrest shook his head as the man staggered away. He looked up at me. "You said you hit the rails to learn some things. You gettin' your education?"

I nodded. I sat in a nauseated daze while Bill and Forrest talked about detoxification centers. Like most men on the road, each had been to at least one; they talked of the drugs given to patients—Antabuse, Librium—and how they "mess up your head." One of them, said Bill, kept you from getting drunk, to a point; the other made you feel violently ill after drinking the slightest bit of alcohol. I knew that some progressive towns, like Denver and Seattle, had decriminalized public drunkenness and redirected funds toward detox centers. The paddy wagons that cruised these towns' skid rows now simply offered free rides to the detox center. Yet it seemed the treatments received at such centers did not work well. I had met so many men who had been in and out, time and again.

I was quiet for much of the rest of the day. Forrest and Bill resumed their bickering as we walked alleys back to the park, but I listened with only half an ear. Life with them seemed suddenly sordid, demeaning and dirty and low. Back at the tree, as the sun went down, the scene under the bridge played back in my mind: the old drunk, tottering pathetically under the bridge, and the face of the loud, younger drunk, wrinkled, sunken, sallow, with no teeth. I looked then at Bill: he had teeth missing. I felt my own teeth, and they were all there, though fuzzy and unexercised. Digging down deep in my pack, I found my toothbrush, slipped it quietly into my pocket, excused myself from the tree and walked into town. In a filling-station restroom, I brushed my teeth until the gums throbbed. Then I washed my face and carefully combed through my hair and beard. The hair was shoulder-length now, and fairly dirty; lately my scalp had developed a fierce itch. I blocked the drain in the sink and washed my hair with a little bar of hand soap, drying it with paper towels. There, I thought: clean and with all my teeth. I *am* different from the tramps.

I wanted now to be a creature about whose identity there was no doubt, no longer a chameleon. A phone booth caught my eye. Telephones were not an element of the tramping life. Not only would I call a friend, I would call a friend collect. I knew people who would *pay* to talk to me. What better proof that I was not a tramp?

My college roommate accepted the charges, and soon I was pouring out my heart to him. Many of my bad feelings about the trip had been dispelled when my friend, searching for more of the bright side, said, "It seems to me that another valuable thing about your experience is that now you know you could survive."

"What do you mean?"

"Just that, if for some reason everything went wrong in your life, or you decided to give it all up, you could rest easy knowing there's a way you could get by. You could just become a tramp!"

He laughed. The remark, only partly serious, had been intended as a comfort, but it had entirely the opposite effect. Hearing someone who knew me propose trampdom as a conceivable destiny for me was utterly depressing. What I needed now was evidence that there were some essential differences between the tramps and me. The thought that Bill in his new clothes could nearly pass for a downtown businessman suddenly scared me. In a complete turnabout from my earlier concerns, I wanted a guarantee that, while I could get close to tramps, I could never really become one, and they would never permanently "rub off" on me. I wanted someone I knew to say that going native sounded more absurd to them that it did to me right now.

My friend's remark met with silence and he tried changing the subject. But I just couldn't pick up my end of the conversation again. With a promise to call again soon, I hung up.

. . .

It was the big pay-off day. We woke early, partly from excitement and partly from hunger. Too many food stamps had been converted to drink rather than food, and we felt it.

"I'm so hungry my stomach's touchin' my backbone," exclaimed Forrest. Bill noticed that he was having a hard time keeping his pants up. "What we oughta do is start up a chain of freight-train weight-loss clinics," he said, "and sign up a slew of them rich, fat broads." We all laughed. It seemed that in the course of last night's bickering Bill and Forrest had worked out some of their differences, and sleep had calmed my nerves. The three of us had things to look forward to today.

But bad news arrived even before we got into the welfare office. The prospect of our impending wealth had gotten Bill excited about the Yukon plan again, and while Forrest and I waited for the welfare office doors to open, he went off to call the gutter company about the job opening. He returned, crestfallen.

"Somebody else already got it."

Condolences were in order, but Forrest used Bill's disappointment to lend credence to his philosophy of work. "See, I told you we couldn't get no work off the street!"

"Fuck you, Forrest! It was just wrong timing is all. I'm gonna go back. I'll find somethin' else."

"Not me," said Forrest, half under his breath. "Hey, Bill, think about it. Why do guys work? They work so they can save up enough money to stop workin', right? They work so they can stop. Well, I think it's time to get smart. I'm not even gonna *start.*"

"Man, Forrest, you're just a lazy bum!" said Bill. "He won't do nothin' if it ain't for free," he said to me with disgust. Forrest stewed, and I noted the irony of Bill's remarks. I also considered the wisdom of Forrest's. Most jobs were, as Forrest put it, just "forty hours and a paycheck."

The welfare office finally opened; called into a back room by a caseworker, we received the bombshell that all welfare payments to single men had been terminated the week before, due to budgetary shortfalls. Forrest groaned; Bill looked at the floor. Fortunately the food stamps did come through, and among us we had just over 200 dollars' worth. They were intended by the government to last a month, but with our disappointment over the welfare money and the final collapse of the Yukon plan, it was decided we would spend the first big chunk of it on drinking. As Bill said, "What else is there to do now?"

Forrest had wrangled a voucher from the Salvation Army good for a small shopping trip in their used-clothing store, and he offered to pick up the wine on his way back. It was dusk when we gathered again under the Waterproof Tree. Forrest's mood had worsened as he had walked clean across Everett carrying three overstuffed grocery bags full of old clothes and wine, two of which had torn open en route.

Plus, there had been trouble. Forrest had gone through the grocery-store checkout line to buy a candy bar with food stamps one too many times, and the cashier alerted the manager, who confronted Forrest. Knowing the store had nothing to lose since it would be reimbursed full value for the dollar, Forrest held his ground and called the manager a "hardass." The argument climaxed when Forrest, all 125 pounds of him, landed his fist in the manager's forehead. The police were called and Forrest was told to leave town by the next day.

"Well, are you gonna?" I asked.

"Hell, no!" said Forrest. "I'm goin' back there and I'm gonna buy another one!" And the next day he did with no ill effects.

But that evening, Forrest was hot, tired, grumpy, and thirsty, a bad combination when there's wine around. He took off his boots and rubbed his feet. As he sorted silently through his old and new clothes, deciding what to keep and what to toss away, Bill said to me in a whisper deliberately loud enough for Forrest to hear, "See, when something goes wrong, he can't handle it!" Forrest remained silent.

The wine began to flow and, for the first time, I drank my share. Bill and Forrest's shortness with each other was making me tired of both of them, but Bill—with his bigoted views, his insistence on winning every argument, his pettiness and disloyalty toward Forrest, and his weird, violent imaginings—had worn especially thin on me. And then there was the whole Everett tramp scene: the dirt, the booze, the sponging, the covetousness, the way nobody seemed to think anything out, and the selfishness. I was getting pretty sick of it all.

Forrest, between sips from one of the three half-gallons of white port he'd bought, scratched his scalp vigorously and pulled out a small something. He flicked it away with distaste toward the other side of the tree where I slept.

"One of them six-legged passengers?" asked Bill gleefully.

"Hey, Forrest, that's where I bed down!" I protested.

Forrest just sulked. It began to grow dark, we kept drinking, and Bill and I decided to trade knives. His was a small hunting knife on a sheath; mine, a Swiss Army knife, was too bourgeois, a symbol of affluence not much good for protection or slicing up kindling. Bill wore his knife on his belt, and I fancied that by doing the same I could assume some of the toughness he projected.

"You said you'd trade it with me!" Forrest objected.

"But you never had anything to trade it for, did you, Forrest?" countered Bill sarcastically. "But here, I'll tell you what. Know those steak knives I carry? I'll play you a game of mumblety-peg. If you win, you get the knives. If I win, you kiss my ass. And I mean *kiss* it."

Bill spoke literally. It was a disgusting prospect, but Forrest agreed. The bottle of wine was set down between them; they would take a swallow between each toss of the knife. I leaned back against the tree, dizzy from the wine and nervous at the prospect of two tipsy tramps tossing knives at each other's feet. My fear multiplied tenfold when I noticed that Forrest was still barefoot. "Don't worry, I can move 'em fast when I have to," he reassured me. But his words sounded slurred. Bill grinned.

The throwing began. Occasionally a knife would smoothly pierce the soil near one man's foot, but usually they were mis-thrown and bounced away. One, two, three times Bill's throws actually hit Forrest's feet, but they landed handle-first and bounced off harmlessly. I sat horrified, waiting to see Forrest impaled on the lawn of the park, tendons and veins in his foot severed. Instead Forrest, by an incredible stroke of luck, vented some of his accumulated rage at the world by landing the blade of his knife in the toe of Bill's work boot.

"Oh, shit!" cried Bill, lifting the foot in the air and hopping frantically on the other one. The knife wobbled from its anchor in the sole of his boot as Bill grabbed for it. Finally he wrapped his fingers around the handle, just as he lost his balance, and his heavy frame crashed to the ground.

"You son of a bitch!" he yelled at Forrest, tossing the knife far away into the shrubs. He would deal with Forrest with his hands. I reached forward and tossed the other knife away, too. The blood inside the toe of Bill's shoe was enough for one night, for me.

Unsteadily, Bill got to his feet, and the two of them squared off, only three feet away from each other. The whole park was beginning to look blurry to me, and I noticed that Bill and Forrest, both now extremely drunk, were barely able to stand up at all. Shouting insults at each other, they circled the tree, and I wobbled out of the way. Since Bill was twice Forrest's size, the outcome of any fight was easily predicted. Even Forrest, in his current state, was aware of that.

"Come on, now, Bill, you know better than that," he said, trying to talk Bill out of his belligerence.

"You better leave, Forrest! Leave the tree and leave Everett! I'm countin' to ten!"

"Now, Bill, come on. You're a big dude, you know I wouldn't mess with you. Ain't nobody messes with you, Bill! So come on, lay off . . ."

Bill started counting but got confused halfway. He put down his dukes and, mumbling, retired to a shrub to urinate. Forrest followed suit. When they were done, up went the fists again. The whole thing seemed surreal to me, but Bill and Forrest weren't joking.

Bill began taking little swings, scaring Forrest. I felt sure I was going to see Forrest's face bashed in and wondered what I could do about it. "'Bye!" Bill began saying, telling Forrest he'd better leave. "'Bye, Forrest!"

"Okay, okay, I'll leave," said Forrest, but didn't.

Bill picked up the ax handle he carried as his main weapon. With terrific might, he whacked it against the trunk of the tree, yelling out that Forrest had better get the hell away. In an anthropology film, I had seen male chimpanzees do the same thing; both then and here, it seemed to work. Forrest turned to run, but promptly collided with one of the tree's stout lower limbs. Bam— the branch hit his face, and Forrest went down on the grass. Bill stood over him with the stick.

"Hey, Bill, take it easy!" I implored. He ignored me completely. Forrest struggled to his feet, stone drunk, and Bill gave him a shove that sent him tumbling backwards again. Then he put down his stick, shook his head hard as though to clear it, and passed out sideways across his bedroll.

But Forrest's troubles were not over. He picked himself up again and, zombie-like, wandered out into the park, where a group of four teenagers, three girls and a boy, had gathered to watch the fun. "Winos! Alcoholics! Cocksuckers!" they shouted. As Forrest tottered by, one of the girls took a wide stance and invited him to come fuck her. He approached, but she ran away chanting, "Ha ha, you can't! Can't fuck me!" There was laughter and the insults continued.

"Hey, Forrest, get back here!" I yelled. But he was under the spell of the girl; now, she had gotten very close and was reaching for his pants. Forrest stood and stared at her, somnolent. From behind her back, she suddenly produced a bottle of beer and proceeded to pour it down the front of his pants. He staggered away, continually on the verge of falling down. The kids' laughter echoed through the park, and all manner of insults continued to be directed at Forrest. He returned none of them; and it puzzled me. The girls tripped him, the guy knocked him down, and I wished desperately I hadn't drunk so much wine. Forrest stumbled over to the frog pond near where they were standing, again lured by the girl. She walked up and pressed herself next to him, and with a sudden push sent him reeling backwards into the vile pool—a total humiliation. Forrest pulled himself out, and this time they followed him back to the tree.

"Going to go sleep with your friend? Are you, faggot? Huh?" Bill didn't stir, and they didn't see me. They came and stood over Forrest. I couldn't take it anymore.

"Get the hell out of here, you fucking creeps!" I screamed from the shadows. The kids jumped, unsure of what lurked there, and then walked quickly away. Tramps were easy targets when drunk, but an angry, invisible tramp who could still talk was a scary prospect indeed. Relieved they had left because I couldn't stave off sleep any longer, I lay back. The last thing I saw before losing consciousness was Forrest, Bill's big stick in hand, thrashing madly at all the bushes, exorcising his invisible demons, vicariously striking the kids and everyone else he could never dare to strike in real life. Leaves flew.

14

I just wanted to get away, the sky was light, but the sun had not yet risen. I did not want to be a hobo anymore. The life was too horrible. And horrible within me was the realization that I had gotten so good at getting along with hoboes that I was having a hard time remembering where they ended and I began. My own unusual talent, as I had thought of it, had turned against me. My hobo identity was now a trap. The only release I could imagine was to be in the presence of somebody who knew who I *really* was. But there was no such person in Everett, or even in Seattle. My hungover head throbbed and I felt miserable. I wanted to be somewhere Forrest and Bill would never go, a place more mine than theirs. Something like college—or a *library* . . .

It was a Saturday, and the public library opened at eight-thirty A.M. I found its address in the phone book and went there to wait. I knew my gear was going to be a problem; in Denver, transients using the library for its bathrooms and to keep warm were often ejected.

I had no idea what time it was. As politely as I could, I asked a woman with a key who was on her way in. It was eight-fifteen, she said. I explained that I was cold, and feeling very poorly, and asked if I might come in a bit early. "All right," she said, "if you will sit quietly." I got my stuff and walked through the glass doors. But from her post at the checkout desk, where she now stood with another, younger librarian, she waved her arms to stop me as I entered.

"I'm sorry, sir, but we cannot allow you to bring your bags into the library."

I explained that they would get stolen if I left them outside.

"I'm sorry, sir, it's library policy that no belongings such as the ones you are carrying—"

"But don't you see, I have no *choice*—"

"I'm sorry sir, library policy . . ." she went on. Frustration welled up inside me, a huge tidal wave of it. I couldn't pretend anymore. My secret was a burden a hundred times heavier than my bags.

"Ma'am," I said, dropping them and looking straight at her, "I'm not the kind of person you probably think I am. I am a student of anthropology, not a bum. I am on leave from Amherst College, living with tramps so that I can understand them better." Aaahh. I felt an incredible surge of relief; it was the first time I had told anybody. "I'm in Everett with tramps I met in Oregon. I had a horrible night with them, and I need to be . . . somewhere else. Could I please use your library?"

The woman just stared at me. Twice she started to speak but stopped.

The younger woman came to the rescue. "Why don't you put your stuff in the closet over there?" The older woman, apparently her superior, turned and looked at her, but she continued. "That's it." She went over and opened the door for me. She had brown curly hair, and a pale, smooth complexion. She sure smells good, I thought to myself as I walked around her with my gear.

"You go to Amherst?" she asked.

"Yeah, that's right," I said enthusiastically. She had heard of it!

"I'm at Lewis and Clark, in Portland. I'm a sociology major, and in one class, we had to live on skid row for three days with no money. It was *so* interesting!" I couldn't believe my luck at meeting this girl. "I'm staying home this semester to earn money for some traveling."

We talked as she worked, and eventually she invited me to her family's house for dinner and a cleanup. It was a wonderful evening. Marla's father worked for the Scott Paper Company and was a student of local history. One of Everett's most infamous incidents was the massacre of a large contingent of "Wobblies" by the local militia, he told me. I remembered seeing a painting recreating the event in the library. Wobblies were members of the Industrial Workers of the World, the radical labor union. The original Wobblies had worked in lumber camps, mines, and mills all over the country. Because they were unskilled, and counted among them many females and immigrants, larger unions shunned them. Their Marxist philosophy scared and angered many Americans, and when a boat of Wobbly sympathizers from Seattle sailed into Everett to demonstrate support for Wobbly strikers, they were shot as they tried to land. The Wobblies, unskilled and displaced, were the predecessors of modern-day tramps.

Marla's mother fixed a wonderful dinner, and afterward we had coffee in their living room. Both parents were interested in finding out just what their daughter had dragged in this time, and I had the floor for about an hour. For weeks I had been listening to hoboes, and now it was wonderful to do all the talking. None of the family had any idea that their town was such a popular spot among tramps. The night grew late and I was invited to stay. Marla's mother washed my clothing, and my shower lasted half an hour.

Two days later, after warm good-byes and a promise to write, I set off from Marla's house. Time spent writing, talking on the phone with Mom, Dad, and my professor, and especially in conversing with Marla had left me more secure again about my identity. Thinking my goal was to become a tramp the way John Howard Griffin "became a Negro," I had come way too close. Now I recognized that unless an awful lot of things in my life went very wrong, I could never really become a tramp. Becoming a tramp apparently meant traveling a hard road of personal crisis, one that began long before it reached the rails. I had gotten to the rails by following a path of curiosity, and it made me a different kind of tramp, if I was one at all. The biggest difference was the one I had just demonstrated: when I wanted, I could return to the place from which I had come. I could meet up with someone like Marla and be invited home.

Bill and Forrest were back on the beach, at our original jungle. Forrest had just set down a bottle when I walked over a bluff and onto the sand; bleary-eyed Bill, with half a case of beer at his side, was tossing pebbles at a moth stuck on its back on the surface of the water, trying to sink it. Empty cans and bottles were scattered around, waiting for the next tide.

I was surprised to find them still at it and still together. They looked puffy-faced and bad. They were only mildly surprised to see me. "I thought you split," said Bill, interrupting the bombardment for a second.

"Sort of." I sat down on my bedroll and turned to Forrest. "Christ, what happened to your eye?"

Forrest had a huge shiner around one eye. The white was red with blood and ooze. "I dunno," he said. "It was that night."

"Oh, I know!" I said. "You walked into a tree branch. Remember that?"

Forrest shook his head.

"Well, do you remember those kids that were hasslin' you?"

"Nope."

"You're kidding!" I filled him in on what I remembered as Bill got up to go take a pee.

"No shit?" said Forrest, laughing. "Well, I'll be damned. No, man, I just felt like gettin' tight that night. It was just somethin' I had to do."

"Bet you're sorry now, though, huh? Shit, Forrest, you coulda lost that eye." I may have been offering Forrest advice, or maybe I was just spelling out for myself another difference between us.

"No! No regrets!" said Forrest, now looking serious. "If you're gonna do somethin' you might regret, then don't do it. But if you do, then don't regret it when you're done." The penal system, it occurred to me, would have a hard time with Forrest if he ever landed there for something serious. He seemed to have a reform-proof philosophy.

"That night in the park," he continued, "that was just somethin' I had to do." He shrugged. "You just gotta let off steam now and then—elsewise you'll be like that old Mount St. Helens, blowin' up."

It had grown hot. Forrest took hold of his white button-down mission shirt just below the collar and pulled hard on both sides. Buttons flew as the shirt came open. Forrest smiled. "Tramp zipper," he said. "I'm gonna swim."

"Sure you are, Forrest," said Bill. "That's Puget Sound, and this is November. I dare you."

The dare wasn't necessary. Forrest took off the rest of his clothes and waded in. Bill screwed the top on his bottle of wine and, with a laugh, tossed it to him. Forrest was waist-deep and had tipped the bottle skyward when I snapped his picture. "Oh man, this is great!" he said, plunging in all the way. "People get civilized and they lose their fuckin' minds!"

On his way back to shore, Forrest checked a fishing line he had found on the beach, tied to a stick, and let out into the surf. The hook was baited with a piece of bacon fat, and for a bobber Forrest had attached an old cigarette package.

"Forrest, that contraption's never gonna catch a thing," Bill had said. "Forget it."

But now Forrest pointed. "Look, guys, it's bobbin'!" He found the line and pulled it in. A small, spiny prehistoric-looking fish wriggled on the end of it.

"A bonehead!" cried Bill. "I fuckin' don't believe it!"

"You know how to fix 'em?" asked Forrest.

"Hell, yes." Bill took out the Swiss Army knife, vivisected and cleaned the fish, and dropped it, still wriggling, on a hot grill over the small campfire. "They taste better that way," he assured me.

After the fish was eaten, conversation stopped. Bill tied together his gear and stood up. Though he and Forrest had not been at each other's throats that day, it appeared something had been decided earlier. Bill was leaving. He looked at me.

"Wanta come?" he asked. "I'm headed east to Williston, North Dakota—now's the time to find a ranch job, maybe puttin' hay out for livestock."

I couldn't imagine being alone with Bill, without Forrest as a buffer. "No, thanks," I said.

"Well, then, here," said Bill, who apparently had been expecting this. He handed me a scrap of paper with an address on it. "This is my sister's. Send her one of your pictures if it comes out, okay? She's got pictures all over her walls of everyone else in the family but me." I promised.

Bill left. There was no good-bye to Forrest, his partner of three weeks, not even a nod. We were quiet for a long time.

"Williston," Forrest finally said in disgust.

"What?"

"That's where he was goin' when I met him. He was goin' to look for work on a ranch. He never did. He won't this time, either."

When the fire had died, we headed for the catch-out point, where the trains slowed. On the way we walked by the huge Weyerhaeuser timber mill which we had camped near on the beach. I asked Forrest two questions I had been turning over in my mind for several days.

"Hey, Forrest, see that factory?"

"Yeah?"

"What would you do if somebody gave you that factory? If it was all yours, and you could do with it whatever you wanted, and change your life however you liked?"

The idea took Forrest a moment to get used to. "You mean if they just *gave* it to me?"

"Yes."

"Shit," he finally said. "I'd call the board together and tell 'em to sell it. What's the use of havin' it if you can't spend it? Shit— owning a company like that, I'd worry myself to death! The guys who do can't enjoy TV or music or nothin'. Yeah, I'd sell it."

I smiled. Then I asked him what he thought he'd be doing when he got old. He wasn't accumulating any nest egg; wouldn't old age be rough?

"Naah." He smiled. "There's always that South Sea island somewhere."

"South Sea island? But there's no freight trains to the South Seas. How're you gonna get there?"

"Oh, I don't know," Forrest shrugged. "Tramp steamer, maybe." I groaned.

We took a seat on a seawall near the tracks. After sitting a while, it occurred to me that neither of us was really sure of what to do next. That had never been a problem before with me and tramps: my companions had always had some idea, some plan of where they'd like to go. But Forrest had none.

"I don't wanta go north—too cold; I don't wanta go south—California!; and I don't wanta go east," he said. Obviously, west was an impossibility. "Well, I guess the thing to do in this situation is sit here and catch the first train that comes by." He plied me for suggestions on what we might do whenever we got where we were going.

I was disturbed to notice that Forrest had begun to laugh at my dumbest jokes and to agree with everything I said, as though I had taken Bill's place as leader. I became afraid that what I would see or observe in Forrest from then on would be a reflection of myself, of what he thought I'd like to see. He would be a fun friend for a while, but I wouldn't learn much. I decided I had better make the disintegration of our trio complete.

"Forrest, I don't think I'm gonna go on with you from here. I feel like traveling alone for a while, spending some time by myself. Is that okay?"

"Okay," said Forrest presently, "whatever you want." This was something he was used to. This was life on the road. "But it's too bad," he added fifteen minutes later. "You don't find many guys like you on the road." He paused. "Or like Bill, either, for that matter . . ."

A lump grew in my throat. "Well, I never met too many guys like you, either, Forrest, on the road or off." We sat on the seawall and talked until sunset, when Forrest landed a creaky eastbound freight. Then I sat alone until around midnight, when another carried me off down the coast toward California. That night I dreamed about Forrest, waist-deep in a warm lagoon on his South Sea island, bottle of wine tipped toward the sky. I hoped the world would make room for him.

15

Buffeted by a sweet, warm, nighttime breeze, I was glad to be in California. Finally, I was back where the weather suited my clothes: Roseville, though it was in northern California at the foot of the Sierras, had palm trees. I lay relaxed on the back of the covered grain car as the train rolled through well-kept neighborhoods toward Roseville's expansive yards, which sat at the junction of Southern Pacific's north-south route through California and Union Pacific's "Overland" line from Oakland to Omaha.

As the train slowed, my pulse quickened. A tramp can feel invincible on a moving train, but back in the yard are his three greatest natural enemies: police, other tramps, and the trains themselves. All three become more dangerous at night.

The engineer cut the air. I dropped off my gear, let myself down the ladder, stretched, and had just taken two steps when a scream pierced the air. I froze, and then scurried for the shadow of a parallel train. All I could see clearly in the eerie glow of the tall vapor lamps above the yards was the train I had just gotten off. A switch engine had been chugging back and forth nearby but now I could only hear it idling. Then I heard shouts, and feet running on gravel. The loud cry sounded again, full of pain. I made my way guardedly across the yard, crossing three trains in the direction of the noise, conscious of the sound of my own footsteps. Swinging over one last coupling, I arrived at the scream's source.

A man lay on his back, curled up and clasping one leg tightly. In the glow of the headlights of a railroad pickup truck that had arrived at the scene, I saw one brakey reaching for the man's shoelaces, while another advised him to leave them alone. Other "rails" stood around; one was talking on the shortwave radio inside the truck. A bedroll lay partly untied on the ground nearby, and not far away rested a torn paper sack, its contents of food, clothing, and a small skillet scattered over the gravel.

I walked quietly up behind one of the railroaders, and cleared my throat. "What's happening?"

He took a good look at me. "It's one of your type," he said. "Must have been crossing that train we were breakin' up, put his foot on the coupling at the wrong time. His heel's crushed. Christ, when are you guys gonna learn? You can't fuck with the railroad—it'll kill you."

The tramp moaned and trembled. I swallowed hard; the railroader was right: railroad yard work, I had read last summer, was the most dangerous occupation in the States. And railroad workers didn't have to carry gear, or worry about staying out of sight. "Keep your wits about you," Portland Gray had said to me, so many weeks ago. This one, perhaps for only a moment, had let his lapse.

I heard an ambulance siren in the distance and saw the yard bull's sedan approaching. While the railroader stood shaking his head, I climbed carefully back over a coupling, the way I had come. Shifting couplings were not the only danger associated with trains in the yard; a switch engine, while breaking up a train, might rev up and send a car or two rolling off by themselves down an open track. Such cars could roll several hundred yards in virtual silence. From campfire talk, I knew that they had been the death of many unsuspecting railroaders and tramps who forgot to look both ways before crossing an "empty" track. The men never knew what hit them.

I returned to my task of catching out of Roseville and realized that the little town had a huge yard. Its size and the inhuman scale of the trains that filled it would have overwhelmed me a few weeks earlier. But though I was on edge that night, I was not lost. Figuring out new yards had become one of my favorite challenges; with resourcefulness, cunning, persistence, and intelligence, a tramp could become master, of a sort, of his specialized little universe.

The first step was to reduce the maze of the yards to a comprehensive system. Much could be learned from an observation of the yards from a bridge or hill or from a brief chat with a friendly brakey. But some things an experienced tramp didn't have to ask. From the location of the tower you had some idea of where the yard's center was; you also knew where the railroad offices, and therefore the bull, would be. The main line, which my train had come in on, was another good reference point: the first track next to the mains was Track 1, the next was Track 2, and so on. More distant tracks had their numbers posted at the switches where they separated from connecting tracks.

Many larger yards also had inbound and outbound areas. From my conversation with two welders working on a brake mount, I learned that Roseville's outbound yard was about a mile away. I had just started my long trek toward it when one of them called out and offered me a lift.

I couldn't believe my luck. They sat me in the middle of their old pickup after stashing my gear underneath a tarp in back. The price of my ride was, as for any hitchhiker, telling my story. The welders were very interested. I remembered when the "rails" had ignored my questions, but lately, they seemed to answer willingly. This good treatment was reserved for tramps whose manner indicated they wouldn't get themselves hurt or interfere with the trains. Given the accident I had just seen, it was an understandable attitude.

En route, the welders used their shortwave radio to locate the train I wanted. They dropped me off just out of sight of its units, with apologies for being unable to take me to an empty—the tracks were too close together for their truck to fit.

I set off. Daytime or nighttime, there is something spooky about railroad yards. Maybe it is because they are man-made, but there are almost no men around them; they have an abandoned feel. The walk I was beginning was my least favorite; between two close freights, at night. The yard lights illuminated only the top edge of one of the freights, leaving the rest of the space in darkness. It was like walking down a dark alley, with the spaces between cars doorways where muggers lurk. Yet it was hard to move quietly: the crunch of gravel under work boots carried between the metal walls of cars gave a long advance warning of my approach.

I walked quickly. The most dangerous yards, I reassured myself, were not in towns like Roseville but in big cities, where thieves from surrounding poor neighborhoods sneak in to loot the freight cars. And the more dangerous parts of yards were the places where cars sat for days or weeks at a time, long enough for tramps to move in—the bad order tracks, where cars waited to be repaired, or the rip tracks, where they were cleaned. Besides, I thought, anyone who would mug a tramp ought to have his head examined. It would take a pretty stupid and desperate guy to—

Suddenly someone swung out from between two cars on my right, landing about six feet in front of me. I cried out in fear, raising my fists in front of me, wondering if I would be able to hear over the pounding in my chest. "Hey, who's that?"

I heard a gasp from the dark figure, who stopped his motion across the gravel toward the coupling of the other train. "Huh? It's me, another guy," he said, regaining his composure and continuing.

"Oh, Christ," I thought to myself, dropping my fists. "Another guy." What a dumb answer. What a dumb question—but what a relief.

I continued on, paying attention now to the kinds of cars that made up the train, hoping to doublecheck its destination. In many parts of the country, experienced tramps could "read" trains to predict their routes. A well-traveled tramp in Spokane, for example, knows that if a westbound train has Canadian National or Canadian Pacific empties in it, it is going to Seattle; if not, it's headed south to Pasco and Wishram. In the fall in the Northwest, refrigerated boxcars—"reefers"—with their compressors running are presumed to be full of apples, and headed out of the Northwest; if the compressors are silent they are probably returning to the region, or heading for California. Anywhere in the Northwest, a train pulling Japanese import cars is probably headed east or south, away from Seattle and Portland—two main ports of entry for the cars. Trains loaded with American cars in any part of the Midwest, likewise, are headed away from Detroit.

But since I didn't know what kind of cars went toward Reno, I was unable to doublecheck. I approached the only empty boxcar I could see, making noise to avoid startling its occupant, if any. Hearing nothing, I shone my penlight around the car: nothing. I was glad; the night had been eventful enough already. Soon I was settled and, just before sunrise, the train pulled out. Another railroad yard conquered.

On the way to Reno I stopped at a resort near Lake Tahoe, where my eldest sister was working for the summer. I eagerly anticipated a day's rest and cleanup, and seeing Pam. Also, my mom had forwarded to her all my mail, including an absentee ballot for the upcoming Presidential election. The chat with Forrest about voting had stuck in my mind. I thought that the tramp interest should be represented at the ballot box, and also saw voting as another way to keep my own identity distinct from the tramps.

The rail line to Reno passed close to Lake Tahoe, but did not stop there. A road map I picked up showed that a highway roughly paralleled the line for most of the route, and I hatched a plan.

As the train made its long, slow climb into the Sierras, I could see the highway running along at the bottom of the valley whose side we traversed. At last, when we were atop a mountain so high that the road was a thin gray ribbon far below, the train slowed and pulled into a hole. I hopped off and ate a quick breakfast; contemplating the view and my long walk down. No sooner had I started off on a dirt road down the mountain, though, than a Jeep carrying two deer hunters and their trophy approached from behind.

"Mind if I come along?" I called.

"If you don't mind sitting on the deer," said the driver. It was a soft, if disturbing, ride down.

It was great to see my sister, and the camp where she worked was beautiful. But it might not have been the wisest stop for me. I was all for a break from the rails, but somehow this was too nice: Stanford University ran the camp, at Fallen Leaf Lake, for alumni, and staffed it with well-scrubbed, amiable, enthusiastic students who were deeply into its several stunningly beautiful acres. The place was a bona fide idyll—but its remove from the "real world" of the rails made the transition too jarring. The risks, deprivations, and uncertainties of the hobo life felt like some kind of dream from there, a hallucination from some other life. I found myself passing judgement on Pam's coworkers; they seemed too self-absorbed to me, too caught up in that gorgeous little world. As I hitchhiked away from the lakes and toward Reno, where trains would take me to the Nevada desert, I felt bad about that—who was I to fault somebody for choosing beauty? Then again, I thought to myself: Did love of wilderness mean you had to close your eyes to the problems of the human world?

I was back on the Southern Pacific, on a night train heading east across Nevada. My long-term plan was to get to Elko, in northeastern Nevada, then switch to the Western Pacific and ride back across the desert to California, up the Sierra Nevada and then down the fabled Feather River Canyon. In the short term, all I wanted was to get off at Elko and find a place to sleep before fatigue completely overcame me and I found myself back in Salt Lake City.

I had been counting stops from Reno, and thought this had to be it. The interstate highway was visible in the distance; flickering lights about a mile away signaled a small town. I left my boxcar, a bit reluctantly: it had been filled to within three feet of the roof with large plywood sheets, and, after I climbed on top of these, the heavy car had given me probably my smoothest boxcar ride of the trip.

The train soon pulled away, leaving me to survey the flat terrain. In the dim light of a moon obscured by clouds, I saw that it was featureless, except for the sage that dotted the fine soil and a few gullies. Neither would provide protection from rain; and a tramp I had met in Reno advised me to stay out of the gullies, as flash floods could kill you in your sleep.

Then I noticed a fence on the other side of the tracks, and a clear area beyond it. Climbing the wooden fence rails I saw that the ground below looked smooth and clean. I unrolled and lay down, my eyes falling shut even before I hit the ground.

I would have thought nothing could keep me awake. But low, breathy noises kept pulling me back from a deep sleep. I lifted my head and looked around: nothing, except for more fence—it appeared I had climbed into a small, empty corral. I resolved not to give the noise any more attention, but the low-pitched snuffles, snorts, and rustling persisted. I hovered in semi-consciousness. Then I heard a thump, and felt little impacts on the ground: footsteps. I sat bolt upright, and looked around again. Across the pen, from a squat, dark shed I hadn't noticed before, came a number of small, dark figures, stout and solid. Dogs? I heard a decided snort, and leaped to my feet. They were pigs—*huge* pigs, trotting now straight toward me. Now, I didn't know much about pigs, but I remembered a scene from *The Grapes of Wrath* in which a pig made its way into a farmhouse and ate somebody's baby. In my sleepy state, I imagined they were coming to have a midnight tramp snack. Killer pigs! I fled over the fence.

The pigs were very intrigued with my gear, and spent a long while poking around it. I heard a couple of them munching on a bag of corn chips I had brought, and then a few others came over to the fence to see what I was all about. My aunt in New Jersey, pig-keeper that she was, would have known how to handle them, but I sure didn't. I waited until they went back to sleep in their shed, and then jumped back in, pulled on my boots, and scooped up my gear.

I found a spot amid the sagebrush and settled down again there. But I never did get back to sleep that night.

The next morning, I discovered I was not in Elko, and had to hitchhike twenty miles down the road. But the tramps I met during my three-day stay in an elaborate jungle just off the Elko yards—a three-room, cardboard, wood, and plastic lean-to built onto the fence of an abandoned corral—were not to my liking. I boarded a westbound freight on the Western Pacific line ("the W.P.," "ol' Wobbly," or "WeePee," tramps called it), and soon found myself back crossing the huge, untracked Black Rock Desert of northern Nevada. According to a map I saw in a gas station, it was the largest continuous chunk of undeveloped land in the continental U.S.—not because the federal government owned it, but because nobody else wanted it. In one direction, the vast white expanse stretched farther than I could see; in another, its limit was barely visible mountains, small lumps on the horizon. I was riding a piggyback, but it was so warm out that the sixty-mile-an-hour wind did not chill me. After several hours, the desert met the eastern Sierra Nevada. The train climbed steeply up Sand Pass, past corpses of hapless cattle that had grazed too near the tracks. The hills became grassy, and finally were covered by dense pine forest.

Then came the dramatic trip from Portola, California, down the canyon from which the railroad had taken its nickname, "The Feather River Route." A twisting chasm of waterfalls, spillways, gray rock, and isolated scrub trees hanging on to the canyon walls for dear life, the Feather River Canyon was inaccessible by car, but, as many tramps had promised me, spectacular by freight train. Halfway down, the train crossed a bridge over the river to follow the other wall of the canyon. The fine view of the gorge which my boxcar had afforded through its one open door was replaced by a too-close view of the rocky canyon wall, and I resolved to find a new car at the next stop. When at last I jumped out, ran several cars back, and climbed the ladder to the back platform of a covered grain car, I couldn't believe my eyes.

"Lonny!"

Lonny jumped at the sudden invasion of his car and reached for his pocket. But then he got a closer look at me and his face broke into a wide smile.

"It's you!" he said, relaxing. "I'll be doggoned."

He was a bit thinner than I remembered him, looked a bit older, and was sitting on a bedroll—I never thought I'd see him with luggage. Most noticeable about his appearance was a huge black eye. After getting over the surprise and joy of running into my first mentor (thank God it wasn't BB on that platform!), I made the mistake of asking, "Where'd you get that shiner?" Lonny didn't stop talking until the train started rolling again a half hour later, making even his shouting inaudible.

Four tramps in Indio, California—near Los Angeles on the Southern Pacific—beat him up, he said. He had approached their camp at dark, asking for a cigarette. ("By the way, you got one on you?" I passed him one, and a light.) Though they were friendly, they had been drinking. He was so tired he rolled out next to their campsite, only to be awakened four hours later by kicks and punches.

"Were they white?" I asked, afraid of what the answer would be. All too many white tramps shared Bill's, Buddy's, and BB's opinion of "niggers."

"I hate to say it, but yes," replied Lonny. As if to emphasize that should not affect our friendship, though, he added, "I saw some black dudes on the way, though, and passed them up—that'd be even worse." He refused to hold a grudge: "That's madness. You flicker yourself out. It was my fault, anyway—I should have been smart enough not to sleep there.

"But that's behind me now," he said, smiling and waving it off. "My thing is to keep on lookin' for what I was seekin'. I been thinkin' of gettin' some dock work down south, maybe Morgan City, Louisiana, on the gulf. That's the best place in the world to work, unless you got a skill. Why you can earn seven or eight hundred dollars a month!"

"Then what're you headed up north for?"

Lonny faltered. "I need some cash to get a start. I thought I'd spend a while in that mission in Oroville, see if they need a cook, then head into Maryville there at the end of the month, pick up them two months' worth of food stamps. That's the only place in the world you can do that, did you know? Show up the last week of the month, they'll give you stamps for the next month, too."

I nodded. We had discussed this many times before, and Lonny's plans had been much the same. What he was seeking, he couldn't put his finger on, and neither could I. "But you went *past* Oroville," I pressed.

"Guess I fell asleep," he said sheepishly. "Yesterday afternoon, I was almost there. But I woke up this mornin' and said, 'Oh, my God! Portola! The coldest place on earth!' "

I took a guess. "Was that what happened that night in Nebraska—in Hastings? I went to sleep in the grass, and you stayed in the boxcar. We were going to meet when the next train came in, but your car was gone and I couldn't find you."

Lonny shrugged. "Guess I just fell asleep again," he said—no apologies, it just happened. I understood then what I had not before: sleep, rather than a fast connection, is the tramp priority.

That satisfied my long-standing curiosity on the matter. But ever since we had parted, I had wanted to know where Lonny, or any of my hobo acquaintances, went next. It was to me one of the hobo life's most foreign, frustrating conventions: the lack of good-byes, the impossibility of staying in touch.

He had followed the route I took, he said, through Denver and Salt Lake City. From there he headed to the Southwest.

"Did you go to Reno?" I asked, remembering that was where his wife and kids lived; he had been planning to get a job there for the winter.

He nodded. I thought to myself, It didn't work out.

Following a long silence, Lonny said, "Somethin's wrong 'tween us, me and my old lady. Every time I go there, we fight. This time, she called the cops—I was in jail for a month." He paused. "We just ain't gonna get along no more."

Our train, still standing, was apparently having brake trouble. Every few minutes, the lines would be repressurized, and then the air would be cut, causing an ear-piercing screech. We covered our ears. "I damn sure wanta have a talk with that railroad," Lonny said, trying to lighten things up.

Finally we were under way. Entering Oroville, the train slowed, passing orchards, suburbs, and then the industrial part of town. We rolled by one of the swish railroad-theme restaurants that one sees near the tracks in some cities, incongruous amid the warehouses. Its plate-glass windows faced the train, and we provided seven or eight seconds of entertainment to those inside, who interrupted their hors d'oeuvres to watch. They were scenery to us as well, and Lonny and I stared back, speculating aloud on the good things they must have been dining on.

But when the train entered the Oroville yards, it was back down to earth. We stopped next to a vacant lot and what unfolded before our eyes looked like a black-and-white photograph from the Depression era. At least twenty-five men were lounging around the lot. All were white, and all had that timeless appearance of men without means: old dusty clothing, caps, bags and bedrolls, whiskers. Smoke rose from a few fires, fading up into the overcast sky. As in most yards, nothing was growing; the scene was practically colorless.

I recognized some of the tramps, but Lonny was timorous after his recent beating, and we didn't stay to socialize. Instead, we headed off through a sizable tract of undeveloped land toward the mission. This, I soon realized, was the real jungle, the one for which Oroville was famous among tramps; those in the empty lot had simply been waiting to catch out. The area was a tramp haven, acres of wooded land adjoining the tracks. Lonny pointed out to me places he had camped, and the spigot where tramps filled their jugs.

Dinner at the mission was over, but Lonny begged us some leftovers—cold fish and hard corn bread. Telling any insider that you were "just in," I realized, was the same as saying to them, "I have suffered." We ate outside the back door, talking quietly. I broached the subject of a medical problem with Lonny.

"It's my scalp," I complained. "It was itching a little a couple of weeks ago up in Everett, but now it's driving me crazy."

Lonny took a look. "Lice," he diagnosed.

"How do you know that?" I demanded, all of a sudden defensive. People like me didn't get lice.

"'Cause, man, you been hangin' 'roun' tramps, you start itchin', and you got 'em. Everybody knows it—simple as that." Apparently, Lonny had much experience in these matters. But it made me feel so . . . defiled. I was a host to parasites.

"You got 'em anywhere else? Armpits, crotch? No? You lucky, then. You oughta get you some of that shampoo, anyway, when you can 'ford it. And take a hot shower—that kills 'em."

A hotter shower I had never taken. Though the Oroville mission was "very accommodating," as Lonny put it, letting us smoke outside and come and go until lights out at nine, it was lacking in hygiene. No pajamas were issued, and men were allowed to sleep with their street clothes on. Waking up in the middle of the night to a concert of snoring, coughing, and hacking, I noticed that my sheets were very dirty and that scattered about them were what appeared to be tiny scabs. I got up and took another hot shower. After drying off, I looked at my clothes and realized why most hoboes were content to sleep with them on: donning the several-days-old T-shirt, undershorts, and socks was just too repellent an experience.

In the morning, I found Lonny's interest in cooking at the mission had waned. I wanted to leave Oroville, and he agreed. After a predawn supply raid on two fried-chicken restaurant dumpsters, we headed south on the Western Pacific. Sacramento was the first stop; after a couple of days there, we continued on, skipping Stockton ("That Stockton's hot, oh, yes—ask a black man! He's the first to know.") and aiming for San Jose. In Milpitas, a town near San Jose, a number of cars were set off; unfortunately, we were asleep in one of them. It was still dark when Lonny woke me with the bad news: San Jose was seven miles away, and we would have to start walking now to be there in time for breakfast at the mission. I suggested hitching.

"Are you crazy? Man, this is California! There's too many weirdos here. Why, that's San Francisco, right up the road. Unh-uh, not here. Not me."

So we walked. This had happened to Lonny before, and he knew the way. We followed the tracks through sleepy suburban neighborhoods, grumpy with each other for the first time since we had met again. Lonny "shot snipes" along the way; when he finally had a whole pocketful of cigarette butts, I had to sit and wait while he rerolled them into one of his used cigarettes. But then the sky grew pink and our moods softened. We passed a grove of walnut trees and sat down to have a snack, pounding the nuts open with rocks. Somebody's garden hose helped us wash down the after-taste. We began to talk again.

Conversation since the first day had been light, limited to matters like television, politics, towns, and trains. Perhaps due to the purposefulness with which we walked now, it became more serious. Lonny talked about why he thought it was important for me to be on the road—about the need for everyone to get away from parents and teachers, to do something on his own, to dis-cover—but almost in the same breath about how eventually I would have to straighten myself out if I were going to amount to anything in this world. Lonny assumed my alienation from society.

I asked him about his own situation. "Well, you know, where I really want to be, I know that'll never work." He was talking about home in Reno, with his wife and kids. His marriage had been a failure, he conceded sadly; but before long his tone had turned from regret to expectation.

"What I'm doin' now is experimentin'. It relieves the pressure that took up eighteen years of my life. That was an experiment, too, but now I know I don't want it. I don't want any more kids. I don't wanta get back into the obligated thing.

"Now I'm gonna do a little livin', the things I want to do. Like

I said, what I'm doin' now—what you and me both doin'—is exper-imentin'. We're experimentin' for knowledge. I think you gotta do it. You a fool not to do it!"

We passed behind a food-processing plant. Lonny picked up a piece of sugar cane and gnawed on it as we walked.

"Way I see it," he continued, "anything beats keepin' up with the same routine. Here, I'm a-learnin' to broaden my mind to the point where I can deal with anything that comes along. It adds to me as a man. Who wants to live like a common vegetable?"

I told Lonny I agreed wholeheartedly, but that sometimes you can get enough of experimenting. Sometimes you want something normal and dependable.

"Well, that's why I'm gonna get that job," Lonny said. "Then I'm goin' back home to St. Louis and see my mama."

"Why don't you just go to St. Louis and see her *now?*" I demanded, tired of having my ears filled with improbable plans.

"Oh, man, you don't understand. My folks put me through school—I had two years of college in St. Louis. My sister went, too. We were the onliest ones in my family, and the onliest blacks at the whole school. And you know, Mama didn't have no school at all. Mama picked cotton in Franklin Parish her whole life. But she wanted me to go to college real bad. And so I did.

"But here I am now, college-educated, and you're sayin' 'Go home and visit your mama'? When I'm a tramp? No way, man, not never! First, I'm gonna get me that van, have somethin' to show for myself."

"Now I see," I said.

Morning had come before we reached San Jose. Lonny thought the tracks would take us right into town, but apparently we missed a turn, and ended up walking through a large upper-middle-class neighborhood. People were awake now, picking up their morning papers and backing cars out of their driveways to go to work. The place reminded me of home and I walked leisurely down the sidewalk. But Lonny felt very self-conscious, especially with his black eye. The last mile to the mission was nearly a sprint.

We spent the day lazing around San Jose, and in the evening joined the long line waiting for admission to the Salvation Army. When Lonny heard the rumor that an I.D. was required for admission, he nibbled nervously on his beard.

"What's wrong?" I asked.

"When I was beat up, they took my I.D."

"Well, then, let's go somewhere else."

"No, no—maybe I can make it. Look, if you get in and I don't, maybe we can meet somewheres in the morning."

"Sounds good to me. How about the post office, at eight?"

"Gotcha."

We were admitted alphabetically; I waited and waited for Lonny Thomas to walk through the door, but he never did. I felt sorry for him, but glad we were meeting in the morning.

At eleven, I gave up.

I felt ditched. Either Lonny was chronically forgetful of his appointments or he had purposefully left me behind. I didn't understand: he had been pleased to see me again and had remembered a number of things about me. Leaving without notice seemed typical of tramps, but I thought we were more than just tramps: I thought we were friends.

Upset, I made my way to a park that Lonny and I had visited the day before and sat down at a concrete picnic table. The park, a short walk across some tracks from San Jose's lovely town square, was overgrown, littered, and avoided by regular pedestrians. Its regular patrons were the local Indian alcoholics, and everyone knew it by the name "Wino Park." The day before, Lonny and I had spoken with some of the older men before they became drunk and, like the others, passed out in the grass. They were Navajo, they had said; some of them even still spoke the Navajo language amongst themselves, clicking their tongues as they articulated the ancient-sounding syllables. Many anthropologists, I knew, would be transfixed to hear such conversation; it was the stuff of monographs, of Ph.D. dissertations, a chance to record the language before it died out completely. Yet although the anthropologists would learn the language, they would forget why it had to be artificially preserved in the first place: the younger Navajos were all languishing here in Wino Park, and couldn't be counted on to learn the language themselves. Anthropologists would save the language, while the Navajos themselves died. As I sat on the hard bench, I felt that an anthropologist was the second-to-last thing in the world I wanted to be. A Navajo was the very last.

I tried reading a newspaper, but Lonny's absence played on my mind. Why did tramps just disappear like that? My disappointment at losing him turned into a general despair with the whole tramp world. It wasn't just Lonny's way to disappear like that, it was Pete's, and Bill's, too, and it bothered the hell out of me. Tramp hello's were very nearly as abbreviated, shorn of the handshaking, embracing, and smiling used by everyone else to say, "I'm glad to see you." Tramp conversation could be animated and genial, but the intimacy that it implied was largely an illusion. In fact, it seemed to me that tramps resisted closeness with each other more than any people I had ever met.

A friend found this a very unlikely observation. "All alone like that, I think they'd really *want* to make friends," he said. I tried and tried to discover an explanation for why it wasn't so, to recall anything a tramp might have said to me about keeping one's distance. I suddenly remembered an incident during my three days in Elko, Nevada.

The jangling of cans and bottles woke me where I was sleeping inside one of the little "rooms" of the jungle in the abandoned corral. Someone had tripped over the alarm, a piece of black nylon cord strung close to the ground at the entrance to the corral. Tied to one end and balanced on a post was an assortment of old bottles and cans that fell off when the line was pulled. I looked up. A tall middle-aged tramp recovered his balance and paused at the threshold of the corral. He gave a little wave.

"Saw your fire when my train rolled in, pardner," he said.

"Okay if I join you for a minute?" I waved him in, coolly. With his brand new clothes, shiny shoes, clean-shaven face, and clean, close-clipped fingernails, he did not look like a tramp just off a freight. But as I put on some coffee water, he explained himself.

He was just in from Salt Lake, and just out of a week-long marriage to a Mormon woman. "Oh, I thought it was gonna be great," he said, talking excitedly. "She wasn't the best-lookin' thing, but she was rich—big old house, nice car. She bought me all this shit," he said, gesturing at his clothing, "—new pants, Florsheims, the works. But after a couple of days, I couldn't stand her."

She was jealous, he said, of the friendliness between him and her mother. She walked the house at night holding a pair of scissors in her hand.

"I could just see her stabbin' me with those things through the sheets, you know what I mean? Those nice satin sheets." He looked momentarily wistful. "But she was takin' pills at night, talkin' to herself—shit, I couldn't sleep either! She messed with my head." Finally, he said, "I put my boot in her ass and split." His bedroll was made up of the covers from their bed.

He talked nervously but without stopping, like one who had had nobody to talk with for a long time, and who had just been through an experience that he desperately needed to share—no matter that the details were intimate, and I a complete stranger.

"I met her in a store three weeks ago," he explained. "I was just shoppin'." That sounded unlikely, but he stuck to it. "I saw her in there a few times, and then I asked her out." Before long, she had driven him to Elko, and they were married in the "Wedding Bells Chapel," a garish storefront wedding parlor I had seen downtown. That part fit anyway.

Since few tramps had stopped by in the past couple of days, I had bought a bottle of wine in the hope that it would help me meet some. Noticing that the gunboat of coffee water had boiled dry, I brought the wine out; the tramp looked very pleased.

"Name's Monty," he said, after taking a very long swallow.

"Sonny," I returned, adding only that I was just in from California. I took a sip of wine and was quiet, having no similar experience to share. But that did not slow down Monty. His talk hopscotched from Louis L'Amour, his favorite author of Western novels, to cotton fields in Texas where he had worked in prison, to movies. Almost singlehandedly Monty finished three-quarters of the bottle and it occurred to me he had probably done so on an empty stomach.

"Wine is a strange mocker," he said all of a sudden. "In the end it stings like an adder."

"Where'd you hear that?" It sounded like the kind of thing they might pound into your head at a detox center. Monty shifted his big frame unsteadily on the small overturned bucket on which he sat.

"Aaaa, I just picked it up," he said, clearly beginning to lose his sense of balance. "That's what got Cleopatra, you know—an adder." He went on to tell me the story of Antony and Cleopatra, speaking more slowly now. "She one day just asked to leave him—started cryin'. That's what gets me—when they turn on the water. Big horse-turd tears." For the first time, Monty was quiet. He looked down at the ground, his head resting in his hands. A tear dropped into the dust between his feet.

Monty reached for his gear and to my surprise produced a bottle from his bedroll. But he had barely unscrewed the top when he began to weep openly.

"I thought it was gonna be great," he sobbed, uncontrollably now. "I thought I found me a brand-new slot." I placed my hand on his shoulder, and Monty really let loose. It was his fourth marriage, he said. What really had happened was she kicked him out. He didn't think he would ever be able to live with a woman. His first wife left him for his best friend, and the second just disappeared one day.

"And now this, now this," he sobbed. "Brother, don't you ever fall in love. Take my advice. It'll getcha too hard when they leave."

Monty slipped off the bucket and landed in the dirt. I helped him up and began dusting off his new clothes, but he regained some composure and interrupted me.

"Nah, don't worry 'bout that," he said woozily, finally locating the edge of the bucket with his rear end. "Them clothes ain't all that good. She didn't buy 'em. I got 'em at Welfare Square, that Mormon place."

Monty pulled long and hard on the second bottle. I didn't object, thinking a good drunk might be what he needed to help him get his grief out.

"I'm a paratrooper, y'know?" he proclaimed to me suddenly. "Hundred and First Airborne Division. I'm a decorated veteran. Silver Star and Congressional Medal of Honor. Oh, and some Purple Hearts." Monty began showing me his scars: a bullet wound on his forehead, shrapnel wounds on his leg and chest. He took pride that all of them were on his front: "I didn't run from anything." It was the Code of the West. "And here I am," he said bitterly, "jungled up in a fuckin' stockyard."

I felt Monty was "messing with my head" now, to use his words. "If you're a paratrooper," I asked, "what're you doin' here?"

Monty paused. "The officers and gentlemen are in Washington," he said. "The heroes are in the gutter. That's 'cause they seen how phony it is."

He finally noticed me watching him quizzically, and his cockiness seemed to vanish. "No, son. Really, I was in from forty-nine to fifty-five. Korean War."

"And you're still thinkin' about it?"

"Hey, man!" he yelled, finishing the last of the second bottle. "That was a *war!* You know what happened there? You hearda Inchon? Pork Chop Hill? I was in 'em. And you know what? They killed my friends." Tears welled back up in his eyes, washing out his anger. "All my friends, guys I grew up with. They're all dead, they're all dead." Monty sobbed. "Why'd they do that? Why'm I alive? They shouldn't've killed them—they was better than me . . ."

"Hey, pull yourself together. That was a long time ago."

"You don't understand, son. Two hundred paratroopers were sent in to rescue some cavalry. Oh, man, oh, man. They cut us down. We couldn't do nothin' right. We died like dogs." He broke down again, losing his balance and landing on me. I pushed him back up.

"You know what then?" he continued. I shook my head but he wasn't even looking. It seemed that he remained upright by pure chance; he was paying no attention to his body. "Know what? They sent in more guys, new guys. But I wouldn't talk to 'em, we wouldn't talk to 'em. You know why? 'Cause you know what's gonna happen. You know they're gonna die, and you don't wanta have ta know 'em then. Oh, they thought we were cold fuckin' sonsabitches. But we knew it was for the best.

"And lemme tell ya, Sonny, you don't want friends after that."

Monty fell down for the last time, dirt sticking to his wet cheeks. I was choked up myself. I propped him against a fence post, rekindled the fire, and refilled the gunboat with water. Meanwhile Monty rambled, weeping off and on.

"I've killed a hundred of 'em—they won't bear arms against us. I hate Chinese. Is that right? No. I got nothin' against 'em. Don't even know 'em. But they killed my friends, murderin' Chinese sonsabitches! And you know what? Now we love 'em!

"I'm a hundred percent American. Paratrooper, Hundred and First Airborne. I'm a hero. Ever seen one? Know what I am? Nothing.

"I'm a killer. I'm not a killer. They made me a killer.

"I'm a misfit. I thought I could make it out here, but I can't.

"I'm a North Korean! I went so far north I'm a North Korean!

"I'm crazy, man. You're crazy, too. You gotta be crazy to live. Asia taught us that."

"What the hell are you talking about?" I demanded.

Monty didn't seem to hear. "I got medals," he slurred. "Congressal Medal, Star of Silver. You know what for? For killin'. I'm a cold shot, and that's why I didn't die. But you know what? It didn't sit too good with my heart."

Upset and confused, I stared at Monty. While much of what he said sounded authentic, his account was overdramatic and exaggerated; the 101st Airborne paratroopers, as I suspected and later confirmed, had not fought in Korea. Still, there was no disputing the fact that, in the war or out, Monty had been wounded. I poured us both coffee. Monty's shaking hand spilled most of his before it reached his lips; but when some did, it burned. He drew the cup slowly, painfully back. I poured in some cold water.

"Oh, man, I'm sorry you have to see me in this condition," he said presently. "I wasn't brought up this way."

"Forget it."

Four or five hours later, Monty left. "I'm goin' into town to round up somethin' to eat," he said. "Will you be here later?" I nodded. "Well, I'll be back then."

But I knew he wouldn't; he was just avoiding a good-bye. That was what had made me think of him in the park in San Jose. One reason he wouldn't come back was that, in his grief, he had told me too much and would be embarrassed to see me again. But the more important reason perhaps lay in the words he had spoken, some of the most meaningful I had heard from a tramp. If tramps avoided using names, didn't do each other favors, seldom inquired after another's well-being, and chose to make theirs a world without good-byes, perhaps it was because they had been hurt. Perhaps, like Monty, they were scared of making friends because they were scared of losing them. When you lost a good friend, you lost a part of yourself. When you lost too many good friends, maybe there stopped being a part of you that could be shared; you just got used up.

I looked out over the figures in the grass at Wino Park. Among the tramps were some real bruisers, that was certain, but there were also men who had been badly bruised.

16

The week in San Francisco did me good. I stayed with Doug and Max, my former college roommates, who had already graduated and were seeking their fortunes in the Bay Area. The first thing I did upon arriving was buy medicated shampoo and purge my scalp of the demon lice. I typed up some notes and, on my friends' advice, trimmed my beard again. We were joined on Thanksgiving by another college buddy who lived nearby, and, after a few long-distance recipe queries to our respective moms, we cooked up a Thanksgiving feast that would have made them proud. After a few days I felt renewed and became downright excited about leaving, when Doug, who was still hunting for a job, asked if he could join me for a few days.

Few of my friends were better suited to a quick apprenticeship. Doug was one of the few people I knew from school who was not enslaved to the hurry habit; he was easygoing and could get along with many kinds of people; he did not believe too much in rules; and he was, in many ways, an experimenter. And since Doug already preferred the unshaven, shaggy look and oversized clothing, the transition to hobo appearance would not be too great. We left the next day.

Oakland was the departure point, a harsh initiation for Doug. "One of the most dangerous neighborhoods in the country," a post-office security guard called the part of town we were in. He pointed to the ten-foot chain-link fences around the parking lots he guarded, and the television monitors affixed to the fence posts. When we asked him directions to the rail yards, he asked if we were planning to pay for our ride.

We told him the truth, and he told us the way to the Southern Pacific yards, and of a good place to catch out. "But watch out— there's cameras set up on the way into there, too."

"You sound like you've hopped a freight yourself," I said.

He smiled. "A long, long time ago."

We walked by burned-out buildings, littered streets, more glass on the sidewalk and more unsavory characters watching us than anywhere I had been. The SP yards in Oakland, Lonny had warned me, were the only ones in the country where the "rails" were encouraged to carry sidearms, to defend themselves against thieves from the surrounding community. I told Doug these things, having come to believe that a little fear often worked to one's advantage in the freight yards.

Yet he was already hypercautious, reminding me of myself a few short months before. He pointed out the No Trespassing signs as though I might have missed them, and tried to stay out of the sight of even the section crews. Somehow we did make it to an empty gondola, where Doug got his heartbeat back under control and we ate a lunch of beer and corn chips.

I thought it would be best to leave the brakemen in this yard alone. I figured out which way the southbound trains left the yard, and Doug and I hopped the first one out—on the fly, so as not to be apprehended by bulls who might search the train before it began rolling.

Doug landed the drag like a veteran, and it was just a few lurching, bouncy miles down the main line that his apprehension changed, as had mine the first time, into a reckless euphoria. "Damn! Damn! This is really it! We're really doing it! I'm on a freight!" he exulted, jumping up and down with excitement. His enthusiasm was contagious.

"Imagine what it must have been like to be on one of the very first trains," I suggested to Doug, "back when nothing had ever gone that fast, or that far. It must have seemed almost like a spaceship would to us today—that big an advance."

We trundled on southward, the train pausing occasionally in holes to let others pass. As was fairly common on California freight lines, one such hole adjoined a large vineyard. No vineyard employees were in evidence, and, taking my cap in hand, Doug and I jumped off to fill it with grapes. To our amazement, we saw the caboose crew pile out to do the same thing, except their containers were grocery sacks.

Back in the boxcar, his mouth stuffed with plump grapes, Doug expressed sentiments about this way of life that not so long ago had been my own: how much fun it was to get really dirty (he was reminded of leading the boys he counseled at a summer camp neck-deep into a swamp one day, just so they'd know how it felt to be utterly filthy), how nice not to have to change clothes at the first indication of perspiration odor, how fine not to have any daily household routines. He added one I had not considered, but certainly agreed with: how good it was not to be constantly confronted with mirrors and the question of your own appearance. The next morning, faced with the dirty, puffy-eyed visage of myself in the mirror of a café men's room, I wondered why we hadn't just cooked up some coffee by the tracks.

Traveling with Doug was unlike being with any of the tramps I had known: he helped me with my bags between trains, made sandwiches for me after making his own, and told stories as a friend would—tailored to my interest, not hobo tales of personal prowess or exploit, told as though the identity of the listener didn't matter.

Yet he was dangerously unschooled in some aspects of tramp life. I explained that in most situations, it was important to strike a tough pose when meeting new tramps. The toughness could be softened once the other tramp was sized up and his trustworthiness assessed, but if he was a bad character, it would help keep him from taking advantage of you. But this seemed so unnatural for Doug: he was forever dispensing pleasantries—hellos, good-byes, thank yous, and friendly smiles—to complete strangers. It really gave him away as a novice, as did his opinion that tramps, like everybody, would show their good side if only given a fair chance. The opposite, I cynically thought, was more likely true: give someone a chance, and you'll see what's bad about him.

We pulled into Bakersfield at the southern end of the San Joaquin Valley, on the evening of our third day out. The rural valley, lush and fertile, had been beautiful to travel through, but the cities did not seem so nice. Then again, the freights always seemed to show you the worst of them. Approaching the yards, we passed a number of small hobo campfires flickering in the dark, and I got the feeling this was going to be a big town for tramps. As it was already dark, I thought it best to stay in the mission, and, just when the train had slowed to jump-off speed, the neon JESUS SAVES sign appeared, right across the street from the tracks. The evangelists knew their clientele.

The long row of men waiting outside—probably fifty all together—had begun to move; we were just in time. An old man with a ruler rapped me on the head as I walked inside. "Take off your hat! You're in the chapel!" Doug tore his off just in time.

Ahead of us was a windowless and brightly lit room with rows of hard wooden pews. Wall placards were the only decoration on the industrial-yellow walls: "Where will YOU spend eternity?" asked one. The placard made the choice clear: on one side were raging flames, on the other ethereal clouds and rays of sun. Another placard had a biblical quotation: ringed again with flames and wraithlike figures writhing in agony, it read, "But the fearful and the unbelieving, and the abominable and murderers, and whoremongers and sorcerers and idolators and liars shall have their part in the lake which burneth with fire and brimstone which is the second death." Yikes, I thought.

Doug nudged me and pointed toward the biggest sign of all, located above the stage. It had a large painting of an elderly woman seated in a rocking chair, Bible in her lap, and the question, HOW LONG SINCE YOU WROTE MOTHER?

"Looks like Grandma to me," said Doug.

The front pews were filling fast; following the sermon, their occupants were excused first for dinner. We took a seat toward the back. Three old Indians sat down in front of us, and next to them sat a tall old white man dressed in a Western shirt.

"Evenin', cowboy," said one of the Indians.

"Evenin', chief," he replied. "Who is it tonight?"

"I don't know. Maybe that young fat dude."

"Oh, Christ, I hope not."

Moments later, the young fat dude strode onto the preaching platform, followed by his smiling wife and two little girls. The wife sat at the upright piano and the little girls, bows in their hair to match their dresses, sat in two miniature chairs. The young fat dude moved to the lectern. He smiled. The cowboy and Indians slumped further in their seats.

"We can tell it must be getting colder outside by the numbers of you here tonight," he began. "Thanksgiving's just gone by, Christmas is around the corner. For most people it's a very happy time of year, but I know for some of you it's a sad time. Are you sad? Rejoice in the Gospel! Let us sing: One fifty-seven."

His little girls caught the cue and stood up; most of the tramps rose creakily to their feet. Some, however, had already fallen asleep. "Get up, goddammit," hissed the man with the ruler to two of them, lifting them up by their collars. The piano started up, but only three voices could be heard singing the first stanza: the preacher's tenor, his wife's alto, and the scratchy bass of the old man with the ruler. Moving into the second stanza, the Indians in front of us joined in with gusto, though in the wrong key.

> Through this world of toil and snares,
> If I falter, Lord, who cares?

Doug, who had been in a school chorus and attended church, smiled at me and sang softly along. But at the hymn's end, the wife made a bad mistake at the piano, prompting several guffaws. The preacher, obviously angered, launched right into it.

"I know what the stagnant swamp of hell that you're living in is like," he testified. The smile on his face didn't seem to fit what he was saying. "Look at those glassed-over eyes. Why, it reminds me of myself because—you know—I had eyes just like that. Yes, I drank all the time! I've been to the detox."

He paused to let this shocking news sink in. I looked at Doug and rolled my eyes. "This is how they all start out," I whispered.

"Yes, I've been in the valleys, and I've been on the hilltops, too. And now I know I've got a mansion on the hilltop waiting for me. Can we sing together? 'Mansion on the Hilltop,' Number ninety-eight."

Some drunken tramps, arriving late, had just been seated in the last row. "Number seventeen!" cried out one.

"Well, all right then, we have a request. Let's all turn to—"

"No, number eighteen!"

"Yes, okay—"

"No! One and a half!" A few men sniggered. The preacher reddened and became stern. "We'll sing Number ninety-eight!" he commanded. " 'Mansion on the Hilltop.' " He nodded at his wife and she started up.

The sermon continued along the lines of the many others I had heard. After telling the audience he had once sunk as low as them, the preacher told the story of his own salvation. His happy family, smiling throughout, was evidence of his spiritual success. But the tramp's choice was not happiness or nothing, it was happiness or eternal damnation. Unsaved, tramps were told again and again, they were "as dead men." In fact, a good half of the sermon was devoted to telling tramps how unhappy they were: the theory seemed to be that only when they were relieved of whatever modicum of dignity they had been able to keep for themselves, only when they had been convinced that they were really a bunch of shits, would they feel the need to accept Jesus.

Underlying the preacher's words—in fact, underlying the whole idea of ministering to tramps in his way—was the assumption that the problems tramps experienced lay not in society but in the tramps themselves. Were they completely responsible for their situation? After meeting men like Bill, Monty, and Pistol Pete, it seemed to me a questionable premise.

The preacher called it quits about an hour later, and the men shuffled into the dining room. As usual, the atmosphere was somber, but while in line for my portions of chicken-skin soup and fallen-on-the-floor cake, I noticed one table that was livelier than others. Doug and I joined it and discovered the reason: a stand-out character, a huge, bearded, jovial, uninhibited tramp who made animated conversation and seemed pleased to talk with anybody about anything. On the table in front of him was his private bottle of hot chili sauce, which he dashed liberally into the soup. His T-shirt bore the slogan: I'D RATHER BE FLYING.

A young fellow, barely older than Doug and myself, was telling him about his recent experiences in the Army, from which he had just been discharged. The bearded tramp interrupted him.

"Wait a minute—how old did you say you were?"

"Twenty-four," answered the younger tramp.

"That's too young to be ridin' the rails," said the bearded one paternally.

"Whaddaya mean by that?" asked the younger tramp, slightly taken aback.

"Yeah, why not?" I joined in. I had been irritated before by older tramps' claims that young men on the rails didn't really know what they were doing, and couldn't really qualify as "good tramps." Probably, it was often true, but I took personal offense. "Why isn't he old enough? When did you start riding?"

The bearded tramp took no offense. "Why, when I was fifteen."

"You were old enough then. What makes him any different?"

"No, man, no. All I meant was, I wouldn't wish it on nobody so young. There's no reason for it. You've got your whole life to live.

There's better places to be—shit, why be fuckin' around here?" He gestured at the dining hall. "I can't stand it. I wish I was some-wheres else."

I was completely taken aback—and had I been anywhere but among tramps, I would have apologized. Here, it would have been overdoing it. I just said, "Oh," and nodded.

Next we lined up for bed assignments, received tokens to exchange for plastic trash bags in which to place our clothing, and filed into the showers. I was struck again by the gruesome sight of the transients with no clothes on. Though some had tanned arms and necks, the rest of their bodies were deathly white. The legs of the man two steps ahead of me were covered with small round sores. Some of the weaker, more derelict men avoided the spray altogether, as though it might hurt them. This was another of the depressing aspects of missions for a tramp: having to take a close look at others like yourself.

Emerging at the other end of the shower room, Doug and I were thrown rolled-up towels. Unrolling mine with a strong shake, I was dismayed to see pajamas come fluttering out, and land on the sopping wet floor.

"Gotta put 'em on," advised the towel thrower, whom I sud-denly disliked intensely.

We entered the bunk room. Double bunks were crowded into the small space, with only two feet between beds. Doug and I, assigned beds three bunks apart, quietly wished each other good night, and lay down. The jovial bearded tramp was two beds over. We nodded at each other: no hard feelings. Between us was a man I had seen in the line outside the mission. He had a long, freshly stitched wound running down the side of his face which, I had heard, he got from slipping and hitting his head on a rail while crossing the tracks drunk. The two of them were talking about how neither could shake their colds, and the big bearded tramp was attributing his drinking to a sore throat.

"My sister asked me why I'm drinkin' so much," he said. "I tell her it's relief, the only relief I can get." The other tramp murmured his agreement. But, as the lights went out, it struck me that drink provided the tramp with relief from more than a sore throat. Wine, the "tramp's blanket," was the fastest and cheapest way of escaping cold, boredom, fear, and other of life's sometimes desperate circumstances. Drinking was simply a second form of hobo travel.

But my concerns that night were more personal. With the beds so close, I worried about homosexual advances; Tiny had told me of waking up in a mission bunk to find another man beside him. The usual snores, wheezes, sniffs, and coughs soon filled the room, though, and, accustomed to them, I drifted off. At one point in the night, one man's fearsome, hacking cough grew loud enough to wake everyone, and several started complaining:

"Go get a glass a' water!"

"Drink some cold water, cough that stuff up."

"Sheeit, he's too lazy to get up and get a drink a' water."

"Get up and get out, man!"

Finally the offender left the room. It seemed like only a few seconds later that the lights came on.

"It's five A.M. Everybody up! Make your bed and make sure you're completely dressed before coming downstairs. Everybody up. *Wake up!*"

I groaned. Outside it was dark, and would remain that way for another hour and a half. It was also cold; anyone who would come outside *not* "completely dressed" was probably crazy. On a patio we were served coffee and old rolls and told to be on our way unless we planned to attend morning Bible class. A large breakfast was the reward, but almost nobody thought it was worth it. Several men were bitter at having to leave so early.

"The Lord wouldn't make us go outside!" complained one.

"Get out!" snarled the mission director. Doug and I laughed to ourselves.

We walked around town a bit and then settled down against the east-facing wall of a warehouse to wait for the sun to hit us.

"You know, I didn't like it there either," said Doug, "but it seems to me those guys are pretty ungrateful. I mean, it *is* free, and they don't have to go there."

I agreed that the tramps were not physically coerced into entering the missions. Yet many had little choice: where else could they find shelter, food, and clothing? The tramps were hostages of their need, and the missions had in them a captive audience.

And almost universally, tramps resented the bargain they made with missions. Many, like Lonny, swore they avoided them— "It's hard to get me into a mission; when I go into one, there's a reason"—although they headed directly for them upon arriving in a town. The price missions exacted in pride and dignity was one reason for the resentment; another was probably stated best by George Orwell in *Down and Out in Paris and London:* "A man receiving charity practically always hates his benefactor—it is a fixed characteristic of human nature." Orwell also described a disturbance he created in a mission with a group of other tramps—"it was our revenge upon them for having humiliated us by feeding us"—and observed that "it is curious how people take it for granted that they have a right to preach at you and pray over you as soon as your income falls below a certain level." I shared these thoughts with Doug. "Still," he said, "they do a lot of work for those guys."

Soon Doug had to return to San Francisco. The rent was due and the job hunt beckoned. We located a spot for him on a north-bound train, and I gave him pointers on how to make his way back. He had passed the tramp apprentice course with flying colors. We talked until the train began moving and I could no longer keep up. Our parting handshake was ended by the train's momentum.

Back at the mission that evening, my attention was caught by the fifteen or twenty Mexicans there. Perhaps I turned to them as a time-tested means of feeling better about something: find someone who had it worse. I felt isolated and alone, but I imagined what it must be like for them: alone in a foreign land, they found themselves somewhere below the bottom of the social totem pole, long miles from their females, families, and a language they could understand. Over dinner, I made friends with Enrique Jarra.

He was younger than I, short, and neatly dressed. His hair seemed to have been recently cut, and, like so many young Mexicans, he cared for it very carefully. Speaking in Spanish, he told me he was 18. His last job, he said, was celery-planting, for which he earned $100 to $125 per week. I told him that didn't sound very good, but he said that in Mexico, a fellow can earn only about $6 a day, or $50 in the best of weeks. And thus come the Mexicans.

After dinner, I helped Enrique get some new shoes from the used-clothing closet, and he took an interest in me, too.

"*¿Estás bien?*" he asked me ("Are you okay?"), looking worriedly at my face.

"*Sí, estoy bien,*" I answered, wondering what the hell he was getting at.

"It's just that you look *ahuitado,*" he said.

"*Ahuitado?* What's that?"

Enrique groped for a way of explaining it, and then said to me, "It's like when you have a girlfriend and she goes away, or when you have been traveling with somebody you like, and you part." I had not told him about Doug.

"*Sí,*" I conceded, admitting it to myself as well. "*Soy muy ahuitado.*"

"Why not come to the fields tomorrow, earn some money?" Why not? Mexican farm workers were the new American hoboes, in my opinion. It would be a chance to see just what life was like for them, and to learn about the immigration problem from their point of view.

"*Simón,*" I said. "Sure."

It was five forty-five A.M. and cold. Enrique and I walked shivering up the dark alley from the mission to "the intersection," two blocks from the mission. Enrique said it was the place where work was found, and the earlier we arrived, the better. Our pockets were stuffed with old rolls from the mission, for lunch.

There was no mistaking "the intersection" once we arrived—the scene could not have been anything else. Thirty or thirty-five men were standing around on two corners. On one, about ten black men sat on the wide front steps of an old drugstore, chatting and smoking. Under the streetlight across the way, by the adult bookstore, were crowded twenty or twenty-five Mexicans. Some carried machetes; these, Enrique explained, were hoping for work in the lettuce fields. Others like Enrique, who had stashed his tools behind a garbage can in the alley, were carrying pruning shears, or *tijeras*. These men hoped for work in the vineyards, doing the late-season pruning of grape vines. Tangerine-picking was another possibility, I heard, as we joined the group of Mexicans. Ours was a conspicuous arrival: I was the only white person there.

The Mexicans were talking, smoking, and shivering. Enrique found two of his friends, Pancho and Pedro, and introduced me. They and some of the others nearby were interested in my ability to speak Spanish—they didn't know any white people could. Several indicated they were interested in learning English. Pancho said the best way was to marry an American woman, and told the story of a friend who met one cherry-picking and did just that: marrying her, becoming a U.S. citizen, and speaking English within a year. The others looked on wistfully.

My three new friends were waiting for an orange pickup truck in which they thought I could get a ride to the fields, too. Meanwhile, every ten or fifteen minutes other trucks would approach and slowly pull up to the curb on the Mexican side. After a decent interval, a few Mexicans would casually approach the driver's window. The drivers, almost always Chicanos, would discuss with them the kind of work and the wages being paid. If the terms sounded good enough, the Mexicans would hop in; if not, the drivers waited for others to walk up and inquire, or drove across the street to the black corner. The blacks, however, seemed more particular: three times I saw men walk away from the drivers, shaking their heads. Only one truck went to the black side first, and I guessed that the employer, for a change, was worried about the law. Almost all the blacks, in other words, were U.S. citizens, and could be legally employed. The Mexicans, mostly illegal aliens, could not, which was the reason all of these dealings took place under cover of night.

A rickety school bus pulled up to our corner and a large contingent of machete-carrying Mexicans climbed aboard. The liveliest of the bunch, a long-haired man with a bright bandanna around his head, handed the last of a joint he was smoking to a man who was staying, and raised his fist in the air. *"Soldados lechugeros!"* ("Lettuce soldiers!")" he shouted defiantly, as though headed off to war, and others cheered.

As it began to drizzle and the sky grew light, the ten or so men who had not been picked up began to drift away. *"Espera,"* Enrique told me. "Wait. He'll come." Sure enough, within five minutes the orange pickup arrived. The driver was at first reluctant to take me, probably worried that bringing a white man would be bringing trouble. "There's no room in front," he warned me.

"That's all right, I'll sit in back," I said stoically, for it was now raining hard.

He finally gave in. "It's two bucks for the ride, but only if they give you work. You got *tijeras?*" I shook my head. He shrugged. "That's your business." Pancho lent me his wool pea coat, and I hunched behind the cab as we drove to the fields.

The expansive vineyards were located at the foot of the brown Sierra Nevada. We passed several work sites where Mexicans were already pruning as we wound through the maze of wet dirt roads to our own. The rain had finally stopped, and Enrique, Pancho, and Pedro got right to work, for they had had rows of vines assigned from the day before, and were paid by the vine. I had to wait for the *patrón,* or owner; meanwhile I watched Enrique to learn how the pruning was done. He was deft and efficient, and would have looked perfectly at home in the fields if it weren't for his nice clothes and neat appearance. I guess I had expected him to change into work clothes before starting, but the Mexicans had no such luxuries.

The *patrón,* who I learned was actually just a contractor,

arrived in a shining white pickup. He, too, was a Chicano, and his bilinguality made him the perfect go-between for owners who relied on Mexicans.

"No *tijeras?*" he asked. "That doesn't matter. Here's a brand-new pair." He pulled the shining clippers from his front seat.

"Oh, great, thanks a lot," I said appreciatively.

"That'll be eighteen bucks," he said, "the cost to me."

I gulped. "I don't have that. Aren't there any used ones?"

He shook his head. "It's no problem, I'll just take it off your paycheck."

"You don't pay daily?" Most farm jobs, I had been led to believe, were "day hauls," which didn't commit a person for more than a day.

"Saturdays," he said. It was Wednesday. It looked like I'd be coming back.

"Any lunch break?"

The contractor shrugged. "Your time's your own," he advised me. "Do what you want with it."

"Is there water? Toilets?" He shook his head, and then assigned me my own rows, long lines of woody grape plants supported by stakes and wire.

I got right to work. With only a short break to wash down the mission rolls with water given me by Pancho, I worked nine and a half hours. When we gathered at the orange truck afterwards, my hands were cramped and badly blistered and my wrists were stiff. I was exhausted but felt proud of the work I had done. I had really applied myself.

"How many vines did you do?" Enrique asked me, with a smile. He was using a handkerchief to wipe the sweat from his forehead, but, miraculously, he was still clean. I noticed that the skin on his palms was thick and callused.

"Let's see," I said, calculating. "I guess about two and a half rows."

Enrique looked at Pancho and Pedro. Nobody said anything. "Well, it takes a while to learn," Pedro said finally.

The driver laughed and spat on the ground. "A while? I'll say a while. Like a year, the rate you're goin'!" He turned toward the others, chuckling, but they didn't laugh along.

"What do you mean?" I asked. "How many did you guys do?"

Again, my three companions said nothing, but the driver planned to milk this for all it was worth. "You know how many they did? They probably did four and half, five, five and a half. I did five myself. Man, this is *easy* work. Let's see: two and a half rows, about thirty-three vines to a row, at fifteen cents a vine . . . You made about twelve bucks. Twelve bucks for a day's work! Man, that sucks."

I calculated it myself. He was right, on both counts: twelve dollars and it sucked. I didn't remind any of them about the *tijeras*, but as we drove back, I figured it out. After four days, once the contractor had subtracted his $18 and the driver his $8, I would have made exactly $22. Divide that by my 38 hours of labor, and my hourly wage worked out to be about 58¢ an hour. I looked down at my stiffening, throbbing hands. Most of the blisters were broken, and one was bleeding. There was no way I could work again soon without risking an infection. I wouldn't be able to clear $22 even if I wanted to. I had just worked a day for free. But it was a great relief to know I was done with the fields.

Enrique, Pancho, Pedro, and I returned to the mission. In the chapel, I noticed that the men slumped in their seats divided into two main groups: the tramps, who were drunk, and the Mexicans, who were just plain tired. Without question, they worked harder than anyone on the road. The sermon began with the preacher thumping the lectern, but my thoughts were elsewhere.

What should our country do with these men? By Mexican standards, work in America was a gold mine. They wanted to stay, and as I had witnessed that morning, they took jobs no Americans wanted. Yet there was not supposed to be a peasant class in America, and surely the millions of undocumented Mexicans constituted one. From my perspective, it was exploitation: our labor demand kept them coming, yet we offered them none of the rights which protected ordinary citizens. Enrique and his friends did not come close to making minimum wage. I knew the thought that would go through my mind the next time I drank California wine: it was cheap, but at what a cost.

Various solutions have been proposed. Force employers to comply with the minimum-wage law, say some, and Americans will seek the jobs now held by Mexicans. U.S. unemployment would decrease, and the Mexicans would stay home. Unfortunately, men like Enrique would then be out of work; also, some Hispanic Americans fear that such a move might result in job discrimination against all Spanish-speaking people, including American citizens.

Others propose stepped-up control of the U.S.-Mexican border. But to seal the border totally is both enormously difficult and politically inadvisable: a penetrable border is recognized by Mexico as an important form of U.S. foreign aid, a sort of pressure release valve for a country with poverty, unemployment, and population pressures of staggering dimensions. Alienating politically volatile Mexico, an important American client state, could have severe long-term effects on American life.

The problem is complex. The only truly comprehensive solution—increasing American aid to Mexico so that its economy can become robust enough to employ its own Enriques, Panchos, and Pedros—would be immensely expensive. So too, however, are the social costs of an unequal America with millions of second-class noncitizens.

I joined the Mexicans at the intersection the next morning, just to watch the remarkable scene again. This time there was another white man present, waiting with the blacks. After my friends were driven away and the crowd had thinned, I crossed the street to say hello.

He was dressed warmly, with a knit hat, a wool shirt with the sleeves cut off over a sweater, heavy work boots, and jeans. He was middle-aged and slightly pudgy. We chatted about the cold, about the diminishing prospects for work today, about how he wouldn't be out here except his food stamps hadn't come through this month. . . .

"Wait a minute," I said, staring at him. "You're a woman, aren't you?"

She smiled, and then I knew for certain. "That's right. You know, pretty many guys can't tell at first. I'm always foolin' people. Guess it's all these clothes I wear." She also kept her graying hair stuck up underneath her cap. She seemed to think it was pretty funny.

The sun rose, the trucks stopped coming, and the two of us crossed the street to sit on a bench in a small park, where we stayed well into the morning. Her name was Sheba, she told me, Sheba Sheila Sheils. Well, actually it was Mary Ann Sheils, but she always liked being called Sheila, and then when she saw a television movie on the Queen of Sheba, "Well, it all came together." Her gear consisted of a small frame backpack; written on the back of it, in grease pencil, were the initials "SSS."

I admitted to Sheba that I'd met very few woman tramps on the road, and none traveling alone, and that if I seemed full of questions, that was why.

"Oh, I don't mind your questions! I'm not like some of these guys—I've got nothin' to hide. Just so the guy askin' questions ain't gettin' creepy about it."

I shook my head. "Don't worry."

"Well, like you said, I don't see too many gals alone, but I do see a fair number with guys. Beats me as to why they stick with some of them!"

"You aren't worried, travelin' alone?"

"Heck, no! Most of the guys treat me real nice."

As if to confirm this, a voice behind us called out, "Hey, sister!" We ignored it at first, but when the man called again, Sheba turned. "Hey, sister, c'mere!" There was a tramp on the bench behind us, alone with his morning quart of beer. "Just a sec," she told me.

I watched as he offered her a sip and chatted with her for a while. Sheba looked up and saw me watching. "That's my friend," she told him. "Why dontcha give him a drink?"

"Sure he is," growled the tramp, but he did give me a swig.

When Sheba felt the visit had lasted long enough, we returned to our bench, and Sheba told me more about herself. She was fifty years old and had three sons, all by different fathers ("I made some mistakes, you know"). The sons were all in their twenties; two were in the military in Texas, and she didn't know where the third was. "I always try and call 'em all at Christmas, though."

She had been dishwasher in a restaurant in Idaho, but got sick of it, and, with the boys gone, had no reason to stick around the house.

"So, I started hitchin'. Did that for a couple of years, but then I decided it was too dangerous, so I started ridin' the trains."

"The trains are safer?"

"Oh, sure, you don't get trapped in a car with some weirdo when you're ridin' freights. And I always ride alone." She had been on the road three years.

I was very surprised to learn she was fifty: she looked ten years younger, even up close, the opposite of what usually happened to the appearance of male hoboes.

"Where do you stay?" I asked. "I haven't seen you in the mission—are you up at The Pipes?" The Pipes, well known in Bakersfield tramp society, were an assortment of large water and culvert pipes strewn around an industrial lot about a half mile up the tracks; they served as an impromptu tramp motel, offering more protection from weather and intruders than did most jungle shelters.

"No, I was there for a while, but now I built me a little place. Wanta see it?"

"Sure."

We walked alongside the yards for a few minutes until Sheba

stopped beside a tire-retreading plant. Tires waiting to be re-treaded had spilled over the tall chain-link fence that separated it from the yards, and several hundred were piled up outside.

"Well," Sheba said, "there it is."

I strained my eyes for some kind of structure, but saw nothing. "Where?"

"Over here!" she said. She walked me toward the piles, and suddenly, amid their randomness, I saw order. Sheba had built a house, of sorts, out of automobile tires. The walls, nearly as tall as the five-foot Sheba, were composed of stacks of tires, six or seven high. Probably 150 tires had been used to construct the entire thing. The front room, which we entered through a gap in the stacks, was for cooking, sitting around the fire, and passing the time. The back room, which had a sheet metal roof, was where Sheba slept. The whole place was carpeted in cardboard. A sheet of Formica lay upon two short stacks of tires, forming the kitchen table, and was covered with food and condiments. Two buckets had been overturned for living-room chairs, with rags placed upon them for seat covers.

"Have a seat," said Sheba. "I'd offer you coffee, but I'm fresh out."

"Here, use mine," I said, astounded by this place. Sheba fanned the fire to life, made the coffee, and sat down.

"How long did this take you?" I asked.

"Oh, just a coupla hours. I made one here back a few months ago."

"How did you think of doing it?"

"Gosh, I really don't know. I think I maybe copied what my sons used to make in the back yard—you know, forts, secret hide-outs."

"Nobody minds that you're here?"

"Boy, I don't think so. Who would mind? Only the tramps can see me. And not even most of them."

We finished the coffee, and Sheba announced it was time for her nap. She had given blood the evening before, and it always tired her out. "You oughta try it, if you need the money. And why don'tcha come back by sometime?" I promised I would.

The blood banks were one part of the tramp experience I had shied away from. In Dallas I had read stories of hepatitis being given to hospital patients by unscrupulous donors, and to donors by unsanitary blood banks. The blood bank there usually had a long line of derelicts stretching out its door and around the corner, waiting to change their plasma into money, which, in turn, would be changed into alcohol and put back into their bloodstreams. Besides, the idea of selling such an essential part of your body was unpleasant to me. "They ain't the Red Cross, you know," Lonny had reminded me. "They sell your plasma to makeup companies; that kind of thing, for ten times what they paid you. I don't need the exploitation."

But I needed the money. Groceries for Thanksgiving dinner had exhausted my traveler's checks, and it was still a fair distance home to Denver. I set my jaw and plodded downtown.

Finding the bank was no trouble; every transient I passed seemed to know where it was. When I was a block away I ran into a man I had met at the mission. He was tipsy, and assumed I would be, too.

"Goin' to the blood bank? I just come from there." He reached into his front pocket and pulled out a roll of breath mints. "Here, take one of these and they'll never know." I sincerely hoped that was not true, though I had heard tales of patients becoming drunk on blood given by inebriates.

The women in nurses' uniforms at the front desk of the bank assured me that could never happen at their bank; the urine and blood tests they took would indicate whether I had been drinking. Still, they asked me if I had: maybe it was the Certs on my breath.

I was ushered into the blood-taking room. The down-and-outers lying on white-sheeted cots looked strangely out of place amid the laboratory equipment and technicians clad in white. It was as though an experiment were being conducted on them. I lay down on the only empty cot, Number 14.

A woman in white started hooking me up to tubes and needles, but I stopped her and asked for an exact explanation of what they were going to do. She seemed surprised that it was my first time. They would take two units of my blood, she said, but as they were only interested in the plasma, the blood would be centrifuged after each unit was taken and the corpuscles returned to my veins in a saline solution. This would leave me stronger than if they kept them, but the trick was that if I got someone else's corpuscles by mistake, I would probably die. "Of course, that almost never happens," she assured me. To avoid it, she gave me a number, to be doublechecked with the number on the bag of corpuscles when she brought them back.

She then inserted a very fat needle in a vein on the inside of my elbow, and taped it down. A plastic bag hanging at my side began to swell with blood; at first I could see it pulsing in. Filling it took a long time. I began to wonder if I would see my stomach or legs start to collapse. My fingertips went numb. Then the woman was back, and presently the flow was reversed as the corpuscles, in the cold solution, flowed back into my bloodstream. My elbow ached, and I could feel the irritating coldness in my veins. I wanted to yank the needle out, but with the size of the hole it must have made in my vein, I feared it would drain my whole body.

It was midway through the drawing of the second unit that my eyes began to lose focus. My head felt tingly and light. "Hey," I said, half to myself, finally realizing that something was wrong. Then, more loudly, "*Hey,*" I called out, looking for the nurse but not seeing anything. My head fell back on the pillow.

The next thing I knew, she was back, holding my head up and offering me a small cup of orange juice. The other donors, interested at the commotion, turned their heads to look at me. My arm was still hooked up, but she had turned off the flow.

"Didn't you eat lunch before coming?" she asked. I shook my head.

"Breakfast?"

"Coffee and a doughnut."

"Well, no wonder," she said, exasperated. After a while I felt better, and she turned the flow back on. I had been wondering where the blood to fill the sacks would come from, and now I knew: my head.

My efforts earned me a ten-dollar bill and a Band-Aid for my arm. Feeling drained and depleted, I walked straight to McDonald's and ate two Big Macs.

I dropped in on Sheba that afternoon, and every day for the rest of the week. Often I arrived with a housewarming gift of coffee or a snack; these she accepted graciously. She didn't want a traveling partner; in fact, she wasn't planning to go anywhere, soon, but the company was welcome. We became friends.

Sheba was not unattractive. Her medium-length brown hair was streaked with gray, her lined face was kind, and her manner was relaxed. But with a couple of her front teeth rotting out, she was no beauty queen either. This did not seem to matter to the succession of suitors who dropped in every day. (Sheba's house, I soon realized, was located on the edge of a major tramp thoroughfare.) Her experiences with them seemed to bear out Portland Gray's report that women on the rails were treated with "a heavy dose of paternalism and a lot of respect." In the tramp's eyes, the two were not contradictory.

Often ignoring me, I guessed because I was so much younger and therefore not competition, they brought Sheba gifts of wine, spare change, food, flattery, and marriage proposals.

"Sheba, baby, how's it goin'?" asked one flamboyant, gregarious tramp one evening. He had never met her before and had learned her name from me just a few seconds earlier, when I left the tire house to refill a jug of Sheba's water.

She looked a little taken aback. "Goin' okay," she replied. "Who are you?"

"Who am I? I'm Freight Train Jack. I wrote the book!"

Sheba looked befuddled. "What book?"

"Oh, you know, the book of trampin'." She didn't get it, so he changed the subject. "Hey, Sheba, where're you from?"

She didn't yet trust this character. "Another state," she replied masterfully.

"Oh, yeah? And where are you goin' when you leave here?"

"One way or the other," said Sheba.

"Hmm," said Freight Train Jack. He would need to try another tack. Reaching deep into his pocket, he pulled out a large handful of change, mostly pennies and nickels.

"Here," he said to her, "I want you to have this."

"Oh, no, I couldn't take your money," said Sheba.

"If you don't take it, I'm gonna throw it all over the tracks!" threatened Freight Train Jack, winding back his arm like a pitcher.

"No, don't do that!" said Sheba in horror, putting out her hands. Jack dropped the change in and smiled. Now he was getting somewhere. He took a seat by the fire.

"Ooh, am I hungry!" he said presently, spying a sack of potatoes on Sheba's Formica counter. "Sheba, honey, I'll bet you're a fine little cook. Fix me up some of them spuds for dinner, wouldya?"

"Forget it!" she replied. Undaunted, Jack made small talk, and observed that the rails were no place for a woman to be alone—a situation he proposed to remedy by having Sheba marry him.

"No way!" she cried. "Who do you think I am, anyway? I just met you!" Their relations deteriorated after that, and Jack was unable to salvage things by promising Sheba he would bring her a ring the next day. When finally she ordered Jack to leave, he did—sullenly, but with hardly a complaint.

Another who dropped in was a Southern black man Sheba's age named PeeWee, who had just returned from picking tangerines. He shared some from a bag he carried under his arm, and I asked how he liked the work.

"It's not bad," he replied. "Sure beats that carrot-snappin'. Man, five weeks of carrot-snappin'll drive a dude nuts!"

"What's carrot-snappin'?" asked Sheba.

"You know, when you buy the carrots in a bag at the store? Well, some's too big for the bag, so somebody got to snap off the end. Lemme tell you, I ain't goin' back to that job for a while." I couldn't believe a job like that existed.

Another visitor was an old hippie with a long gray beard, who, like Sheba, had switched to the rails from hitchhiking. His name was Diamond. As we talked, he mentioned another reason he thought the rails were better: "The hitchhiker's a beggar. He asks for a ride. That tramp doesn't ask. The tramp just takes it!" Most tramps, I thought, would agree.

I didn't think Sheba and Diamond would get along, but when I returned after a couple of hours they were sharing a joint. Sheba seemed embarrassed about the joint, but I told her it was nothing—how many middle-aged women, I thought to myself, led lives as interesting as hers?

Even the immigration officer, scouring the yards for Mexicans, would stop in late at night while on his rounds to give her cigarettes, said Sheba.

Some tramps asked her to mend or wash their clothing; others, drunk, tried to kiss her. In their eyes, these were the things a woman was for. But Sheba declined all requests and advances more or less firmly, depending on how well she liked the tramp. And, true to her claim, the tramps didn't seem to cause her any trouble. Chivalry and the rarity of her kind on the rails were one reason they didn't. Another was probably fear. Women on the rails were notoriously adept at looking out for themselves. In her "bedroom," Sheba kept a butcher knife and a hatchet, and I had no doubt that she knew how to use them. As one passing tramp noted to me, "You don't see nobody else's scars on Sheba."

From the vantage point of the tire house, Sheba and I watched the small waves of tramps dropping off every southbound freight, fifty or sixty tramps a day. Typically, Bakersfield was just a rest stop on the birdlike migration south, and after a day or two the tramps would catch out again. Their flight had a pull on me, a contagious momentum. Christmas decorations I saw in shops in Bakersfield somehow heightened it: there was a place I wanted to get to as well, a place families should be at Christmas—home, together. Sheba's company, and her talk of her sons, reminded me of it. Time was short, and I had a long way to go.

One afternoon, I knew it was time. I told Sheba good-bye and gave her a hug brought with me from life before the rails. It surprised her, but she was used to surprises, and smiled. I located a shallow gondola on the next train out, and was rolling toward Los Angeles as the sun went down.

The ride took me "over the Hill," as the tramps call the Sierra Nevada. On the far side lay the Mojave Desert. The night was cold and low clouds, lit by a thin moon, mostly obscured the dry, bare hills. My gondola was near the front of the train, though, and the powerful head beam of the front unit cut through the mist. The engineer also had on the oscillating beam, which, following a woozy figure-eight pattern, lit up the hillsides, high and low, left and right, on either side of the train. The momentary glimpses of weird stone formations shrouded in mist set me on edge; the twisting light gave life to the strange rocks and contours, and the hillsides seemed peopled with stone giants.

It was a relief when the warm lights of Los Angeles came into view below, and we descended to the steadiness and predictability of the desert. And I felt lucky when the train did not roll directly into Los Angeles, whose yards and skid row were supposed to be extremely dangerous ("I'd rather be naked in a pack of baboons than in skid row, L.A.," Lonny had told me; "walkin' into that place like walkin' into hell"), but stopped instead in the big yards of suburban Colton.

Yet, as I got to know the Colton yards, the creepy feeling returned. I tried to leave briefly, to buy food and a cup of coffee before continuing my journey. But after walking nearly two miles without finding a break in the twelve-foot fence, I learned from a sullen brakey that the yards were sealed at night: there was no way past the gates for non-railroad personnel. Next I looked for a tree or shrubs to rest under until dawn, but all of them had been removed. One large field, in the light of the mercury lamps, looked like the surface of the moon. The winter tramp problem was bad enough in L.A., the brakey said; they didn't need the trouble in Colton. The yard, as a result, was probably the starkest, most lifeless place I had ever seen. Nothing was natural: not the light, not the sounds of metal banging harshly on metal, not the air, full of diesel fumes. My nervousness grew, and I caught out of the spooky yard on the next train.

Friendly company would have been welcomed at that point. Instead, when the train was out of the yard and picking up speed, a tramp who had apparently been unable to enter the yard appeared alongside it. Oblivious to the possibility of other passengers, he barely noticed me standing in the doorway of my empty as he prepared to board on the fly. I shouted at the man to grab another empty. He ignored me and began to run. His bag flew in the door, and he placed his hands on the threshold. He was about to leap in when I set my boot down on his fingers, hard. With a yelp, he disappeared. I looked out the door and back; he had fallen down. After waiting a while, I tossed his bag out.

I leaned back against the boxcar wall and took a deep breath. I was surprised by what I had just done, but even more by my attitude: I felt no remorse. The man had breached the tramp rule about asking before you come in, and gotten what he deserved. If the same thing had happened at the beginning of my trip, and I had had the guts actually to throw the guy out, I would have felt guilty, illiberal, and brutish.

But now I was living by the rules of the road. I had done what I had to do. Lying down on cardboard, I fell asleep.

17

Temperature aside, Yuma, Arizona, was hot. As the few tramps who beat their way back north from there to Bakersfield would attest, too many southbound tramps had landed there and chosen to stay the winter. The result was an overloading of the city's welfare system and goodwill, and a crackdown on tramps through arrests for victimless crimes they perpetrate as a way of life: trespassing, vagrancy, loitering, public intoxication, public urination. The penalty for all of them was a ten-day stint in Yuma's inhospitable jail, something the tramps I had met—including Sheba—recommended strongly against. The heat put a strain on relations between tramps as well, and word had filtered up to Bakersfield of at least two recent murders of tramps by tramps in Yuma, in one of which the killer also knifed his victim's dog. Yuma was a place to avoid; unfortunately my route home required a stop there.

Yet rumors could be exaggerations. I paced nervously about the boxcar as the train approached Yuma, looking forward to asking someone who was actually there about the situation. I did not have to wait long for my chance. A bridge over the river marking the California–Arizona border came into view, and I stuck my head out the door to take a look at Yuma, on the far side.

"Get off here!" yelled two young tramps at me as I did. "Get off and walk across! Stay outa the yard!" But it was too late. The train was on top of the bridge, and the yard came immediately after.

Dusk had fallen. The train stopped. Hesitantly, I dropped off, but then immediately jumped back on. At each end of the train were sedans, moving on opposite sides toward the train's middle, where I was. Small spotlights on the cars played through the doors of the empties and anywhere else there might be a rider; the headlights lit up the only escape route. Panic surged inside me, but I tried to control it. I would be discovered for sure inside this empty; the grain car right behind me offered a better chance. I let myself down from the car, slowly this time. Crouching low, I moved under the overhang of the boxcar back to the grain car, praying that the bull's eyes would be turned in another direction. Meanwhile his car proceeded methodically up the line. I squeezed myself into the cubbyhole in the grain car's frame, and sat very still. The bull pulled up, shined his light quickly around the platform, and went on. Either the cubbyhole was too hard to check, or he didn't even know about it. I sprinted out of the yard.

I took a seat under a highway overpass, high over one end of the yard, where I could watch what was happening. I wanted out on the next train, no matter when it left.

My edginess increased because there were no tramps around, and there ought to have been. I had escaped the police menace for now, but the tramp menace had not been met yet, and was possibly even worse. You could see the police coming. The trouble with tramps, especially if you were asleep, was that you often could not.

I turned on my transistor radio for company. To my surprise, I tuned in a Denver radio station. Excitement raced through me as I realized how close I was getting to home. Then, however, the national news came on, and the lead story stunned me: former Beatle John Lennon had been shot in the back and killed. I was shocked at first, but then a fearful feeling crept over me. *Lennon had been shot by someone he didn't even know.* That was exactly what I feared most about the rails: not that someone like BB, whose temper I understood, would hurt me, but that someone from out of the blue, someone with impersonal, unpredictable motives would hurt me to get money, or for no reason at all. The first kind of violence you could prepare for by keeping your wits about you; the second kind, you could not. It was what kept people in big cities from being friendly with each other, the kind of violence you avoided thinking about, because you could do nothing about it. And it could leave you dead.

Perhaps it was the combination of the frightening experiences of the trip over the hill from Bakersfield, the emptiness of the Colton yard, and the malevolence of the atmosphere in Yuma that made me so frightened I began looking all around for that evil someone, even behind me into the one cubic yard of space between me and the bottom of the overpass where no one could possibly have concealed himself. Or maybe it was the cumulative experience of my trip, of acting bravely when really I was scared, of sleeping deeply when the risk didn't justify it, of being alone and exposed, that finally caught up with me. At any rate, the fear attached itself to me and stuck, from Yuma to Tucson to El Paso and southern Colorado. At college in Massachusetts, sitting in the ivory tower, I had been frustrated by the remoteness of the "real world." There had been times when I couldn't imagine what it was like outside of school. Now, though, as I gazed from my boxcar to the light dusting of snow on the Colorado Rockies and tried to remember the stars I had seen the night before, I found I barely could. Losing myself in pleasant thoughts on the rails was almost as difficult as imagining the "real world" had been before. There were too many things in the real world that a tramp had to look out for, too many bulls and couplings and tramps like the ones that, without provocation, beat up Lonny. You just couldn't relax.

The cold, from which I retreated to the units of the trains in southern Colorado, the Christmas lights I saw at night in Pueblo, or possibly the sheer fatigue of carrying my extraordinary fear for so long helped me recover my normal state of mind shortly before I reentered Denver. I was almost home, and very excited about it.

I dropped off the end unit of the Burlington Northern at a point convenient to downtown. Though glad to be stretching my legs, I felt a twinge of nostalgia as I let go of the railing of the unit's back stairs; I was tired of that train, but not tired of trains. At last I understood how they worked, how the network of rails fit together, how to take advantage of them. I knew I would return to the rails— although from a different direction, on a different path, maybe just to enjoy a midsummer's ride over the Rockies and across the desert to Salt Lake City.

I stepped lightly over the forty pairs of tracks that lay between me and downtown proper. It was late afternoon, a cool but sunny December day. In El Paso I had picked up an overcoat at a used-clothing store, and I wore it over my sweater, fur collar turned up. An old, hand-knit watchman's cap was pulled down over my ears; from underneath it spilled three or four inches of curly blond hair that had not been there when I began.

The viaducts overhead marked my way across the tracks. One of them had been the scene of my arrest, not so long ago; the memory still made me bitter. Today, though, I felt older and much wiser. I understood the tramps' need to be invisible, why they walked the alleys instead of the streets, and the yards instead of the public viaducts. Even if they had done nothing wrong, they were safer there.

I crossed Larimer Street, no longer a frightened tourist in a foreign land. In the past few months I had learned the skills necessary for survival in such a place. I had gained a feel for the respect I could command for myself, a feel for my place and power. A great confidence grew within me; I had undertaken something difficult, and was nearly done. I walked to 17th Street and, as the sun sank low, caught a bus for home.

Some neighbors stared hard as I walked down the pleasant street to our house, but by now it hardly bothered me. Part of my immunity was the hard-won knowledge that people like the one they thought me to be were really a lot like them; another was the fact that, really, this was my neighborhood. Up our front walk, my excitement still growing, I put down my gear and rang the doorbell. I had not told my family when I would arrive.

My sister Beth opened the door, looking out into the half-dark. "Yes?" she said, through the screen.

"Um"—I had hoped for this—"is, um, Mr. Conover there?"

She looked at me as one would regard an odd and interesting stranger, then turned and began to walk back down the hall toward the living room. Halfway there she stopped and turned back around.

"Ted?"

"Mm-hmm," I confirmed.

"Oh my gosh, it's Ted!" she hollered, and this time there was much commotion in the living room. The beagle barked and the rest of my family came quickly around the corner into the hall. Our reunion took place there, but when the initial excitement died down Mom ushered me back outside and around to the back yard. Though I was welcome inside, she explained, handing me my bathrobe, my clothes were not.

"But, Mom, I got rid of the lice!"

"Can't be too careful," she replied. I was somewhat amazed, as I undressed in the dark, to discover that underneath the over-coat were six layers of T-shirts, long-sleeved shirts, including the black polyester one from Everett, and sweaters. The innermost layers conformed to my body so well I thought for a moment they might be attached. But it all came off, including my work boots, with new holes under the toes. Despite the squares of cardboard I had placed inside the shoes, my feet were damp. Three paper bags were filled with my clothes before I was done.

My family coddled me during the next few days, and I didn't resist. While on the rails I had missed them more than ever before. The transition back to the ease and amenities of home was strangely uncomfortable—it bothered me to be living so well—but the transition back to an atmosphere of love was not. Never had I felt so lucky to have sisters and parents.

Other changes were simpler. I took pride in my weathered hands, tanned and tough, and in my sunned and windburned face. Five pounds lighter, my body felt lean, relaxed, and strong; life outdoors had agreed with it. Sharing all those bottles of wine with tramps, drinking from water jugs found by the side of the tracks, sleeping irregularly, and eating with dirty fingers had, luckily, not hurt me at all.

Eventually, of course, the weathered look faded. I clipped my nails, cropped my beard, and got a haircut. But even as the hobo trip receded in time, some of its lasting effects became apparent. I would hear train whistles across town, for example, that companions could not hear even if they stopped to listen. And stop we often did, for the sound transported me involuntarily from whatever activity I was engaged in to the mood of weeks before. I also found I had grown impatient with friends complaining of life's difficulties: minor problems of health, unpleasant people at the office, or meals not quite properly prepared at a restaurant all seemed so petty compared to Pete's hand, Enrique's poverty, or Monty's wracking memories. People absorbed in their own worlds, unconscious of the drama of other people and places, lost interest for me.

In my free time at home, I read a book by Herman Hesse about a wanderer who led a merry and carefree youth, but to whom life was harsh in his old age. In the last scene the tramp has collapsed on a hillside and is breathing his final breaths; God comes to him, and they have one last talk. The embittered tramp asks why he was put on earth at all. God explains, "You were a wanderer in My name and wherever you went you brought the settled folk a little homesickness for freedom."

The words struck a chord in me. In the beginning, the idea of tramps had made me homesick for freedom—from bosses, routines, and the expectations of others, the freedom to go when and where I wanted. Among tramps, I had found these things. I had learned how to exploit a system—the railroads—not created with my convenience in mind, had sampled a life where first-class rides were purchased with experience, not with cash and a ticket agent. The individual and his survival savvy were what counted on the rails. In contrast to large cities, factories, or universities, where people can feel like ciphers, numbers in a computer, the rails are a place where, as one songwriter guessed, "numbers live like men."

I hit the rails to learn and because, as Lonny said, when you become afraid to die, you become afraid to live. Confronted by the prospect of entering a laid-out and set-up life largely devoid of the need to be resourceful, I had desired an activity with an unpredictable outcome. Risk-taking, in a way, seemed its own reward. "Well, at least you got the best of life/Until it got the best of you" a song consoled a hobo who fell off a train one night and died. Few could claim as much, I thought; I wanted them to be able to say that about me.

But for real hoboes such as Pistol Pete and the tramp who had been stoned by children at Wishram, "risk" and "romance" often translate into "hardship." Up close, the hoboes' freedom seemed more like poverty: isolated from the American Dream, tramps had no social mobility, no safety, nobody to count on, nobody to love. Tramps were strangers wherever they went. Living with them had made me homesick, period.

It also had taught me some things about the society I had stepped out of. Life on the edge showed me what I might have guessed that morning outside Britt, trying fruitlessly to thumb a ride to the Hobo Convention: ordinary people respond very differently to the romanticized, folkloric hobo than to a real one, asking them for help. Real ones we don't like to look at or think about. Forrest's comments on unemployment suggested to me a reason why: perhaps we compel the existence of hoboes, not only because the welfare "safety net" has holes in it (and is often demeaning), but because we make impossible demands upon some people.

To understand tramps, in other words, you have to understand the idea that people cannot always do what they are told. Maybe you are told to get a job, but there aren't any; maybe you return from a crazy war and are told to carry on as though nothing ever happened. Maybe you live in a small room on a smaller pension, spending each day doing nothing. Demoralization and disgust come easily then. Many tramps' careers on the road began when the tramp told society, "You can't fire me—I quit!"

The existence of tramps who don't want to be tramps—and there are many, many of them—lessens all our lives. One Bible verse absent from the mission walls was these words of Christ in Matthew: "Inasmuch as ye have done it unto one of the least of these my brethren, ye have done it unto me." We are no richer than the poorest among us. If we are not going to make room for tramps inside society, we can at least make allowances for their presence outside it. We can repeal laws against victimless crimes such as public intoxication and vagrancy, and we can make sure that no one is denied food, warm clothing, and shelter, all of which are basic human rights.

That these things have not been done already can be explained by the way most of us still see hoboes as a race apart, strangers whom we have no need to know and no way of knowing. But I believe this attitude is mistaken. If I violated the hobo's privacy in these pages, it was in order to share those glimpses of his life and character that taught me my greatest lesson: that the hobo is not "one of them." He is one of us.

ALSO BY TED CONOVER

COYOTES

A Journey Through the Secret World of America's Illegal Aliens

To discover what becomes of Mexicans who desperately slip into the United States, Ted Conover walked across deserts, hid in orange orchards, waded through the Rio Grande, and cut life-threatening deals with tough-guy traffickers in human sweat. This electrifying account is the harrowing vision of a way of life no outsider has ever seen before and an enduring contribution to our national debate on immigration.

Travel/Current Affairs/0-394-75518-9

NEWJACK

Guarding Sing Sing

At the infamous Sing Sing, once a model prison but now New York State's most troubled maximum-security facility, Ted Conover gets a job as a gallery officer, working shifts in which he alone must supervise scores of violent inner-city felons. With empathy and insight, *Newjack* reveals a harsh, hidden world and describes the conflict between the necessity to isolate criminals and the dehumanization— of guards as well as inmates—that almost inevitably takes place behind bars.

Current Affairs/0-375-72662-4

WHITEOUT

Lost in Aspen

Irreverent, poignant, and revealing, *Whiteout* is a meditation on wealth and the vainglorious quest for paradise in Aspen, Colorado. Even as Ted Conover describes how he crashed Don Johnson's Christmas party, or what it was like to sit in on the taping of John Denver's holiday video, he is turning the lens of his craft upon himself and is documenting his own seduction by the Aspen mystique. The result is journalism with the laser moral focus of enduring satire.

Travel/0-679-74178-X

VINTAGE BOOKS
Available at your local bookstore, or call toll-free to order:
1-800-793-2665 (credit cards only).

Printed in the United States
by Baker & Taylor Publisher Services